SWEET
SPOTS

SWEET SPOTS

In-Between Spaces in New Orleans

Edited by Teresa A. Toulouse and Barbara C. Ewell

University Press of Mississippi / *Jackson*

Funding for permissions and reproductions was provided by the
Dorothy H. Brown Distinguished Professorship (Loyola University
New Orleans) and by the Department of English, University of
Colorado, Boulder, and the Department of English, Tulane University.

www.upress.state.ms.us

The University Press of Mississippi is a member
of the Association of American University Presses.

First printing 2018

∞

Library of Congress Cataloging-in-Publication Data

Names: Toulouse, Teresa, editor. | Ewell, Barbara C., editor. | Heard,
Malcolm, dedicatee.
Title: Sweet spots : in-between spaces in New Orleans / edited by Teresa A.
Toulouse and Barbara C. Ewell.
Description: Jackson : University Press of Mississippi, 2018. | Includes
bibliographical references and index. |
Identifiers: LCCN 2017051514 (print) | LCCN 2017053011 (ebook) | ISBN
9781496817037 (epub single) | ISBN 9781496817044 (epub institutional) |
ISBN 9781496817051 (pdf single) | ISBN 9781496817068 (pdf institutional)
| ISBN 9781496817020 (hardcover : alk. paper) | ISBN 9781496818577 (pbk. :
alk. paper)
Subjects: LCSH: Space (Architecture)—Louisiana—New Orleans. |
Architecture—Human factors—Louisiana—New Orleans. | New Orleans
(La.)—Buildings, structures, etc. | New Orleans (La.)—Civilization.
Classification: LCC NA2765 (ebook) | LCC NA2765 .S88 2018 (print) | DDC
720.9763/35—dc23
LC record available at https://lccn.loc.gov/2017051514

British Library Cataloging-in-Publication Data available

For Malcolm "Mac" Heard (1943–2001)
Architect, teacher, colleague, friend

Contents

Acknowledgments

This book has evolved from an interdisciplinary course, New Orleans as a Cultural System, originally team-taught at Tulane University from 1990 to 2000 by Mac Heard and Teresa Toulouse. The volume reflects the broader aim of that class: to bring together diverse students from architecture, business, and arts and sciences to explore intersections among different spatial and cultural phenomena in New Orleans. For support for that original course, we thank the deans of the Tulane School of Architecture, Ron Filson and Don Gatske, the dean of the Faculty of Liberal Arts and Sciences at Tulane, Teresa Soufas, provost James Kilroy, and Tulane University presidents Eamon Kelly and Scott Cowan. In January 2014, seeking to honor Mac Heard and to develop his ideas about in-between and interstitial space in an interdisciplinary collection of essays, the editors organized a seminar of interested scholars at Loyola University New Orleans, with generous support from its Department of English.

For their assistance in this undertaking, we are particularly grateful to Michael Kuczynski, chair of the Department of English at Tulane, and William Kuskin, David Glimp, and Ruth Kocher, chairs of the Department of English at the University of Colorado, Boulder. Teresa Toulouse would also like to acknowledge the help of Lia Pileggi of the Visual Resource Center and Vicky Romano of the Department of English at the University of Colorado. Barbara Ewell would also like to thank John Biguenet, chair of the Department of English, Kate Adams, and the rest of her colleagues at Loyola University New Orleans for their support and inspiration.

For their assistance in finding and acquiring crucial images and texts for this volume, we would like to thank the helpful staff members at the Louisiana Collection of the Howard-Tilton Memorial Library at Tulane University, the Historic New Orleans Collection (especially Rebecca Smith), the New Orleans Public Library, and the Office of the Clerk of Civil District Court of Orleans Parish. We also thank the staffs of Norlin

Library at the University of Colorado and of the Howard-Tilton Memorial Library at Tulane University.

A number of individuals contributed to the realization of this volume through their insights and encouragement. We particularly thank C. Errol Barron, Emily Clark, Sylvia Frey, Jessie Poesch, Lawrence Powell and Ellen Weiss, all of Tulane University, and Katherine Eggert, Katie Little, and Richelle Munkhoff at the University of Colorado. We also gratefully acknowledge the advice of historian Ed Dimendberg (University of California at Irvine), architects Ben Ledbetter and Charles Sanders, and architectural historians Ann Masson of New Orleans and Gary van Zante (curator of the MIT Museum's Architecture and Design Collection). More personally, we thank Beth Willinger, Andrea Ewell Cox, Lynne Koch, Minrose Gwin, Ruth Salvaggio, Pamela Menke, Sheila Geha, and Mary Beth Rose.

At the University Press of Mississippi, we would particularly like to thank our editor, Craig Gill, assistant-to-the-director Emily Bandy, project editor Valerie Jones, and the entire press staff. We are also grateful for the careful copyediting of Joseph Muller, and we acknowledge with appreciation the perceptive comments of our anonymous readers.

There would be no book at all without our contributors, some of whom participated in the original course, many of whom are colleagues and friends, and all of whom have persisted in their confidence and enthusiasm throughout this process. We thank each one, especially Barbara Brainard, whose allusive cover image adds her own subtle graphic commentary on interstitial space. Barbara Ewell would especially like to thank Teresa Toulouse, her longtime friend and colleague, for inviting her to share in this labor of love. Teresa Toulouse would particularly like to thank her coeditor, Barbara Ewell, for her irreplaceable role in this collection. There would be no sweet spots without her.

We gratefully acknowledge the indispensable contributions of our good friends and husbands, Michael Zimmerman and Jerry Speir, not only for their reading, re-reading, and smart editorial suggestions, but also for their refereeing, good humor, and apparently endless patience. Teresa Toulouse is also grateful to her daughter, Liz Zimmerman, for her exceptional forbearance during this long process.

Alicia Rogin Heard has been friend, supporter, and invaluable contributor to this collection. Without her, it simply would not have happened. From the very beginning, she took the students and many of the participants of the course into her heart—and into her and Mac's incomparable Bywater house. We acknowledge with gratitude and affection Alicia, Lucy, and Wendell Heard.

We gratefully recall the many illustrious and generous New Orleanians who provided the guest lectures and on-site experiences that so deeply enriched that first course. And, finally, we thank the outstanding students of New Orleans as a Cultural System.

Our dedication attests to our inspiration and to our greatest debt. For Mac.

Introduction

—Teresa A. Toulouse

In-between—interstitial—spaces famously abound in New Orleans. From the high ceilings and the hidden staircases to the passages functioning almost invisibly within individual houses; from the balconies, porches, stoops, courtyards, walls, and *portes-cochères* separating houses from the outer world and connecting them to it, to the accidental spaces formed by dense stylistic juxtapositions of elements along downtown and uptown blocks; from the spatial possibilities for hidden gardens and little-known neighborhoods, to the shared public life of local markets that materialize anomalously out of the city's original gridded plan, New Orleans emerges as a place where different dimensions of the interstitial have been clearly and richly expressed.

Other colonial cities located around the Caribbean rim share what Tulane University geographer Richard Campanella in this volume calls "high-grain interstitiality"—an urban texture "spatially heterogeneous," dense and diverse in its structural elements. In New Orleans—a city often viewed as an island floating dreamily above the south coast of North America, somewhere between the United States and Latin America—interstitial spaces have contributed both to a complex historical self-understanding and to a shared sense of place. They have also played a major role in the way New Orleanians themselves have long imagined, explained, and marketed their city's so-called mysteries to outsiders. In the essays that follow, as the city approaches its tercentenary, still in the midst of its development after Hurricane Katrina, we take a moment to pause and to place at the center of attention a range of interpretive responses to the city's in-between spaces, both for what they reveal about certain intersections between New Orleans's lived and imagined pasts and for the insights they offer about the city's possible futures.[1]

Derived from the Latin *stare*, "to stand," and *inter*, "between," the adjective *interstitial* most literally describes something that stands between other things. The term has long been used in physics, chemistry, and biology to describe structures of relationship either within a given phenomenon (an atomic structure, chemical bond, organ, or tissue) or between such structures. Only in the early 1960s did the term migrate to the fields of architecture and urban design.[2] For many at the Tulane University School of Architecture, it was Mac Heard, the late architect and faculty member to whom this collection is dedicated, who helped to broaden understandings of *interstitial* in the late 1980s. Heard saw the concept as one that could be usefully expanded to interpret a wide range of in-between spaces and provide a new lens for cultural inquiry into certain distinctive features of New Orleans.

As comments in his *French Quarter Manual* (1997) suggest, Heard was interested in how in-between spaces worked within the interiors of particular structures. He was thus concerned with "interstitial space" as referencing what John Klingman, his colleague and friend at the School of Architecture, defines "as a certain kind of spatial/structural infrastructure, often invisible, that allows for enhanced building capabilities without disturbing essential use." At the same time, given Heard's own earlier training by such Tulane architects as Bernard Lemann and Samuel Wilson, Heard was also intrigued by spatial relations between and among buildings and streets, especially in the French Quarter. Describing the distinctive spatial "energy" he finds permeating the Quarter, for example, he attributes it to the "tension between the clear street grid and the idiosyncratic spaces stacked and wedged and hung in interstices" along a given block.[3]

Heard's use of an architect's terms like *energy* and *tension* to describe spatial relations of buildings to one another and to their streets raises a question that perennially intrigues architectural historians, theorists, and practitioners alike: how do experiences of space move so readily to larger philosophical, aesthetic, and social discussions of feelings associated with, or evoked by those spaces?[4] As a student of English literature as well as architecture—he majored in English and studied with Eudora Welty at Millsaps College in Mississippi—Heard was well aware that New Orleans's in-between spaces affected those who experienced them, often through the media of story, fiction, and visual representation. Running throughout his *French Quarter Manual* is a fascination with the ways that spaces, often in-between spaces, come to take on and shape stories that promote certain consequences, not only for those who live in them but also for those who only observe or read about them. Heard commented appreciatively on how interstitial spatial features encouraged narratives that then, in their turn, encouraged the literal replication of imagined features in real spaces. Two of his favorite examples were the ways that locals and tourists read the spaces of a particular French Quarter house, Madame John's Legacy, through the lens of George Washington Cable's eponymous short story, and the ways the wrought-iron balconies displayed on the *Yancy Derringer* television show of the late 1950s influenced a range of suburban buildings inside and outside of New Orleans. With wry amusement, Heard noted the process by which banana trees and courtyards featured in stories end up in actual court-yards, images of which, in turn, circle back to inform more stories using courtyards. If this is true at the level of individual structures, the stories accreted around neighborhoods like the French Quarter, Congo Square, and, more infamously, Storyville and Bourbon Street suggest how the significance granted to in-between spaces, variously experienced, his-torically affected understandings and practices in wider areas of the city.[5]

Heard's fascination with New Orleans's interstitial spaces, whether within individual structures or without, and with the dense cultural meanings that such spaces come to shape and are in turn shaped by, has directly influenced both our own approach and the title of this collection: *Sweet Spots.* The phrase *sweet spot* aptly invokes the weaving together of both feeling and physical space. In New Orleans (and elsewhere), jazz musicians have used the phrase to refer to that elusive spot between musicians and their audience—or later, their audio equipment—where the sound resonates most pleasingly. While identifying these particular spots as in-between highlights the spatial ways that musical production and reception can be interpreted, calling these spaces sweet highlights their emotional power. Aligning these musical sweet spots with inter-stitial spaces, our title asserts that spaces of in-betweenness possess agency—they do something to those who experience them.[6]

The use of the term *sweet*, however, is by no means intended to imply that encounters with or practices of spatial in-betweenness in New Orleans are saccharine. Indeed, the phrase *sweet spots*, with all its tonal innuendo, complicates rather than simplifies the meaning of *sweet*. What or who grants sweetness to these New Orleanian spots? Between what kinds of structures–physical, historical, aesthetic, eco-nomic, or social—are they understood or imagined to stand? How do sweet spots affect these structures—and how are they, in turn, affected by them? Given New Orleans's long and fraught racial history, might not the personal or group experiences expressed or shaped in sweet spots vary, depending on the invisible as well as visible structures associated with their in-betweenness? If in certain registers, sweet spots promise licit and illicit pleasures or even utopian possibilities, how might such spaces, in other registers—anxious, nostalgic, tragic, or apocalyptic—uncannily limn pleasure's absence or even threaten social or natural implosion? If the phrase *sweet spots* thus grants power to the concept of interstitial space, it also implies how such power involves a surplus of multiple, con-flicting, and often controversial associations with the in-between.

While the essays here draw on Mac Heard's spatial idiom of the "interstitial," they also push it outward to encompass a variety of cultural phenomena: sweet spots in New Orleans that slip between the material, the physical, and the metaphoric. Heard often noted this relationship of in-between spaces and stories, but he admitted that his architectural "taxonomy" of the French Quarter could not fully encompass the area's "experiential and associational" aspects.[7] In contrast, many of our contributors are particularly interested in asking how historical and imaginative associations, positions, and competitions—of race, gender, class, and other categories—consciously or unconsciously contribute to understandings and practices of in-between space. In raising questions about the complex desires and meanings crossing through and constituting specific sweet spots, their work intersects both the work of scholars who have sought to rethink the category of space in political and social terms and the scholarship of those who have examined the rich spaces of the southern United States and New Orleans.

Our essays complement theoretical conversations initiated by sociologist Henri Lefebvre, who explored the notion of space as a socially constructed, historical meaning-making process—not merely a container of human activity—and by scholars such as American geographers Edward Soja and Yi-Fu Tuan. Both men advanced the perspective of what is called postmodern geography by elucidating the role played by humans' feelings and interactions with their environments in constructing space. British geographer Doreen Massey has countered and given nuance to such claims by arguing for the ways in which constructions of place are always competitive and heterogeneous, possessing global as well as local dimensions.[8]

Scholars including historian Lawrence Powell, environmental historian Craig E. Colton, and geographers from Peirce Lewis to Richard Campanella have painstakingly traced the inescapably entangled, shifting human and natural histories involved in the making of the space that became New Orleans.[9] Drawing on the work of such historians and geographers, cultural studies critics like Thadious Davis and Barbara Eckstein have sought to understand the nature and ongoing consequences of collective stories responding to southern and especially New Orleanian physical and social environments. Davis examines how marginal enclosures of segregation have been reimagined and rewritten in African American folk stories and practices and in the novels of major twentieth-century African American writers. Such narratives have reframed and newly related the story and "place" of African Americans in the making of the South and of New Orleans. Concerned with what it might mean to "sustain" New Orleans environmentally as well as culturally, Eckstein was uncannily prescient in articulating how urban design and planning must take into account competing stories and cultural practices in the often-feminized city, even as, in the aftermath of Katrina (just as her book appeared), some local narratives were being undermined and discounted.[10]

The essays collected here pose related questions about place and story, but our inquiries emerge from the earlier, specific concerns of a practicing architect, Mac Heard, as he contemplated the types, uses, and tangible and intangible qualities of a particular kind of space in New Orleans: in-between or interstitial space.[11] Our focus is thus not explicitly on general theories of space, but on the critical purchase afforded by exploring instances of a distinctive kind of space; not on the South as region, nor solely on the bounded area of New Orleans, but rather on a range of sweet spots that have historically emerged out of the city and helped to shape certain urban practices and narratives in the city. We explore and meditate on some of the different processes—national, international, and local—by which in-between spaces come into being and accrue associations from a wide variety of positions. In so doing, we seek not to answer unequivocally but instead to complicate questions about how diversely conceived sweet spots in New Orleans have historically furthered, exposed, disputed, expanded, or celebrated assumptions, hopes, or anxieties about race, gender, class, community, history, and even nature itself.

A collection like this cannot possibly address all types or dimensions of interstitial space in New Orleans, nor can it provide, other than indirectly, comparisons with the in-between spaces of other cities. As atlas makers and urbanists Rebecca Snedeker and Rebecca Solnit have recently observed, whatever one says about New Orleans "requires more elaboration."[12] We hope that our conversations will invite elaborations from still other perspectives. We are scholars of architecture, art history, English, African American studies, geography, the history of jazz, philosophy, sociology, and women's studies. Our essays incorporate architectural history, architectural practice, literary texts, paintings, drawings, photographs, music, dance, and statistics. Our styles differ. Seeking to address a broad audience, contributors use the personal essay, photojournalism, the manifesto, or, more commonly, critical and cultural analysis. Still, we share a common goal: to explore how Mac Heard's insightful understanding of in-between space can serve as a productive lens for describing, revealing, interpreting, and relating distinctive sweet spots in New Orleans whose significance might otherwise be missed.

The structure of this collection is loosely analogous to the concept it explores, using brief editorial interspaces to comment on associations between and among essays in each of the text's six sections. We begin by literally and purposefully situating the concept of in-between space in features of New Orleans's history, topography, and housing types and then turn to different kinds of practices and stories that have developed in relation to specific spaces. We end with a broader philosophical meditation on New Orleans itself as an interstitial space, apocalyptically balanced between catastrophe and revelation, destruction and reinvention.

NOTES

1. See Richard Campanella, "Seeing the Elephant," chapter 7 of this volume.

2. Architecture scholars Stephen Verderber and David J. Fine define "interstitial" historically in terms of how architects responded in the postwar period to rapidly developing technologies and practices that were making traditional hospitals and scientific laboratories obsolescent. They define "interstitial space" as "a plenum, between two occupied floors that housed all the anatomical support systems of building (HVAC, electrical, and materials transport systems)." Interstitial spaces separated so-called human spaces from service spaces. A premier example in the United States was Louis Kahn's Salk Institute for Biological Studies (1960–62) in La Jolla, California. See Stephen Verderber and David J. Fine, *Healthcare Architecture in an Era of Radical Transformation* (New Haven: Yale University Press, 2000), 63. Architect Peter Eisenman defines the term more generally, commenting that the interstitial "could be considered as a formal trope, as a solid figuration known as a poché. Poché is an articulated solid between two void conditions, either between an interior and exterior space, or between two interior spaces." While this definition bears initial similarities to that of Verderber and Fine, Eisenman then broadens it in more theoretical directions to consider how a reconceived "interstitial" might both manifest and contest social relations of power. For Eisenman, "interstitial" space should be apprehended in its "*affective* difference from its condition as articulated presence between spaces." His reformulation encourages us to start thinking about what he dubs the revolutionary power of spacing, as opposed to forming. Eisenman's notion of the "interstitial" bears suggestively on several essays in this volume, especially that of John Clark. See Peter Eisenman, "Processes of the Interstitial: Spacing and the Arbitrary Text," in *Blurred Zones: Investigations of the Interstitial: Eisenman Architects, 1988–1998*, ed. Peter Eisenman et al. (New York: Monacelli Press, 2003), 94–101.

3. For Klingman's expanded definition and his own practical applications, see his "Harmony Street," chapter 4 of this volume. For Heard's comments, see *French Quarter Manual: An Architectural Guide to New Orleans's Vieux Carré* (Jackson: University Press of Mississippi, 1997), 7, hereinafter *FQM*. Mac Heard's teacher at the Tulane School of Architecture, Bernard Lemann, famously articulated a view, shared with his colleagues, Samuel Wilson Jr. and John Lawrence, that the New Orleans French Quarter should be conceived not as a collection of individual buildings but as a *tout ensemble* whose spatial interrelations were central to the area's aesthetic effects and cultural meanings. For Lemann's elaboration of this view, see *The Vieux Carré—A General Statement* (New Orleans: School of Architecture, Tulane University, 1966).

4. The question has an immense interdisciplinary history. In this volume, the focus is often on the intersection of the social or political and the phenomenological.

For one preeminent modern touchstone often taught in design classes at the Tulane School of Architecture, see French phenomenologist Gaston Bachelard, *The Poetics of Space*, trans. Maria Jolas (Boston: Beacon Press, 1969). For a recent critical discussion of Bachelard's influence, see Joan Ockman, "*The Poetics of Space*, by Gaston Bachelard," in "Representations/Misrepresentations and Reevaluations of Classic Books," special issue, *Harvard Design Magazine* 6 (1998). See also "Learning from Interdisciplinarity," special issue, *Journal of the Society of Architectural Historians* 64, no. 4 (2005), particularly the introduction by Nancy Stieber, 417–18. Architect Adam Scharr draws on Marxist cultural theorist Raymond Williams in his "Introduction: A Case for Close Reading," in *Reading Architecture: Researching Buildings, Spaces, and Documents* (London: Routledge, 2012), 2–12. For a reading using psychoanalytic theory, see Catherine Belsey, "Quality beyond Measure: Architecture in the Lacanian Account of Culture," in *Quality Out of Control: Standards for Measuring Architecture*, ed. Allison Dutoit, Juliet Odgers, and Adam Scharr (London: Routledge, 2010), 188–97. For a philosophical perspective integrating Marxist, phenomenological, and psychoanalytic theory, see Slavoj Žižek, *The Parallax View* (Cambridge, MA: MIT Press, 2009). For a specific architectural commentary by and on Žižek, see Slavoj Žižek, "Architectural Parallax: Spandrel and Other Phenomena of Class Struggle," lecture delivered at the Jack Tilton Gallery, New York City, April 23, 2009, as discussed by Lahiji Nadir, "In Interstitial Space: Žižek on 'Architectural Parallax,'" *International Journal of Žižek Studies* 3, no. 3 (2009), 1–19. See also the scholars discussed in the notes below and in the bibliography.

5. See Heard, *FQM*, 8, 18–20. *Yancy Derringer* was set in New Orleans during Reconstruction and ran on CBS television in 1958–59. Mac often joked about its unexpected architectural influences in his classes. Bernard Lemann also mentions the show and comments on its effects on the city's suburban architecture. See Lemann, *The Vieux Carré*, 29.

6. See jazz historian Bruce Boyd Raeburn's description of "sweet spots" in chapter 10 in this volume.

7. Heard, *FQM*, 8. "A book such as this Manual, principally analytical, shows only part of a picture, an intellectualized taxonomy of pieces. But it is obliged to acknowledge the other realm of the associational, the experiential."

8. Lefebvre's most influential work was *La production de l'espace* (1974). *The Production of Space*, trans. Donald Nicholson-Smith (Oxford: Oxford University Press, 1991). Soja is best known for *Postmodern Geographies: The Reassertion of Space in Critical Social Theory* (London: Verso Books, 1989) and for the concepts elaborated in *Thirdspace: Journeys to Los Angeles and Other Real-and-Imagined Places* (Oxford: Basil Blackwell, 1996). Yi-Fu Tuan developed his notions of "humanistic geography" and "topophilia" in several works, most famously *Space and Place: The Perspective of Experience* (Minneapolis: University of Minnesota Press, 1977). Doreen Massey, concerned with the politics of meanings granted to space, especially in the inseparability of global and local, has also written about space and gender. See especially *For Space* (London: Sage Publications, 2005), 1–8 and 177–95; and *Space, Place, and Gender* (Minneapolis: University of Minnesota Press, 1994).

9. See Lawrence Powell's comprehensive history, *The Accidental City: Improvising New Orleans* (Cambridge, MA: Harvard University Press, 2012); Craig E. Colton, *Unnatural Metropolis*, Baton Rouge: Louisiana State University Press, 2006); Peirce Lewis, *New Orleans: The Making of an Urban Landscape*, 2nd ed. (Santa Fe, NM: Center for American Places; Charlottesville: University of Virginia Press, 2003); and the many important studies of Richard Campanella, including *Geographies of New Orleans: Urban*

Fabrics before the Storm (Lafayette: Center for Louisiana Studies, 2006); and *Bourbon Street: A History* (Baton Rouge: Louisiana State University Press, 2014).

10. See Thadious Davis, *Southscapes: Geographies of Race, Region, and Literature* (Chapel Hill: University of North Carolina Press, 2011), especially her introduction, 1–21. See also Barbara Eckstein, *Sustaining New Orleans: Literature, Local Memory, and the Fate of a City* (London: Routledge, 2006). Our contributors share Davis's and Eckstein's concern with how different stories and practices of space can be critically used to sustain New Orleans.

11. Heard's development of ideas about interstitial or in-between space came from his own training at Tulane (see note 3), his architectural practice, and his teaching and writing, especially his *French Quarter Manual*. He expanded his exploration of the cultural meanings associated with interstitial or in-between spaces in New Orleans as a Cultural System, a course he team-taught for a decade with Teresa Toulouse. The class, which included students from then Tulane and Newcomb Colleges, the Freeman School of Business, and the School of Architecture, was featured in the *Chronicle of Higher Education* in March 1994.

12. Rebecca Snedeker and Rebecca Solnit, "Sinking in and Reaching Out," in *Unfathomable City: A New Orleans Atlas*, ed. Rebecca Solnit and Rebecca Snedeker (Berkeley: University of California Press, 2013), 1.

SWEET
SPOTS

INTERSPACE ONE ❖ *City Palimpsest*

Scott Bernhard and Ruth Salvaggio begin this volume by reading contemporary New Orleans as a palimpsest, revealing in its layers a range of uneven agricultural and urban breakdowns and choices that result in spatial configurations both intended and surprising. A scholar and practitioner of architecture, Scott Bernhard explores past and current possibilities for dwelling, community, and visual pleasure opened up by the need for certain city streets to adapt to an entangled human history and to a winding river. Salvaggio, a literary critic, explores how the breakdown of the plantation system eventuated in a range of available new spaces that became cultivated as urban gardens by formerly enslaved peoples and immigrants. Arising out of the fragmentation wrought by urban change and war in the nineteenth century, these small, dense, sometimes hidden gardens become for her an image of social and cultural renewal for the city in the protracted moment after Hurricane Katrina.

CHAPTER ONE

Interstitial Urban Space

Inhabiting the Pleats and Notches in the Urban Fabric of New Orleans

—Scott Bernhard

Pleats and Notches

The curious and sometimes perplexing street pattern of New Orleans was generated by the successive overlay of three circumstances—unique riparian geography, idiosyncratic agricultural subdivisions in the eighteenth century, and a tumultuous expansion of population throughout the nineteenth century. The historical exigencies that created the city's alternating sequence of ordered neighborhoods and the jumbled zones between them are as intricate and variable as the delta landscape itself. Positioned adjacent to the dramatic undulations of the Mississippi River, the pattern of streets in the city is, as many careful observers have come to know, a nearly indecipherable manifestation of discrete orders layered simultaneously, one upon another. Each layer in this system is the trace of an effort to reconcile an urgent need of the moment with a rich but ambiguously soft land.

As will become evident in this essay, a combination of factors—from the organization and land-use patterns of plantations to the conflicting geometries of orderly grids and irregular curves—conspired to produce the complex urban landscape of New Orleans. As the order of streets and neighborhoods in the city unfolded, seams and interstitial zones appeared in the irregular collisions of regular parts. The order of streets and avenues in New Orleans produced nearly as many contorted and irregular urban blocks as it did regular ones, but as the building stock of the city adapted to the irregularities of the system, valuable landmarks and important urban spaces emerged that helped to lend a revelatory clarity to the more conventional and regular areas of urban growth.

Two of the most common anomalies in the pattern of New Orleans are the pleats and notches in the urban fabric of the city. Pleats formed when the regularly platted blocks of one former agricultural plantation crashed into an adjacent sliver of plantation land on a different geometric orientation. Notches were generated when oddly stretched city blocks developed fissures, allowing access deep into the normally private inner areas of the block. While the triangular pleats sometimes generated neighborhood green markets, small parks, and small institutional buildings on otherwise unusable parcels of ground wedged between former plantations, the notches often generated tiny streets or alleys occupied by small-scale houses—comprising an interstitial world of compact living. A closer examination of the Upperline Street pleat with its neighborhood green market and the Martinique Alley notch with its four tiny houses will open a window to the rich urban life occupying the interstitial zones between stretches of the more rational and regular urban grid of New Orleans.

Part I
A Crescent of High Ground

New Orleans is known as the Crescent City due to its location on the quarter-moon-shaped strip of relatively high ground deposited by the Mississippi River along its banks. As it nears the Gulf of Mexico, the Great River writhes and twists, forming dramatic curves along its path. Each season, in the time before artificial levees, the river would overtop its channel and deposit rich sediment along its banks. Over many years, the deposits of sediment created higher ground along the river's edge, forming ridges along the course of the water and creating some of the only high ground for dozens of miles in all directions. The French Quarter (the original city of New Orleans) was located on this curving strip of land along the river. Agricultural plantations then stretched up and down the river from the French Quarter, following the arable land of the riverbank.[1]

The Organization of Plantation Properties

Each plantation along the Mississippi River was configured as a narrow slice of the riverbank, extending from the edge of the river back into the low-lying cypress swamps beyond the arable land. A plantation property was described as a length of river frontage measured with the French unit *arpent* (one arpent—when used as a measure of linear distance—is

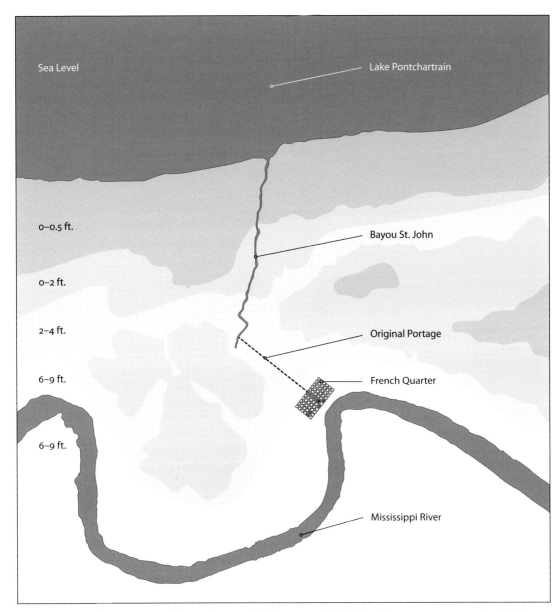

Figure 1.1. New Orleans was originally a small street grid adjacent to the Mississippi River, near an access point to Lake Pontchartrain. Since the mouth of the Mississippi was difficult to navigate, most vessels entered Lake Pontchartrain from the Gulf of Mexico and transferred their cargo across the thin band of land between the lake and river. All cargo moving up or down the Mississippi passed through New Orleans, making it the gateway to much of North America. This advantageous position came at a cost, however, since this narrow strip of high ground beside the river was surrounded by low-lying swamp. Drawing by Scott Bernhard, Catherine Nguyen, and Anne Peyton.

about 192 US feet or 58.5 meters).[2] Plantations upriver from the French Quarter were typically between three and twenty-three arpents wide. When the river frontage of a property was determined, property lines were extended back, away from the river, to establish the long side

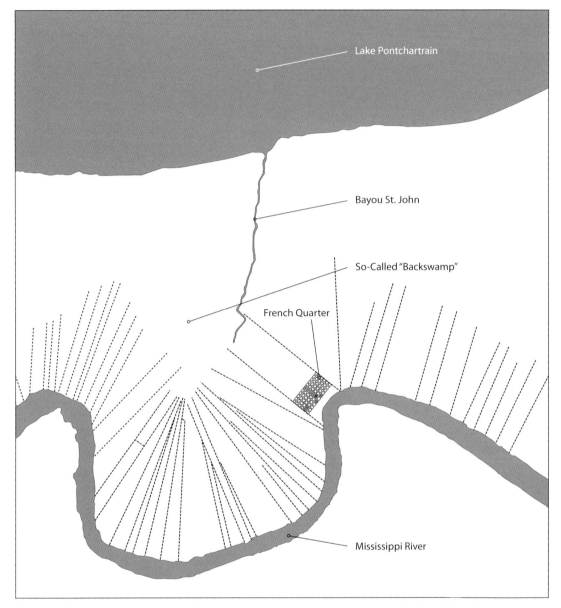

Figure 1.2. The radiating property lines of eighteenth-century plantations are depicted with dashed lines. Each plantation had river access, creating long, thin slices, as of a pie, up and down the Mississippi River from the city. Since the Mississippi represented the front of each plantation, the area of low, swampy ground toward Lake Pontchartrain was the back; hence the phrases "backswamp" and "back of town." Drawing by Scott Bernhard, Catherine Nguyen, and Anne Peyton.

boundaries of the plantation. When the river curved, however, some complexity emerged since the lines extending from the river's edge were perpendicular to the tangent of the curving river at any point. Thus, when the river made convex curves, plantation boundaries became shaped like a long, thin slice of pie—tapering from the wide river-front-age back to a point of convergence often lost in the low-lying swamps beyond. When the river made a concave curve, the plantation boundaries would splay outward from the river's edge, growing wider and wider until, again, they were lost in the cypress swamp.

Along most of New Orleans's riverbank, the Mississippi makes a convex curve, and the plantations were arrayed like slices of a large, somewhat irregular pie. Each plantation property had its essential riverfront exposure to support commerce and provide a point of reliable water access. Plantation houses were constructed at the front, or river edge, of the property and typically faced the river as a house would face a street. This configuration positioned the plantation house on the highest ground, closest to the river. Agricultural buildings, servant or slave housing, and planted areas were organized toward the lower-lying land at the back of the property.

Platting and the Subdivision of Agricultural Land

As the population of New Orleans grew throughout the nineteenth century, new land was needed to accommodate the new arrivals flooding into the expanding city. Plantation owners and their heirs came to find themselves in possession of land that was originally outside the city boundaries and that was, suddenly and advantageously, located very close to the growing urban network as it spread up and down the Mississippi from the French Quarter. As it became more profitable to organize agricultural land into streets and lots than to continue with farming, each plantation was eventually platted in an orderly grid of streets and the land sold in small residential or commercial lots. When superimposing a street grid upon each pie-shaped plantation, surveyors would first establish a wide central boulevard and then create standard, square blocks at right angles to that central boulevard's axis. As the rectangular grid moved outward toward the tapering edges of the pie-shaped plantation, the regular geometry of the blocks would collide with angular boundary lines and yield residual blocks with triangular and trapezoidal shapes.[3]

To add to the geometric complexity of the boundary areas, the sequence of plantation platting was not as contiguous or sequential as it might have been. In the 1834 map by Charles F. Zimpel, for instance, we can observe a series of platted and unplatted plantations continuing up the river from the French Quarter with only one road (St. Charles Avenue) connecting the urbanized areas across the intervening and still agricultural plantations. Thus, when each plantation became a gridded city segment, it did so in isolation from the other segments that proceeded and followed it. Each newly urbanized plantation was described as a faubourg or suburb of the city, and some were even towns in their own right, albeit briefly. Later, when all of the plantations had succumbed

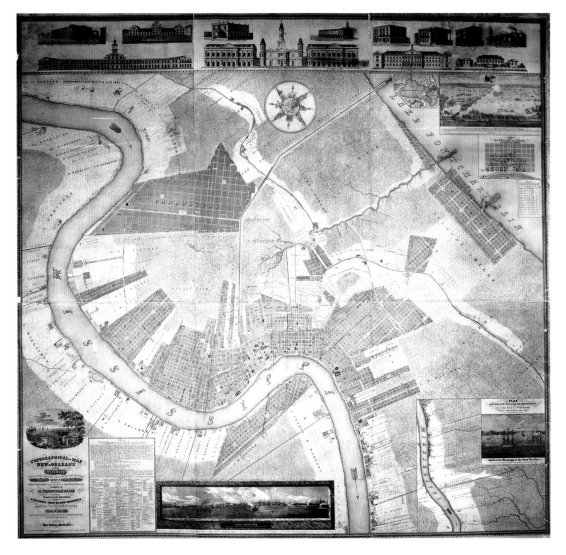

Figure 1.3. The Charles F. Zimpel map of 1834 reveals the incremental and discontinuous process of supplanting the former agricultural order of New Orleans with an urban order based on individually platted (gridded) plantations. Historic New Orleans Collection, acc. no. 1945.13. i–xix.

to the expanding needs of the city, the former plantation boundaries became the awkward joints between the faubourgs, generating irregular block geometries and discontinuous streets.[4]

The Faubourg Bouligny

One such plantation converted to an urban street grid was known as the Faubourg Bouligny.[5] In 1816, Gen. Wade Hampton purchased 23.5 arpents of the former Avart Plantation—a large wedge of land near the

Figure 1.4. Detail of the 1834 Zimpel map, which highlights the street grid or platting of the Faubourg Bouligny. Many resulting irregular blocks can be seen at the edges of the former plantation where the new urban order abuts the site's former agricultural order. Historic New Orleans Collection, acc. no. 1945.13. i–xix.

center of the crescent. General Hampton ran the plantation under the name of the Cottage Plantation until 1829, when he sold the agricultural land to Louis Bouligny. Bouligny and two business partners had the property platted in 1834 and then mapped by cartographer Charles F. Zimpel. The resulting neighborhood at the heart of the crescent city was called the Faubourg Bouligny. Zimpel's plan for the streets presented an almost perfectly symmetrical organization of blocks arranged in mirrored formation around a central spine named Napoleon Avenue. With its grand central avenue and regular blocks extending upriver and downriver, the new faubourg was a clean, formal system of organizing property—until one reached the tapering edges of the former plantation. General Taylor Street formed the downriver boundary of the faubourg, and Upperline Street, named for the uppermost property line of the former Cottage Plantation, formed the other long boundary. As the system of regular blocks intersected the diagonal lines of the boundaries, streets would periodically merge with General Taylor or Upperline Street, creating a succession of tapering blocks until a final triangle emerged, as the "lesser streets" were absorbed into the former plantation boundary lines. This gathering of the urban fabric at former plantation edges created what could be described as pleats as the columns of full blocks tapered to a point.

On Orientation in a Crescent

Streets stretching from the Mississippi River back toward Lake Pontchartrain formed the straight and radial (if somewhat irregularly spaced) spokes of a large wheel. Streets parallel to the river formed faceted curves following the turns of the Mississippi. Those faceted curves also became intermittent as they encountered the unplanned intersections of the former plantation boundaries, and numerous jogs back and forth are necessary when one travels on these streets upriver and downriver from any point in the older parts of the city. Of course, St. Charles Avenue and a few other important streets continued parallel to the river without the sporadic jogs in their course, but even in those continuous streets, the old plantation boundaries can be discerned in the kinks or faceted turns, as when the avenue changes direction by a few degrees at each former property line.

In the Crescent City, one's direction of movement can be identified by examining the street; if the street is straight and continuous, it is likely a radial moving from the Mississippi River toward Lake Pontchartrain; if the street is faceted or discontinuous, it is likely that one is moving along a course parallel to the river. In fact, directions in New Orleans are rarely described as north, south, east, or west—but rather as upriver (or uptown), downriver (or downtown), toward the lake, or toward the river. This system of directional terms adapts our orientation to the distortions of the urban grid. In New Orleans, one's sense of direction is linked to the very same geological features that generated the order and pattern of the landscape originally. This system of reckoning by means of fundamental qualities of the landscape and the systems of organization resulting from it is helpful in a city where it is possible to be on the east side of the Mississippi River and simultaneously due west of the river's western bank.[6]

Strangely, although New Orleans is located adjacent to and defined by its proximity to the river, from almost all vantage points within the city, the water itself is hidden from view behind levees and floodwall protection systems. Some familiarity with the urban systems of the city, however, allows the river to be sensed through the orientation of blocks and streets in the urban system. This orientation makes the river a constant, though often unseen, presence in the life of a New Orleanian.

The Palimpsest of Systems

As we have seen so far, the street fabric or network of New Orleans was created through a variety of discrete efforts that attempted to superimpose a regular, rectangular grid of blocks on an underlying plantation system, and not directly onto an undisturbed, natural topography. Understood in isolation, each of the individual systems that generated the urban pattern of New Orleans seems a perfectly logical way of organizing the landscape, adapting a cultural need for clear and repeatable systems of geometric order and subdivision to a specific geographic condition. But when one logical system of order becomes superimposed upon another, and geometric discrepancies and irregularities result, many of the complexities and fascinating idiosyncrasies associated with New Orleans's urban fabric ensue. Like a palimpsest of ancient writing on parchment in which traces of writing once erased emerge ghost-like from the cellular structure of the lambskin, so the agrarian orders of New Orleans's territory rise up at the interstitial seams in the superimposed street patterns of the contemporary city. Time and circumstance, benign neglect and historical drift have picked away at the edges and gaps between the discrete geometric logics of plantation and platted city, creating a fascinating array of unique instances—fertile ground for exploiting the possibilities of meaningful anomaly.

Part II
Along the Upperline Pleat: The Prytania Market

One phenomenon produced by the unreconciled geometries of the plantation wedges and the grid of regularly platted streets is the pinched or pleated blocks occurring along the former plantation boundaries. When one examines a street map of the crescent city, the triangular wedges of streets and blocks are clearly visible. In each pleat, radial streets are

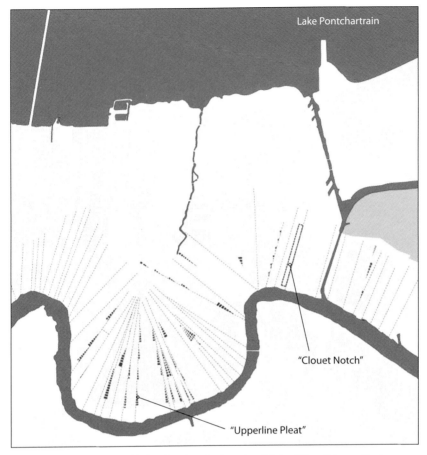

Figure 1.5. This drawing highlights the pleats in the urban fabric of New Orleans. Pleats negotiate the discordant geometries of city parts that were established at different times within the boundaries of a former plantation. Each pleat terminates in a slender triangle of land between merging streets. Difficult to use for conventional purposes, many of these acutely angled properties have become small parks or other urban amenities. Drawing by Scott Bernhard, Catherine Nguyen, and Anne Peyton.

absorbed into a former plantation boundary, merging at acute angles with the dominant boundary street. This confluence of streets produces tapering blocks with narrowing widths until a final, triangular block is created and the lesser radial street is absorbed. This final, triangular block is often a sliver of land too small in area and too acute in geometry to be used as a conventional bit of real estate.

One such triangular pleat of ground lies at the intersection of three streets on the boundary lines of the older Cottage Plantation (Faubourg Bouligny) tract where it borders the smaller, more recently platted F. R. Avart Plantation. Fittingly, the upriver boundary line of the Cottage Plantation became Upperline Street, which, as the dominant radial street, merges with four lesser streets as it moves from the river to the

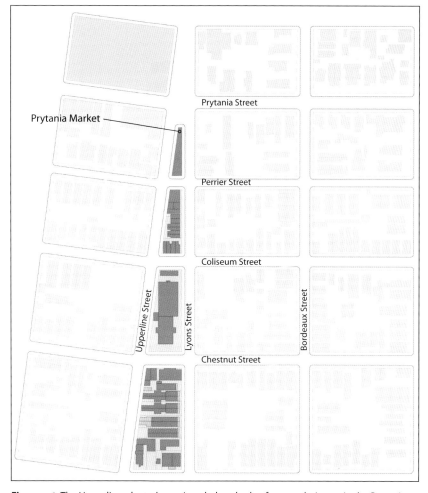

Figure 1.6. The Upperline pleat, shown in a darker shade of gray, culminates in the Prytania Market structure. Ordinary homes occupy the pleat until the shapes of properties become too acute for normal use. Drawing by Scott Bernhard, Sam Levinson, and Catherine Nguyen.

former back swamps of the city. The first of these mergers occurs when Lyons Street ends, merging with Upperline Street just as they both intersect with Prytania Street, which runs nearly perpendicular to the merging radials. Because this intersection occurs at a former plantation boundary, the street parallel to the river, Prytania, is faceted (or kinked) at this point. Thus there are streets arriving at the intersection from four distinct geometric orientations. Of the three streets passing through this intersection, only Upperline Street emerges without an alteration to its geometry.

Prytania Street is an intermittently commercial thoroughfare running parallel to St. Charles Avenue, just a few blocks closer to the river. As such, it forms a significant path though several city neighborhoods

Figure 1.7. The Prytania Market, circa 1920. The oddly elegant market building, dating from 1915, occupies the last sliver of triangular property in the Upperline pleat. The location marks the confluence of Upperline, Lyons, and Prytania Streets. Because Prytania Street jogs at Upperline, the tower becomes a prominent terminus as the market is approached from five different directions. This building was replaced in the 1930s by an enclosed structure, which was demolished in the 1950s with the advent of supermarkets. The Charles L. Franck Studio Collection at the Historic New Orleans Collection, acc. no. 1979.325.3980

and crosses through many former plantation tracts. The four-block area around the intersection of Prytania and Upperline is one such commercial segment, possessing numerous shops, restaurants, and service businesses that line the street up and downriver from Upperline. The triangular parcel at the intersection described above is, today, a small park in the midst of the busy commercial activity. It was once, however, an elegant little green market known as the Prytania Market, and it formed a central hub of activity in the area from the late nineteenth century to the mid-twentieth century.[7]

There were once dozens of open-air municipal markets in New Orleans. Every neighborhood had a market, and most were owned and managed by the city. The Prytania Market was typical of such venues, selling meat, fish, and produce in market stalls though a carefully regulated system that controlled sanitation and fair access for vendors at family-owned stalls under the large market roof. Sanborn insurance maps made in 1895 depict the presence of the Prytania Market, and it was likely on the site for many years prior, though its precise origins are not recorded. The building was photographed in 1915 and the surviving image reveals a wonderful view into the clever design of the market structure, which blended perfectly with its irregular site and made intelligent use of its somewhat awkward and irregular location.

Like most of the municipal markets of the city, the Prytania Market was composed of a large roofed area, open on its sides to the available breezes and sheltered from the sun and rain. There was also an enclosed portion of the market for the sale of meat and fish. In the era before mechanical refrigeration, the meat and fish were sold very fresh or not at all, preserved for short periods by blocks of ice from the nearby icehouse. At the narrow end of the triangular building, a tower rose above the roof, marking the location of the facility and addressing the need for some civic identity in this city-owned neighborhood amenity. The roof and tower were supported by slender iron columns located at the perimeter of the property just inside the inner edge of the surrounding sidewalk. These minimally intrusive supports were ideal for allowing the open area under the roof to merge almost seamlessly with the space of the sidewalk and street in fine weather. Here, at the narrow end of the property, the openness of the structure allowed flexible use of the space that would have been too narrow if enclosed by walls. The enclosed areas of the market were located at the wide end of the site where more conventional techniques of space-making were workable.

The triangular block formed in the Lyons/Upperline pleat has an area of only 1,875 square feet. A typical block in New Orleans measures 300 feet on each side and contains about 90,000 square feet. Typical residential building lots on a standard block are thirty feet wide and 120 feet deep, or 3,600 square feet. Since the pleated blocks became so small and so oddly shaped, they have been very difficult to use for traditional residential structures or small retail buildings. Appropriately, the city took ownership of most of these tiny parcels and, in times past, found ways to convert such unworkable fragments of the urban order into modest amenities for the community. The Prytania Market, among many others, was one such municipal use for an anomalous urban fragment.

Though emerging as the leftover elements of a more formal urban vision, the pleats do have one unexpected characteristic that helps to establish them as significant components of the urban system. As one moves along a street parallel to the river, oblique views of houses or commercial establishments at the kinks in the street create a bounded condition—making the street a comprehensible space rather than a perceptually continuous system. This condition of visually bounded streets places emphasis on those buildings located at the turns, making odd landmarks at some of the most informal junctures in the urban fabric.

When it stood, the Prytania Market, with its tower at the point of the block, was visible as such a bounding landmark. The market served as an obvious amenity in the neighborhood and, fittingly, as a landmark and bounding device at a turn in Prytania Street. The tower of the Prytania Market was visible for many blocks in both directions of Prytania Street not because of its great size or splendor but because of its position at an interstitial seam in the city fabric.

Sadly, the introduction of supermarkets to the New Orleans area throughout the 1950s made the open-air green market seem obsolete, and most of them disappeared shortly thereafter. Of the dozens of markets active in the late nineteenth century, only the French Market in the French Quarter remains under municipal ownership today (though more as a tourist attraction than as a true green market). The Prytania Market disappeared with the rest. The point of the Upperline/Lyons pleat is now a small, simple park within the busy commercial district of Prytania Street.

Part III
In the Montegut-Clouet Notch—Martinique Alley

The history of plantation boundaries is more complex in the parts of the city downriver from the French Quarter (or "below" the French Quarter) than in the band of systematic plantations above it. Still, it was the original organization of agricultural property in the downriver neighborhoods of the Faubourg Marigny and Bywater that generated the geometry of their streets and blocks. Downriver from the French Quarter, agricultural properties were platted along a concave stretch of riverbank. This produced splaying boundary lines in some places and created two new kinds of grid distortion in their wake. The first of these anomalies is identical to the pleat discussed previously—but positioned in reverse. Here the pleat presents its narrow end to the river and opens to low swampy ground beyond. Instead of closing the street grid and gradually eliminating streets as they merge with boundary lines, the pleats below the French Quarter open the grid and add new streets as they continue. Once the boundary line of the Faubourg Marigny, the Franklin Avenue pleat began at Chartres Street and created new streets as it traveled along: first St. Roch Avenue emerged, followed by Music, Arts, and Painters Streets. Over the course of the nineteenth-century urban expansion of the city, this process continued as four more streets were added until the system eventually disappeared into the marshy land beyond the current Florida Avenue.

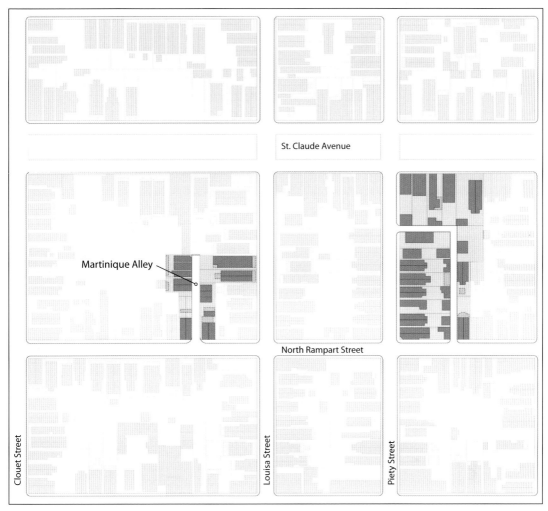

Figure 1.8. The small homes of Martinique Alley, once part of the Faubourg Clouet and now in the Bywater neighborhood, are indicated in darker shades of gray, indicating the handful of properties adjacent to this intimate public way. Two homes fronting on North Rampart Street bracket the entrance to the alley. Drawing by Scott Bernhard, Sam Levinson, and Catherine Nguyen.

More interesting than a pleat in reverse, however, was the emergence of several wide blocks, occasioned by the oddly sporadic platting of downriver plantation properties in very small increments. In particular, many blocks of the former Montegut and Clouet Plantations were configured with a typical depth of about three hundred feet, but with a much greater width than the conventional three-hundred-foot block of the city. These wide blocks of the former Faubourg Montegut and Faubourg Clouet are cut with notches in several places—allowing semi-public streets to venture into the normally private world of the inner block. Such a street or alley exists in a block near the former boundary of the

Figure 1.9. Three small homes on Martinique Alley can be seen here fronting the narrow alley. No fewer than a half-dozen cats are normally observed in this secluded inner-block world at any time. Photograph by Scott Bernhard.

Faubourgs Montegut and Clouet in a short street segment called Martinique Alley. Here, the expansion or stretching of the systemic urban fabric yields an unexpected gap exploited by several small houses operating in the interstitial zone between the scale of the traditional street and the much smaller scale of the outbuildings of a block interior.

The platting of the downriver plantations to create the neighborhood now known as Bywater was accomplished in much finer increments than those of the larger upriver plantations such as Bouligny.[8] Still, the pattern of converting agricultural land to urban tracts was much the same. In 1804, Joseph Montegut purchased a plantation just downriver from a landmark cotton press facility (now Press Street), and sometime later his heirs platted the two-and-one-half-arpent tract to become the Faubourg Montegut in about 1830. Similarly, the De Clouet family gradually amassed a seven-arpent tract just downriver from Montegut between 1801 and 1809 that became the Faubourg Clouet. Uniquely, a street did not mark the boundary line between the Faubourgs Montegut and Clouet; the dividing line merely passed through the middle of the blocks between Montegut and Clouet Streets. For reasons no longer clear, this resulted in the first of three rows of longer blocks in rows moving back from the river. Each of these long blocks (the last two separated by a rather diminutive block) was occasionally penetrated by a narrow alley or a strange *T*-shaped lot allowing access to the large block interior.

The center of most New Orleans blocks is populated by abundant greenery, small out buildings and, in the case of the grander houses, servants' quarters. Since the buildings of the city typically front the sidewalks with little or no setback, the blocks' interiors are almost always rather open, even somewhat naked. In the case of one long block between Clouet and Louisa Streets, the block interior is uncharacteristically exposed through the introduction of Martinique Alley. As the alley penetrates the block interior, it moves between two typical houses on North Rampart Street. The alley then begins to engage the back buildings and appurtenances of the street-fronting lots and finally arrives at the first of four diminutive homes near the block interior. The size of the lots and of the buildings fronting Martinique Alley is necessarily small, since the properties use the narrow width of a standard lot as their length. Thus the properties of Martinique Alley range from about sixteen hundred to eighteen hundred square feet, while the one-story houses are correspondingly small, with interior spaces of nine hundred square feet or fewer.

The intimate scale of the Martinique Alley homes compounds the already tight proximity of most New Orleans houses and begins to merge the tiny world of the alley with the quirky array of service buildings on the adjacent properties. A shed at the rear of one typical property stands next to an alley house, inviting a comparison of size and revealing the shift in scale occasioned by the interstitial occupation of the block interior. The close proximity of the homes in the alley makes for a small community within the community of the block, and the homeowners of the alley are a tight-knit group quietly going about their lives on a seldom-noticed street. (In fact, some digital mapping systems omit Martinique Alley entirely from their images of the city.)

Martinique Alley was originally called Josephine Alley and was cut fully through the block in an *L* shape to emerge around the corner on Louisa Street. On another stretched block two streets away, Rosalie Alley forms a mirror image of the former Josephine Alley, populated by a few tiny cottages and merging identically with the surrounding block interior. Passing through these alleys one has the peculiar feeling of an accidental interloper. The shift in scale of the environment, the tight proximity of each structure, and the intimacy of the dwellings create an atmosphere of privacy and of a closed community encountered by invitation only. Visitors to the alleys experience a place between the normative city and the hidden back-lot realm of gardens and service spaces. Once again, the overlay of land-use systems has yielded a strange, interstitial condition, exploited in this instance by a semi-private and miniature neighborhood.

At Martinique and Rosalie Alleys, we find a direct inversion of the conditions described at the Prytania Market. Where the upriver urban pattern at the market conspired to aggrandize a modest structure and present it with maximum exposure to the commercial street, the pattern of fissures into stretched blocks downriver serves to conceal a discrete segment of the city, merging it with the tranquility of the block interior well away from the activity of the street grid. That something as prosaic as the organization of properties and the geometry of a curving river can create such disparate and distinctly textured environments within an otherwise orderly and continuous system is fascinating.

Of System and Anomaly

Though there are a few instances of conventional urban hierarchy in New Orleans, such as the intersection of major radial boulevards like Napoleon Avenue with continuous perpendicular boulevards like St. Charles Avenue, on the whole, the street grid of New Orleans is a patchwork of discrete systems held together by the anomalous seams. Unconventional and even unorthodox in many ways, the Crescent City celebrates and exploits its moments of hierarchical order and quirky, circumstantial anomaly with equal vigor. Landmarks emerge by intention and by curious accidents within the complex palimpsest of systems. A deeper understanding of the multi-layered urban orders afforded by a knowledge of the city's history allows the confusing and seemingly disordered patterns of the street network to become a cogent system with simultaneous reference to the geography, the agricultural past, and the contemporary street pattern.

The richness of the urban geography of New Orleans emerges through two acts: in the adaptation of an abstract system of agricultural division to a given topographic situation, and in the juxtaposition and overlap of platting logics. These actions create unexpected hybrid conditions born of logic but manifesting multiple simultaneous orders and the collisions between them. Such conditions may emerge as extroverted, public artifacts—making modest circumstances into valued cultural amenities such as green markets and parks—or as introverted enclaves of intimate dwelling set within the nominal system. In either case, perhaps the layered and circumstantial way of an urban unfolding is valuable beyond its prosaic aims and expedient resolutions. In the Crescent City a potent and richly complex environment has been born of just such unconscious means.

NOTES

1. Peirce F. Lewis, "The Stages of Metropolitan Growth: The Street Pattern," in *New Orleans: The Making of an Urban Landscape*, 2nd ed. (Santa Fe, NM: Center for American Places, 2003), 47–49.

2. Richard Campanella, *Time and Place in New Orleans: Past Geographies in the Present Day* (New Orleans: Pelican, 2002), 85–86.

3. See Sebastian Velez, "Evasive Ground: Axioms of New Orleans' Morphology" and "Fragmentation" in *New Orleans: Strategies for a City in Soft Land*, ed. Joan Busquets and Felipe Correa (Cambridge, MA: Graduate School of Design, Harvard University, 2005) 86.

4. Richard Campanella, "Why Prytania Jogs at Joseph," *Preservation in Print* (October 2013): 18–19.

5. Richard Campanella, *Time and Place in New Orleans*, 93–94.

6. Ibid., 108–9.

7. Ibid., 356–57.

8. Samuel Wilson Jr., *The Creole Faubourgs*, vol. 4 of *New Orleans Architecture* (New Orleans: Pelican, 1974), 19–21.

CHAPTER TWO
The Broken Plantation and the Sweet Space of Gardens

—Ruth Salvaggio

The epigraph that Tennessee Williams chose to open his signature New Orleans play, *A Streetcar Named Desire*, comes from lines written by a young poet who would ultimately commit suicide by jumping into the Gulf of Mexico—"And so it was I entered the broken world."[1] The lines could have been uttered by any of the people who arrived in the city some three centuries ago by way of the gulf, more often than not under the worst of conditions. Or, some three centuries later, the lines might have been uttered by people who managed to survive a great modern flood and came back to pick up the pieces. But in Williams's play, the person who enters this "broken world" is an imaginative yet delusional woman, Blanche DuBois, who rides the Desire streetcar and ends up at a congested corner of Elysian Fields Avenue, between the train tracks and the Mississippi River. In the early colony, this exact site was where the Marigny Plantation stood, surrounded by orange trees and gardens and the river levee. The site had already served as a brewery, a brickyard, and a sawmill before Bernard Marigny subdivided his plantation into streets and residences that would form one of the oldest faubourgs in the city. He named the street where Blanche would eventually arrive the Champs-Elysées, "Elysian Fields." When Blanche enters New Orleans at this precise place, she is stepping into a historically dense and complicated space—not only the site where an actual plantation once thrived, but also where it came undone, where it was transformed into a neighborhood heavily occupied by refugees from the plantation island of Saint-Domingue, especially free women of color, and where its main avenue recalls the mythic gardens of Elysian Fields.[2] Add to this complicated scene the fact that Blanche is arriving from a plantation in Laurel,

Mississippi, and you begin to realize that the space where Williams has set his signature New Orleans play takes root in deeply troubled yet rich soil—in the rapacious plantations of the south, but also in the looming promise of the gardens of Elysian Fields.

Precisely here—between plantation land and Elysian Fields—I would like to situate the gardens of New Orleans, gardens that have cropped up in the midst of plantation breakdown and that have grown all along and within the tightly wedged architecture of the historic city. Because of their interstitial placement within the tight confines of the city's land-scape, these gardens emerge as a special kind of sweet spot in New Orleans, and not only because they crop up on the terrain of so many former sugar plantations. In the place of expansive sugarcane fields and ravenous plantation economies, these gardens have historically offered fertile ground for sustainable and often quite aesthetic plantings. It might not have turned out this way. Vast sugar plantations north of the city and along River Road as far as Baton Rouge have since become Louisiana's toxic petrochemical corridor known as Cancer Alley. And plantations all across the US South have hardly been reclaimed by gardens, emerg-ing instead as monoculture croplands controlled by agribusiness with its own toxic brew of fertilizers and profits, or as pockets cleared for subur-ban development and sundry shopping malls or, along the East and Gulf Coasts, for beach houses, tourist enclaves, and casinos. The fate of plan-tations forms a historically compelling topic all its own, often setting the stage and the stakes for how we use and abuse land on an increasingly fragile planet.[3] I intend to take up a small part of this topic by looking at the historic emergence of gardens on parcels of land that were once plantations in New Orleans—a city that has managed to transform its sugar-saturated plantation soil into sweet spots for replanting.

To enter these gardens, we need to do something like what Tennes-see Williams describes in the epigraph of his play—we need to enter that broken world. I invoke the play *Streetcar* not because "that rattle-trap street-car that bangs through the Quarter, up one old narrow street and down another," as Blanche calls it (scene 4), will necessarily take us to some idyllic reincarnation of Elysian Fields by the river. Instead, the very narrow streets and in-between spaces that we encounter in *Streetcar*, if not in the path of Desire itself, show how some particularly transforma-tive gardens do not replicate the plantation structure at all but emerge instead in the narrowest wedged-in spaces. New Orleans remains a city noted for its grand public gardens—stretching across time from the colonial Place d'Armes to the late twentieth-century Besthoff Sculpture Garden in City Park, and including a host of historic gardens that have marked the city's geography—Lafayette and Coliseum Squares, Tivoli

Gardens, the Carrollton Hotel and Gardens, and the historic Garden District itself, to name only a few. Yet most gardens in the city find their place tightly wedged into the cramped and curving spaces that define this urban topography. Here we encounter the greenery and trees of neutral grounds that meander between city streets, creating miniature habitats where at least one species of South American parrot has taken up residence. We encounter gardens draping down from balconies, sprouting from pots on front porch steps, extending along narrow alleyways between shotgun houses and elongated lots or nestling at their farthest end, and creeping along back sheds and fences. Gardens "in back" seem apocryphal in New Orleans, ranging from the back of the house to the back of the town and historically centered on the backwoods known as Congo Square.

Such gardens are a far cry from plantations built on landscapes cleared and cultivated by enslaved people. Something about the varied gardens of this city—perhaps their relentless tropical growth, their extending vines and tree roots, or the way they can at times become intensely clustered in the tightest spaces—gives them a certain creative and invasive energy that pervades the city. Historians have often noted that the diverse Creole community that shaped the city's culture also shaped its agriculture and food markets, informing a distinctly Creole horticultural tradition that proved to be generative, adaptive, and resilient. This pervasive vegetative energy may be what continues to save the city in the wake of disaster after disaster, in the way, for example, that vegetation often grew uncontrollably around flooded houses and ruined yards after Hurricane Katrina, in the impressive number of community gardens that have reoccupied the narrow lots of flooded and demolished houses, and in the area in City Park known as Grow Dat, where vegetable plots abound. Whatever the source of their vegetative vitality, the city's gardens have converted the addictive monoculture crops of plantations—sugar being the most prominent in Louisiana—into remarkably aesthetic, sustainable, and sustaining grounds.

If Blanche DuBois shows us how to enter what is at once the broken plantation and the city that grew within its pieces, it remains for another woman in *Streetcar*—the unnamed, blind Mexican woman who appears along the city's streets near the play's end—to show us how to enter gardens that both recall the past and sustain a future. I invoke these two women from *Streetcar* not to offer another interpretation of a drama that has taken its place as a classic of New Orleans literature, but to use the space it occupies for casting the dramatic history and possibilities of gardening in New Orleans. As I hope to show, gardens that emerge from the bits and pieces of broken worlds can offer much more than beautiful flowers. They present us with sweet spots primed for replanting grim landscapes and for potentially transforming their legacy of human and environmental exploitation.

Plantations have a long history, one that is thought to go back at least to early Mediterranean cultures and is firmly established throughout the modern Atlantic world. New Orleans occupies a special place in this history, its landscape formally and continually divided, along with much of the French colony, according to the European arpent system of elongated parcels of land that offered fertile growing conditions in increasingly narrow spaces. These narrow plots, or groups of them, would typically run from the Mississippi River to the interior landscape, with smaller gardens often occupying the back sector. Not all such parcels of land served as monoculture plantations, but many did, notably for sugar. These extended along the river above and below the original French Quarter settlement—downriver following the original King's Plantation at Algiers Point, and upriver from the Marigny and the Quarter along the original Chapitoulas Coast, present-day Tchoupitoulas Street—each narrow parcel fanning out from the sustaining waters of the river, radiating like a folded paper fan spread open. From the Jesuit Plantation that spanned the area within and beyond what is now the Central Business District, to the Macarty Plantation at Carrollton, these properties provided the skeletal structure for the city as it took shape atop their breakdown. Plantation subdivision commenced from 1788 at the latest, when the Gravier Plantation was parceled into the Faubourg Sainte Marie, to the early years of the twentieth century, when the Burthe Plantation was subdivided into tracts of land that would eventually form Audubon Park and its neighboring communities.[4]

But well before the Central Business District took shape on the grounds of a sugar plantation, the original French settlement was surrounded by a more extensive system of plantations that spread throughout the US South. Laurel, Mississippi, for instance, where Blanche "lost" the family plantation of Belle Reve, marked only one site where cotton plantations covered the landscape, from the Carolinas all the way to Texas. Blanche brings Laurel's sad story to New Orleans, but New Orleans already had deep investments in cotton. While sugar, not cotton, became the prized crop of the city's immediate surrounds, it was King Cotton that was shipped through New Orleans, generating profits reaped by merchants whose home bases extended as far as Philadelphia, New York, and major European cities.[5] Taken together, sugar and cotton shaped New Orleans into one of the wealthiest cities in the United States, at a staggering cost to those field workers whose labor made this wealth possible. New Orleans, too, became the center of the horrifying internal slave market, where millions of enslaved Africans were shipped downriver to be auctioned and sold for work on the vast network of cotton plantations in the surrounding states. When Blanche describes the long parade of deaths on her family plantation in Mississippi, she might as well be talking about a cult of loss and death that pervaded plantation life throughout the modern Atlantic world. She tells her sister: "Why, the Grim Reaper had put up his tent on our doorstep! . . . Belle Reve was his headquarters!" (scene 1). If the Grim Reaper set up his tent on that cotton plantation in Mississippi, he also stalked the streets of early New Orleans where the booty arrived and the profits were gleaned.

Yet New Orleans was also the place where such grim landscapes became vulnerable, and where small gardens *within* the vast plantation structure would provide some of the first sites for plantation breakdown in the emergent urban landscape. The Marigny Plantation, for instance—marking the site where Blanche steps into New Orleans and forming today one of the hippest neighborhoods in the city—at once served as a grand plantation and as a kind of Elysian Fields on which smaller gardens took root. An early drawing of this plantation gives a glimpse of a few small garden plots on the grounds, and a glimpse, too, of a different kind of garden that would eventually become planted across the expanding city. Among these were small gardens tended by slaves for themselves. We know of the existence of such gardens not because pictures of them have been safeguarded in museums and collections, as photos of the Marigny Plantation were, but because we know the history of laws that allowed slaves to grow their own produce and sell it at their markets on Sundays. One might imagine the kinds of fertile gardens that grew in such small spots—fertile not only in the sense that they provided food, but also that their sale generated sufficient profit for slaves to achieve some autonomy and at times purchase their own freedom. Based on information about the large numbers of enslaved people who did precisely that, we can assume that such slave gardens formed a special kind of replanting within plantation economies that in fact inverted the very exploitive labor on which plantations relied.

At least one image of an early slave encampment, across the river from the French Quarter on the King's Plantation at Algiers, is based on a design by Le Page du Pratz, remembered today as the author of the three-volume *Histoire de la Louisiane* published in 1758, but who was also the manager of the King's Plantation in the earliest years of the colony. Although no gardens are identified here, the spatial design of this "Camp des Negres," which separates slave housing from the actual plantation grounds, also shows ample space for gardens that could be wedged between each housing unit.[6] While the spatial separation of the huts actually reflected efforts to monitor and control the people who lived there, it also offers a glimpse of the kind of interstitial space where gardens could be planted, as we know they were in fact planted, both on and off the plantation grounds as well as throughout the tight spaces of the urban French Quarter during the eighteenth century. Emphasizing the importance of these gardens, Lawrence Powell explains how the "self-provisioning" of slaves made the early colonial city into a "veritable African market town" where produce from slave gardens, along with other foods and herbs traded by nearby Indians, proved crucial to sustaining the early colony. Well into the nineteenth century, enslaved Africans continued to till their gardens and fill their markets. Congo Square, known primarily as the place where African song and dance shaped lyrical traditions that would ultimately give the world jazz, was, as well, a world market where the produce of slave gardens was exchanged and from which the city itself was sustained.[7]

Such small, interstitial garden plots take their place among myriad interstitial spaces in New Orleans, as this volume of essays details. Among them are sites and structures wedged into the setting that Williams describes for the opening of *Streetcar*, where Blanche both arrives from and enters into a broken plantation. Here, as the stage directions indicate, we encounter "rickety outside stairs and galleries and quaintly ornamented gables," themselves situated in a section of town where "you are practically always just around the corner, or a few doors down the street, from a tinny piano being played with the infatuated fluency of brown fingers." As if this brown hand reaches out to us from around the corner, or from the recesses of history, from a plantation or maybe from a slave garden, we are pulled into the narrow streets that curve around corners and each other, the sounds of the piano seemingly squeezed out of these same spaces. Even the path of Elysian Fields Avenue, we are told, "runs between the L&N tracks and the river," its interstitial placement both confined between two structures and within the river's curve.

Elysian Fields emerges as a space—on the very site of a former plantation—where gardens take root between streets, alleys, apartments, and houses. And precisely here, plantation afterlife becomes possible. In Greek myth, the Elysian Fields served as the abode of the dead. Ancient writers typically described a place infused with flowers and gardens, wreaths and garlands and shady groves and crystal streams. But they also described a contained, liminal landscape. Plutarch envisioned the Elysian Fields as two islands separated by a narrow strait, as if something needed to be in between the two flowery spaces to make them so profuse and abundant. We might pause to consider the connections that link interstitial space with generative sites—the fingers that produce music on narrow keys of the piano, or the force within the green fuse that drives the flower. But whatever the implications of such a narrow divide, the proximity of Plutarch's islands could well guide us through the confined yet generative spaces of the city's gardens. We get only a sense of the presence of such gardens in the opening stage directions of *Streetcar*, where houses squeezed into the tight constraints of the Quarter are nonetheless cushioned alongside "river warehouses with their faint redolences of bananas and coffee," as if the plantations that produced all these bananas and coffee are recast as a sheer odor, a faint redolence of something far off that is now undergoing transformation. Banana plantations in Honduras and Guatemala thus assume a kind of afterlife in the French Quarter and throughout the city, where banana trees flee the plantation to take up residence in patios and backyards or along alleyways, where their rhizomes spread out from the tightest of intersections. Who could imagine gardens in New Orleans without banana trees? They may not look like they come from the Elysian Fields, but they play their part in the plantation afterlife in New Orleans.

Beginning in the confines of the original French settlement, and then following the river's curve toward Elysian Fields Avenue, we can trace fairly precisely the shaping and development of gardens in the early colonial city and its extending surrounds. In his richly documented book *The History of Designed Landscapes in New Orleans*, Lake Douglas describes the very first drawings of gardens in the French colony, found, of all places, in a set of memoirs that were rendered in epic verse—the first, but hardly the last, alignment of gardens and poetry in the city. One of these drawings, dated around 1730, shows the gardens of the author, Dumont de Montigny, at his own lodging, where we can see "a small house with a detached kitchen and 'pavillion' (privy?), a house and kitchen for 'negroes' (*cuisine ou maison les nègres*), a hen house in a willow tree (with a ladder for access), a trellis, vegetable garden, and orchards in the rear."[8] Another drawing, of the Chouachas Concession, which was established below the city very early in 1719 and was considered one of the most important downriver plantations, shows a similar plan and a garden surrounded by orange trees. Whether or not these designs reflect the reality of the day, they do give us some indication, as Douglas suggests, of the intended, if only partly realized, layout and features of the earliest of gardens within the Quarter and on nearby plantations. Dumont de Montigny's gardens show how much is squeezed into the tight spaces of small square blocks in the original Quarter. In the city's nineteenth-century Notarial Archives, containing watercolors and legal descriptions of such plots of land, this same design is repeated throughout the developing city, often indicating the precise placement

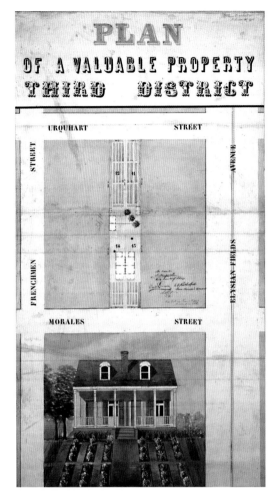

Figure 2.1. "Plan of a Valuable Property, Third District" (1858). Situated between Frenchman Street and Elysian Fields Avenue, this site would be in the Marigny Plantation and the eventual subdivision, very near where Blanche arrives in the city in *A Streetcar Named Desire*. Plan Book Plan 48.64, F. Nicolas Tourné & de L'Isle, June 7, 1858. Courtesy Dale N. Atkins, Clerk of Civil District Court, Orleans Parish, Notarial Archives Division.

of gardens, notably on the oblong parcels that often fostered gardens both in front and in back of the house.[9]

Especially important to observe is that while these gardens reflect aesthetic design, they are also intended to produce sustainable vegetation. It was not until well into the mid-nineteenth century that domestic gardens began to shift from functional to more ornamental modes. Letters and journals from this time indicate a plethora of vegetation that such gardens generated: purple broccoli, pomegranate, asparagus, beets, peaches, plums, lettuce, beans, quince, and oranges.[10] Africans made the most significant contributions to sustainable vegetable gardens in the city, often by cultivating distinctive plants like okra, but also through their expertise in cultivating major crops like rice, the grain that arrived in New Orleans along with a shipment of African slaves who were skilled in its cultivation and who subsequently made rice a reliable source of food in the struggling colony. What we glean from these early descriptions and drawings, then, are the first in a long series of multifaceted gardens in New Orleans—not the plantings and profits of sugar cane, but small sweet spots cropping up everywhere.

Varied kinds of urban gardens thrived. Some reflected the careful designs of colonial planners, but more often, gardens would simply take shape as the city itself evolved—within the compact spaces of the Quarter and then extending into former plantation lands. As Shannon Lee Dawdy has documented, the early city was often a "rogue colony" where the schemes of administrators, including plans for gardens, were always being undercut, improvised, or simply ignored in the tumultuous daily life of early settlement. While urban planners made sure there would be space for gardens that could help sustain its colonial population, and while a "mini-Versailles" sprouted up in the wealthier parts of town, Dawdy reminds us that the sheer effort of maintaining "these gardens against the exuberance of Louisiana's native plant life" gave the city a "disorderly appearance"—and probably sketched the uneven design of exuberant interstitial gardens where almost anything could grow. One can only imagine the task of weeding and pruning on rich river soil once covered by a profusion of tropical and swampy vegetation, where plants sprang up in every available space, and where "garden fancies" needed to be tempered to suit the dense environment. As a result, Dawdy explains, subsistence gardens in the early colony "departed from both the feudal and emerging capitalist models of settled agriculture," the latter a context where the southern plantation loomed large. Colonial gardens, like much early civic design, had to adjust to the "local terrain."[11]

The local terrain turned out to be at once exceedingly fertile and increasingly cramped into smaller and smaller plots of land—which is exactly where interstitial gardening took root. Interestingly, the spatial model for such gardens may have come from the distinctive layout of plantations in French Louisiana. Lawrence Powell offers some important observations about the arpent system whereby each plantation extended from narrow slivers of riverfront to even narrower backwoods. These French concessions in and around New Orleans were not only "tightly packed" but also "close to town." Especially in these regions, "plantations seemed more like an extension of urban life," Powell explains. "Most of the colony's slaves lived within thirteen miles of the center of town," which both "enhanced sociability for *les grands*" and also afforded an "ecology" that "enabled mixing among the slaves."[12] This proximity of plantations and people, intensified on landscapes that were continually subdivided into smaller and smaller units, generated an unusual amount of interchange between people of decidedly different status. Dawdy suggests that these structures affected both people and gardens. Instead of

the large estate, "a *métis* version of rural subsistence arose that readily combined French, African, and Native American practice" governed
by "the necessity of subsistence" in all aspects of life, and especially
in "tending gardens." The small garden plots scattered throughout the
early city, on plantations, and eventually on their subdivided landscapes
became a mélange of gardens that reflected a diverse people living in
close proximity and bringing to their gardens a vibrant mixture of cultivation practices. Dawdy summarizes: "Agriculture was not limited to
the plantation zone, but dominated concerns in New Orleans as well.
French New Orleans was a city of gardens that combined subsistence
and aesthetics." She cites an early engineer who staked out some of the
elongated lots that derived from the narrow arpent structure and who
pointed out "that each and every one may have the houses on the street
front and may still have some land in the rear to have a garden, which
here is half the life."[13]

Half the life of the early city, we might say, grew around interstitial gardens—increasingly wedged into diminutive spaces, sustainable,
beautiful, and reflecting a distinctly Creole culture of diverse inhabitants. If these early gardens produced vegetation cultivated by both
indigenous peoples and Africans, without whose expertise the early colony surely would have starved, the city's gardens also owe a profound
debt to the many migrant populations who continued to arrive in New
Orleans and make it their home. German immigrants, whose vegetable gardens included small farm plots both upriver in the Carrollton
area and downriver in the present-day Ninth Ward and Bywater, left an
especially indelible imprint on both vegetable and flower gardens in the
city. An 1860 census shows that nearly half of those who classified their
profession as farmer, gardener, or florist came from one of the German
states.[14] Along with the influence of these hearty Rhinelanders, horticultural contributions came from virtually every single immigrant group
to arrive in the city—Irish, Sicilian, Honduran, Vietnamese, Mexican,
and even "American" (whose numbers increased significantly after the
Louisiana Purchase), to name only the most prominent. The original
French Market boasted one of the first thoroughly multicultural displays
of vegetation and people in North America. Early descriptions mention a plethora of produce: sassafras root, leaves of plantain, potatoes of
all kinds, bananas, oranges, sugar cane, apples, carrots, corn, rice, and
coffee. Cross-cultural fertilization permeated the city's arpents, garden
plots, and market stalls. On the grounds of former monoculture plantations, a thoroughly Creolized horticulture flourished.

We can trace the legacy of these early gardens into our own times,
often at quite auspicious locations. Tree-filled City Park was once the

Figure 2.2. Poetry featured at the Audubon Zoo, formerly part of the Boré Plantation. Photograph by Ruth Salvaggio.

Allard Plantation, and the present-day New Orleans Botanical Garden, with its historic Rose Garden, remains as one of the few lasting WPA public gardens in the United States. Once a backwater swamp beyond both the city and its riverfront plantations, the park now forms its own interstitial space between Bayou St. John, the modern neighborhoods near Lake Pontchartrain, and the cemeteries, which once marked the city's farthest edge. Tree-filled Audubon Park, site of the former Boré Plantation, where sugar was successfully grown and granulated on a large scale, once featured beautiful gardens around the principal residence—gardens "with magnificent lanes of orange trees," ramparts covered in clover, "retreats of myrtle and laurel," flowers, orchards, and "an abundance of juicy grapes."[15] The place where that garden once stood is now wedged into the landscape of Audubon Park, which now has its own zoological garden. Between and among the dense vegetation that now forms these gardens, poems have recently been dispersed on signs and fences, along walkways and inside fountains, hanging like flowers from the rafters—the result of a project initiated by the National Poetry Foundation. They recall at once the colonial garden described by Dumont de Montigny in the early French settlement, which he rendered in verse, and also the gardenic market of Congo Square, where sung poetry and food sustained the early city.

Congo Square remains the most important poetic garden in New Orleans, the first garden to take shape in the back of town, across Rampart Street, which divided the French Quarter from the backwoods and the outspreading cypress swamps. Here is where Africans sang

the songs that formed the city's lyric traditions and poetic legacy, and
where people exchanged their garden produce at a great world market—the most enduring evidence of the abundance of slave gardens in
the early Americas. The gardens that fed Congo Square, the stalls where
food was exchanged, and the kitchens where that food was prepared,
were all dominated by African women, who thus shaped the interstitial
spaces where marketing took place. As Freddi Williams Evans explains,
marketing commenced along "sidewalks and alleys," "at doors of houses
and businesses," on levees and street corners, with women often "carrying their 'shops' on their heads, calling out their wares with melodic
chants."[16] Among these were the "calas women," whose rice cakes (calas)
were marketed in and around Congo Square, helping to transform rice
from a subsistence product, as it was in the early colony, into one of the
city's evolving Creole cuisine's first delicacies.

The voices of these women calling out their wares—fruits and vege-
tables and flowers and rice cakes—further transmute their markets and
gardens, squeezed along sidewalks, alleys, and corners and seeming to
sprout from their colorful tignons, into an audible resonance that pervades the city and its history. This resonance in turn anticipates what
Tennessee Williams describes as a "faint redolence," a sweet scent that
weaves gardens into the very aura of New Orleans. And it anticipates
the unnamed Mexican woman calling out her wares at the end of *Streetcar*—"Flores. Flores. Flores para los muertos."—flowers for the dead.
Williams portrays her as a ghostly presence, but she is no Grim Reaper.
She is the gardener who bears flowers from the city's broken plantation
landscape. She offers them to Blanche, another woman who bears the
burdens of the plantation but who remains unable to transform that burden into a garden. No wonder that Blanche, both inheritor and victim
of a horrifying plantation history, descends into total delusion—believ-
ing that a Texas oilman will soon arrive to take her on a tour of the
Caribbean. The Caribbean, after all, is where the whole sordid story of
the plantation has its beginnings. And oil empires are exactly what got
built atop the sugar plantations that ran north of New Orleans all the
way to Baton Rouge. The Mexican woman appears dark and deathlike in
Streetcar, selling what Williams specifies in his stage directions as "those
gawdy tin flowers that lower class Mexicans display at funerals and other
festive occasions" (scene 9). Thankfully, in New Orleans, people of different social status were all cramped together in tight spaces where their
varied flowers and vegetation converged as a mélange of gardens permeating the urban landscape. The tin flowers of the Mexican woman, like
the tinny sound of the piano at *Streetcar*'s opening, exude the pervasive
redolence and resonance that issue from the city's gardens.

Figure 2.3. *Woman in a Huipil* (1981) by Mexican sculptor Enrique Alférez, in the New Orleans Botanical Garden in City Park, once part of the Allard Plantation. Photograph by Ruth Salvaggio.

In the swampy backwoods that became City Park, this Mexican woman presides over the New Orleans Botanical Garden as a sculpture carved by Mexican artist Enrique Alférez, entitled *Woman in a Huipil*. Here she is nestled in a garden, staged not as some deathlike premonition, but as a figure almost spinning among flowers. She knows that in the Mexican Day of the Dead commemorations, flowers are a medium of transformation between death and life that have served generations of diverse people in New Orleans who bring flowers to the cemeteries on All Saints' and All Souls' Days. Here in City Park, on the grounds of a former sugar plantation, flowers grace this historic rose garden—a sweet spot all its own, a sign of the enduring presence in New Orleans of plants that crop up everywhere and manage to transform entirely the city's culture and cultivations.

New Orleans is a city that always has needed to transform itself, and its continual outcroppings of gardens have no small significance in our own troubled climate. As we ponder the fate of environments everywhere that have, it seems, been all but ruined by exploitive economies, we might learn a few things from a city that has managed to make space, within the broken world of plantations, for gardens. What can be planted at the back of the house or in the side alley that might grow and prosper? What beckoning sounds can be heard from around the corner, and what scents offer some promising redolence? And what market women, delivering produce and flowers from the city's gardens, might take center stage in a play that recasts the ruin of plantations into zoological gardens that sprout poetry, or into a narrow space between the train tracks and the river where we can reinvent the Elysian Fields? Despite the massive rush of brackish water that poured into the city after Katrina, greenery still sprouted up everywhere, even downriver from the Marigny and throughout the Ninth Ward, where German gardeners once set up their farm plots before an Industrial Canal and the Agriculture Street Landfill brought blight to this area, which is where I grew up. Yet all sorts of exuberant vegetation are growing here amid the remaining desolate, forgotten parcels of land[17]—including the Ninth Ward Community Garden, one of several sustainable vegetable gardens supported by NOLA Green Roots. On this organization's list of over thirty community vegetable gardens in the city, we encounter Word Wise Community Gardens, located in Mid-City, featuring art and poetry, and sustaining a tradition that extends at least from Congo Square to the poetry-infused Audubon Zoo.

Post-Katrina gardens now seem especially devoted to both the aesthetic and functional labor of sustaining a fragile city. Among the myriad replantings across the city's flooded landscape, the water garden is emerging as a site where vegetative growth might be able to sustain a city that is fast going under. New Orleans filmmaker Rebecca Snedeker, looking at the city today, sees it as a "cement lily pad" sinking deeper everyday into its spongy alluvial landscape. As it currently exists, the city is simply unsustainable. Still, Snedeker offers us a different conception of the city, imagining it as floating on water like a water lily. Drawing on the visionary work of architect David Waggoner, she describes how New Orleans's urban landscape can only survive by embracing, not fighting, its encircling waters. Rather than draining the soil, she explains, allow the earth to hold in water in "pockets, crevices, runnels, and depressions, of all scales, in yards, alongside roads, in parking lots, in neighborhood parks."[18] Gardens dispersed throughout the city have always served this function, breaking apart the paved-over urban topography and allowing water to seep in. In another sense, what Snedeker imagines here is an urban water garden all its own—an alluvial city filled with interstitial fluid spaces where water is absorbed "to nourish a variety of plants," and where the city itself is kept afloat: "Imagine New Orleans as an emerald green lily pad, a healthy circulatory system with the vitality and structure that come with hydration. A floating city, with skin that breathes, within a delta coast."

Her description echoes Plutarch's version of the Elysian Fields as flowery islands floating on water. If we imagine the city resembling the namesake of one of its main avenues, then precisely on Elysian Fields Avenue in the Marigny we might visit the American Aquatic Gardens, a small shop whose specialty is combining water and plants. Located where a plantation once thrived before it was broken down, it is not far from where Blanche stepped into a broken world. Here, we might pick up a few supplies for water gardening, along with a few select species of water lilies. Planted throughout the city, in choice little interstitial crevices and pockets that are amply hydrated, water lilies would give shape to the latest in a long line of adaptive Creole gardens that have continually sprung up in this fluid city. And the distinctive lily flower—the fleur-de-lis—would become transformed, yet again, from the perfectly etched design of French heraldry to a Creole flower in an historic garden city that, despite all odds, and often in the midst of them, manages to stay afloat.

NOTES

1. The poet was Hart Crane. See Tennessee Williams, *A Streetcar Named Desire* (New York: New Directions, 1947), opening epigraph. All citations to *Streetcar* are to this edition and will be noted in the text by scene number.

2. See Lawrence N. Powell, *The Accidental City: Improvising New Orleans* (Cambridge, MA: Harvard University Press, 2012), 347–49, for a discussion of the historical shaping of the Faubourg Marigny.

3. Plantation economies have been extensively studied by historians and cultural critics. For a general overview, see Philip D. Curtain, *The Rise and Fall of the Plantation Complex: Essays in Atlantic History* (Cambridge: Cambridge University Press, 1998). While the fates of former plantations vary widely, the transformation of plantations into tourist economies built on the notion of gardenic paradise remains pervasive throughout the southeastern United States and the Caribbean. See, for example, Ian Gregory Strachen, *Paradise and Plantation: Tourism and Culture in the Anglophone Caribbean* (Charlottesville: University of Virginia Press, 2003).

4. For identification and detailed discussion of the layout of these plantations, see Richard Campanella, *Time and Place in New Orleans: Past Geographies in the Present Day* (New Orleans: Pelican, 2002), 88–98. For an explanation of the arpent system of land design, see Campanella, *Time and Place*, 86, and Powell, *Accidental City*, 71–73.

5. See Sven Beckert, *Empire of Cotton: A Global History* (New York: Alfred A. Knopf, 2014), on the fertile land that shaped cotton's vast network of production and exploitation in the Deep South.

6. See Shannon Lee Dawdy, *Building the Devil's Empire: French Colonial New Orleans* (Chicago: University of Chicago Press, 2008), 147–50, for a discussion and an image of the "Plan du Camp des Negres" on the King's Plantation in the late 1720s. The drawing shows a rectangular parcel of land, smaller rectangles within for each camp site, and an open space in the center.

7. See Powell, *Accidental City*, 95–100 and 334–39. On Congo Square as a crucial

early market for the exchange of food, see Jerah Johnson, *Congo Square in New Orleans* (New Orleans: Louisiana Landmark Society, 1995), 5–10, and Freddi Williams Evans, *Congo Square: African Roots in New Orleans* (Lafayette: University of Louisiana at Lafayette Press, 2011), 109–14. Also see "Horticultural Economy of Enslaved Populations" in Lake Douglas, *Public Spaces, Private Gardens: A History of Designed Landscapes in New Orleans* (Baton Rouge: Louisiana State University Press, 2011), 144–45.

8. Douglas, *Public Spaces*, 103–4. Also see Dawdy, *Building*, 83–86, and plate 2.

9. See Douglas, *Public Spaces*, on the Notarial Archives, and also his reprint of twenty color plates from the archives, 123–25, and inset imprints.

10. See Douglas's discussion of early colonial domestic gardens, *Public Spaces*, 105–13.

11. Dawdy, *Building*, 97–98.

12. Powell, *Accidental City*, 72.

13. Dawdy, *Building*, 82–83.

14. Douglas, *Public Spaces*, 177.

15. Ibid., 110, and Campanella, *Time and Place*, 134.

16. Evans, *Congo Square*, 109–110. Also see Powell's description of markets dominated by women, *Accidental City*, 269–70, and my essay, "Eating Poetry in New Orleans," in *Southern Foodways*, ed. David Davis and Tara Powell (Jackson: University Press of Mississippi, 2014), 105–23.

17. See, for example, Nathaniel Rich, "Jungleland: The Lower Ninth Ward in New Orleans Gives New Meaning to 'Urban Growth,'" *New York Times Magazine*, March 21, 2012, 32–48, 56.

18. Rebecca Snedeker, "The Cement Lily Pad," in *Unfathomable City: A New Orleans Atlas*, ed. Rebecca Solnit and Rebecca Snedeker (Berkeley: University of California Press, 2013), 158.

INTERSPACE TWO ❧ *Interstitial Systems*

This section features two architects, Carrie Bernhard and John P. Klingman, who consider structural and architectural features of nineteenth- and early twentieth-century houses and city blocks that developed in response to New Orleans's topography and weather, on the one hand, and to the city's changing patterns of urban growth, on the other. Carrie Bernhard traces how—from the eighteenth-century plantation house to the Creole cottages, shotguns, and townhouses of the nineteenth and early twentieth centuries—architects and builders, while attempting to create comfortable conditions for private domestic life in a hot, humid climate, simultaneously fashioned what she calls an urban "interstitial system" that not only was aesthetically rich and visually pleasing but also staged possibilities for diverse forms of social relations. As a practicing architect living in a nineteenth-century house, John Klingman takes us on a meditative tour of the in-between features, old and new, inside and out, of his own private home in the Garden District. Detailing the kinds of physical and social experiences made possible by living without the now ubiquitous air conditioner, Klingman makes a case for the pleasures and values of "interstitial living."

CHAPTER THREE
Connection, Separation, and Mediation
Interstitial Systems in Traditional New Orleans Architecture

—Carrie Bernhard

The traditional architecture of New Orleans is widely appreciated as one of the city's greatest treasures. The Creole cottage, the Creole townhouse, and the shotgun are three distinct house types that formed in New Orleans during the nineteenth century and that survive today throughout the French Quarter and its surrounding faubourgs, where much of the historical urban fabric remains intact. The venerable age and ubiquity of these traditional house types is unusual for an American city, as is the unique nature of the architecture itself. From the perspective of the observer on the street, the traditional house types of New Orleans are often admired for their picturesque aspect, particularly the overall impression of balconies, galleries and other overhung spaces that layer the fronts of houses and consistently line the city's streets. Visually, these elements cast shadows, create contrast and depth, express hierarchy, and articulate entrances. Spatially, they define an area between inside and outside that buffers the building and its occupants from the harshness of the environment, and they often share this protection with passersby on the street below. Perhaps less noticeable than balconies, galleries, and other overhung spaces, however, are the interstitial spaces that regularly accompany all traditional New Orleans house types but whose importance often goes unrecognized. These are usually very humble and sometimes lowly spaces, such as the crawlspaces between a building's floor and the ground below, the narrow gaps between adjacent buildings, or the shadowy passages that cut through contiguous buildings. Such interstitial spaces are actually part of an entire network of spaces that wraps and sometimes perforates a building in order to amend it to its surroundings. Historically, interstices were integral to

the success of early buildings, tempering the otherwise harsh relationship between the building and its hot, humid environment. Eventually
whole systems of interstices developed to correspond with a specific set
of house types that developed in and are distinctly associated with New
Orleans. Not only do these interstitial systems fulfill crucial functional
requirements within a given building, but they also help to modulate its
formal, spatial, and experiential qualities and mediate the nature of both
the building's habitation and its urban interactions. Taken individually,
interstitial spaces are mere architectural components, but, as a matrix of
systems, they are indispensable constituents of their typologies: vitally
effective, discreetly ubiquitous, and in the range of their variability,
beautifully sophisticated. During the heights of their production, interstitial systems were vital to the original success of New Orleans house
types and remain so even now, constituting much of the enduring appeal
and relevance of traditional New Orleans architecture.

Architectural interstices can be understood in a number of ways
depending on scale and perspective. In contrast to the interstices that
comprise the intervening voids between the structural components of
a building, the interstices examined here involve the intervening spaces
that are both habitable in scale and adjacent—but subordinate—to a
building's principal interior spaces. The sheer variety of such interstices
can be observed to form an entire taxonomy based on their relationship to the main volume of the building, whether they are integrated or
applied, open or enclosed.[1]

The original necessity for interstices as a building strategy is illustrated in the early construction efforts of the French colonists in Louisiana during the beginning of the eighteenth century. Applying the same
building methods of their temperate homeland to the swampy terrain of
hot, humid southern Louisiana, early engineers constructed buildings
either of heavy timber framing on sills laid directly on the wet ground
or of exposed brick-between-post construction using weak bricks made
from the local clay. Compromised by deterioration and undermining, a
large number of these early buildings failed within the span of only a few
decades.[2] Such harsh and exacting conditions necessitated new strategies to adapt Old World building traditions.

During this period of French colonization, most ships passed through
the West Indies before arriving in Louisiana, and it is likely that colonists
assimilated the tropical building strategies they observed there and gradually learned to apply them.[3] The principles of building in a hot, humid climate are simple but imperative. The basic aims are these: (1) to minimize
heat gain by providing shade, (2) to maximize ventilation by promoting
air pathways, and (3) to manage water by controlling its movement and

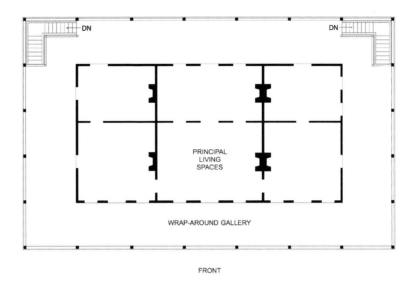

Figure 3.1. Plan of the principal floor of Destrehan Plantation, a colonial plantation house in St. Charles Parish, as it was built in 1790. The generous interstitial space of the covered open gallery entirely surrounds a compact inner core of principal living spaces. Illustration by Carrie Bernhard based on survey drawings from the Historic American Buildings Survey, 1989. Courtesy of the Library of Congress.

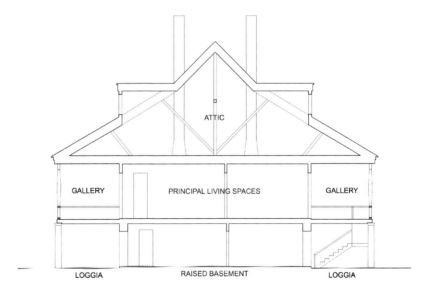

Figure 3.2. Transverse section cutting through the central front entry of the plantation house. The core of principal living spaces is lifted high off the ground by a raised basement and is surrounded on all sides by a wrap-around lower loggia, a corresponding gallery above, and a large vented attic. The core is protectively suspended within a deep layer of interstitial spaces. Illustration by Carrie Bernhard based on survey drawings from the Historic American Buildings Survey, 1989. Courtesy of the Library of Congress.

creating barriers. Accordingly, in the new colony, buildings of greater success sat atop raised brick foundations that distanced them from the wet
ground and allowed for the movement of air.[4] Their increased height also
provided better access to cooling breezes, and their openings grew correspondingly larger. Galleries and overhanging roofs shielded the buildings'
walls and guarded their openings and materials from the assault of intense
sun and torrential rain. The resulting in-between spaces provided sheltered areas for work and living, measurably cooler and considerably more
pleasant than spaces either fully inside or out.

These new strategies essentially lifted the building up and sheathed
it in an interstitial layer of protective space. Effectively, the point of interface between the building and its environment became once removed.
As systems for shading, ventilation, and water management, interstices
not only safeguarded the integrity of the building, they moderated the
extremes of the environment for its inhabitants. Their use significantly
changed the relationships between the building, its occupants, and its
surroundings from one that was harsh and immediate to one that was
substantially more nuanced. Interstices were the key to both the viability
and livability of buildings in the new colony.

The early plantation house, built between the mid-eighteenth and
early nineteenth centuries, demonstrates the rapid assimilation of interstitial spaces into the established mode of building in colonial Louisiana.[5] It is an early example of the regular integration of interstices as an
essential and defining characteristic of its form and organization. The
typical organization of the early plantation house consists of a simple
core of principal living spaces surrounded by a series of secondary, interstitial spaces (see figures 3.1 and 3.2).

These spaces typically consist of a wide wrap-around gallery or
a gallery along one or more sides often combined with a cabinet-gallery-cabinet assembly[6] along the rear. Together, these spaces form a
perimeter that is incorporated under the main roof of the house. The
steeply hipped roof sheds water efficiently and forms a spacious cavity
for a vented attic, another in-between space, that exhausts rising heat
from the living spaces below and the driving heat from the sun above.
The building's principal living spaces, forming a compact inner core, sit
high off the ground either on piers or a raised brick basement and are
usually oriented to face the accompanying breezes of a nearby waterway.

In larger plantation houses, a row of thick masonry columns typically supports the wrap-around gallery on the principal floor above
while defining a corresponding loggia on the ground floor of the raised
basement below. These covered outdoor spaces surround and protect
most of the building while also functioning both as external circulation

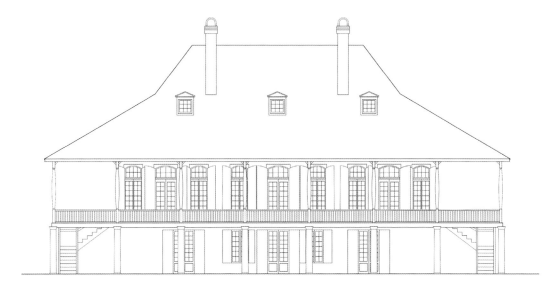

Figure 3.3. Elevation of the front facade. The massive protective framework of secondary interstitial spaces is immediately legible as the dominant formal expression of the colonial plantation house. Illustration by Carrie Bernhard based on survey drawings from the Historic American Buildings Survey, 1989. Courtesy of the Library of Congress.

corridors and as open-air rooms in themselves for eating, sleeping, work and leisure. Thus, the essential idea of the early plantation house consists of a core of principal interior spaces deeply ensconced within a protective framework of secondary interstitial spaces—an idea that is very legibly expressed in the building's form.

The formal and organizational relationships of the early plantation house demonstrate the interweaving of two contrasting architectural traditions; the organization and proportion of the core interior rooms reflect the European heritage and preferences of its builders, while many of the surrounding interstitial spaces reflect newly adopted building strategies from the hot, humid Caribbean.[7] This particular marriage of Old World and New World gives birth to an entirely new architecture often described as Creole. This blending of elements from disparate sources later characterizes the traditional architecture of New Orleans as a whole and is a dominant reason for its singularity. The particular house types that formed in New Orleans during the nineteenth century are unique amalgamations of mixed elements, shaped by various forces at various times, that eventually regularized and finally became recognizable as a distinct set of house types amid their rich array of variations. What remains constant, however, is the original concept of a building core surrounded by the indispensable, mediating layer of interstitial spaces. What emerges is a diverse range of interstitial systems that inter-

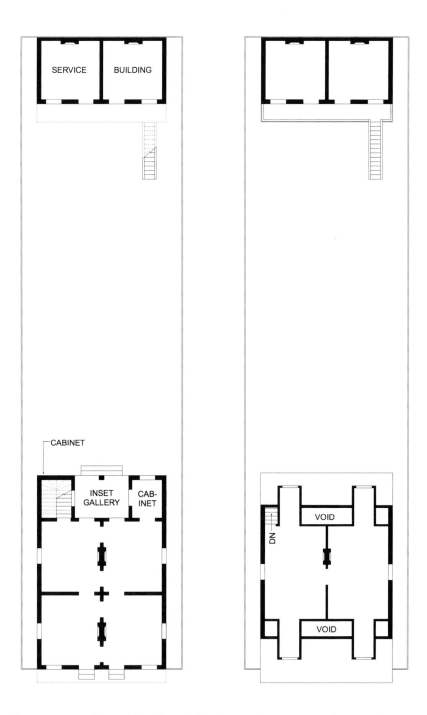

Figure 3.4. First and second floor plans of a four-bay Creole cottage. Typical interstitial spaces include an abat-vent along the front facade, narrow side alleys created by close adjacencies, a cabinet-gallery-cabinet assembly along the back of the building, and a rear yard (or court-yard) often bounded by a balconied service building. Drawing by Carrie Bernhard.

Figure 3.5. Transverse section of a typical Creole cottage. As in the colonial plantation house, the principal living area is entirely surrounded by a protective layer of interstitial spaces. However, within the dense urban context, some of those spaces are now shared with the street and adjacent buildings. Drawing by Carrie Bernhard.

act symbiotically with their associated house type, often of dissimilar origin but ultimately selected by local and contemporary forces and, as a working whole, inextricably joined.

During the early nineteenth century, New Orleans flourished, growing from a swampy colonial outpost to a vibrant and culturally diverse metropolis. The tremendous need for housing to supply the burgeoning population and the wide-ranging needs of a broad demographic spurred the refinement of three distinct house types, each with their own set of variations.[8] During the first half of the nineteenth century, the relatively modest freestanding Creole cottage developed concurrently with the comparatively grand party-wall Creole townhouse. In the second half of the century, the economical and highly modifiable shotgun proliferated to become the most common house type in New Orleans by the century's end.[9] Today, the Creole cottage, the Creole townhouse, and the shotgun all survive in abundance, dominating the housing stock of the French Quarter and the older faubourgs. Despite their formal, organizational, and material differences, each of these types employs the same basic building strategy of a core of principal living spaces surrounded by a protective layer of interstitial spaces, just as in the early plantation house. Unlike the massive interstitial framework typical of the rural plantation house, however, the interstitial systems of New Orleans house types, reflecting the density and shared infrastructures of their urban environment, are necessarily more varied, multifunctional, and compact.

The Creole cottage, for example, maintains many elements of the early plantation house but also introduces a new set of interstitial relationships. Like the early plantation house, the basic organization of the Creole cottage consists of the familiar core of principal living spaces with a cabinet-gallery or cabinet-gallery-cabinet range along the rear, as in figure 3.4. Instead of sitting atop a raised basement, however, the one to one-and-a-half-story core of principal living spaces typically sits above a crawlspace of only one-and-a-half to three feet. This distance

Figure 3.6. A row of three typical side-by-side Creole cottages. A passerby walks within the shade of their overhanging abat-vents, a protective interstitial space shared by the building and the public realm. Photograph by Carrie Bernhard.

separates the structure from the damp ground and permits airflow, but keeps the principal living spaces low enough to allow easy entry from the banquette, or sidewalk, which the building fronts with little to no setback.

A stoop of two to four steps, either bare or flanked by box-like platforms, provides both access and an informal seating area. The overhanging extension of the roof, called an *abat-vent*, defines an in-between space, shielding the front wall of the house, the front stoop, and even a portion of the public sidewalk, offering shade and shelter to strangers as they pass by. The interposition of the overhang defines an interstitial space that connects the building with the street at the same time that it separates both from the elements. In such a harsh climate, the gesture of the overhang is one that is not only economical in its multifunctionality but also distinctly civic, and highly gracious, in nature.

This expressly urban notion of the shared interstice is integral to the traditional house types of New Orleans, not only in the relationship of individual buildings to the street but also in the relationship among multiple adjacencies. Sitting on typically narrow lots, the Creole cottage maximizes its lot width, leaving tight intervals of only three to six feet between adjacent buildings.

Figure 3.7. A typical side alley: two three-foot-wide setbacks combine to create a six-foot interstitial space between the houses. Side alleys are often, but not always, divided by a shared fence or wall and typically gated at the street, as seen here. Photograph by Carrie Bernhard.

Figure 3.8. Some side alleys are narrow to the point of delightful absurdity, as between this townhouse and Creole cottage in the French Quarter, with just enough space to permit access, provide essential light and air, and aid in water management. Photograph by Carrie Bernhard.

This interstitial space forms a narrow side alley that permits access between the front and rear of the house and also directs water runoff toward the street. This separation between buildings also provides interior rooms with vital access to light and air and forms a channel that facilitates air currents. At the same time, the closeness of the separation essentially links consecutive buildings together—a propinquity that enables a reciprocal system of protection as adjacent buildings shade one another from low morning and afternoon sun and laterally buffer one another against storm-driven wind and rain. The shared interstices of the Creole cottage constitute a mutual system for addressing common exigencies. As a consequence, buildings are effectively connected by the very spaces that separate them, essentially joined by their interstices.

This shared relationship among buildings is a fundamental departure from the paradigm of the French colonial period. Urban buildings of that era, sharing many features with the early plantation house, such as overhanging hipped roofs, raised basements, and galleries,[10] were

1731

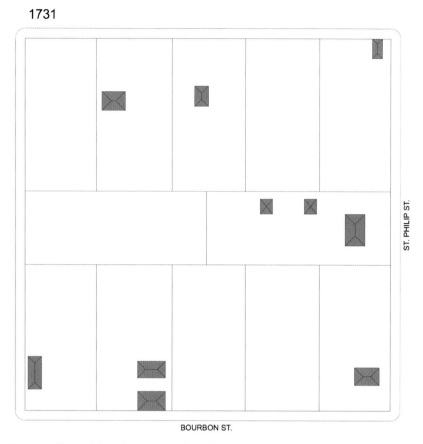

Figure 3.9. The roof plan of square 76 in the early city during the French colonial period (1731). Largely self-contained houses featuring hipped roofs sat far apart on spacious lots, exhibiting little relationship to one another. Drawing by Carrie Bernhard based on a detail from Gonichon's *Plan de la Nouvelle Orleans*, 1731. Courtesy of the Library of Congress.

independent objects in the round: spaced relatively far apart, wrapped within their own protective shell and largely self-contained.

In the early nineteenth century, however, as the population of New Orleans more than doubled, the demand for housing forced buildings to sit closer together. As the density of the city intensified, the relationships between buildings, their occupants, and the environment became increasingly complex, and a more collective formal identity among buildings eventually took shape.

Among these tighter adjacencies, roof forms, such as that of the fully developed Creole cottage, changed their slope to drain exclusively toward the front and back rather than to all four sides as with the hipped roof of the French colonial era.[11] This change from hipped to side-gabled also expanded the usable square footage of the attic and, with the inte-

1885

ST. PHILIP ST.

BOURBON ST.

Figure 3.10. By 1885, a roof plan of the same French Quarter block illustrates the results of increasing density. Among tighter adjacencies, roof shapes changed to slope to the front and back, and the addition of dormers expanded livable square footage. Newly defined interstitial spaces between buildings assumed multiple functions. Drawing by Carrie Bernhard based on Sanborn fire insurance maps, 1885, in *New Orleans, Louisiana,* vol. 2 (New Orleans: Sanborn Map Company, 1885), p. 2, cross-referenced with images from the Vieux Carré Digital Survey (Vieux Carré Commission, New Orleans), and Google satellite images of extant buildings (DigitalGlobe, US Geological Survey, USDA Farm Service Agency, Google).

gration of interstitial dormers to provide essential light and ventilation, made it habitable. With its side-gabled roof, the side facades of the Creole cottage extended upward and became purposefully flat and spare as the protective and circulatory functions of overhangs and galleries were assumed by the newly established propinquity among neighboring buildings and the narrow bands of space between them. Not just leftover space, this shared interstitial space of the Creole cottage's side alleys is a careful balance between economy and function: between maximization of buildable area per lot and optimal performance and livability. They are a vital component of the formal and organizational feasibility, and

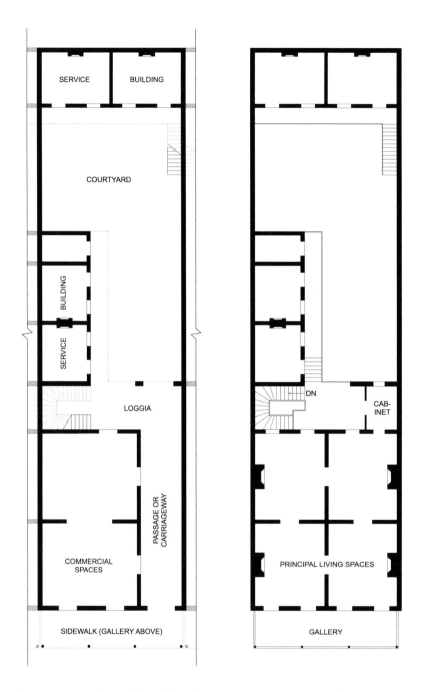

Figure 3.11. First- and second-floor plans of a typical Creole townhouse. The first floor shows the party-wall relationship with its contiguous adjacencies and the resulting need for interstitial spaces to provide light, air, access, and opportunities for water management. The ground floor was traditionally—and often remains—for commercial purposes. Drawing by Carrie Bernhard.

Figure 3.12. A row of Creole townhouses in the French Quarter. The open grilled transoms above the *passage* doors connect with open courtyards beyond and allow for air movement. Galleries overhang the full width of the sidewalk and provide protection to both the building facades and pedestrians. Photograph by Carrie Bernhard.

continued longevity, of the fully developed Creole cottage type within the dense contextual fabric of New Orleans and its climate.

The Creole townhouse type, which developed in New Orleans at the same time as the Creole cottage, likewise relies on interstices as an integral component of its building concept but in an altogether different way. In contrast to the freestanding Creole cottage, the Creole townhouse occupies the full width of its lot and abuts its neighbors directly with common walls.

Adjacent buildings are arrayed contiguously so that their brick sidewalls, problematic in a hot, humid climate,[12] are subsumed entirely within the collective mass. Thus the longest, most vulnerable sides of each building are sheltered internally, leaving only the relatively narrow front and rear facades exposed. These, in turn, are protected with a plaster coat and usually shielded by a balcony or gallery on the front facade (often extending over the public sidewalk) and usually by a loggia on the rear facade facing the courtyard. Extending the length of the building is a partially open through-space, called a *porte-cochère* or *passage*, that connects the street with the loggia and open courtyard to the rear. Thus the interstitial side alleys that would adjoin the sides and rear of the

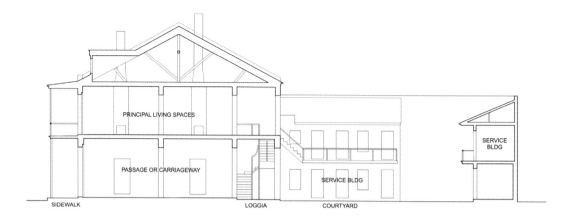

Figure 3.13. Diagrammatic section cut through the *passage*. The transverse sectional relationships of the Creole town-house's main house are nearly identical to those of the plantation house (see figure 3.2). Photograph by Carrie Bernhard.

Figure 3.14. The *passage* of a Creole town-house, a partially open through-space between the street and rear courtyard of this contiguous row house. This interstitial space functions essentially as a side alley that has been subsumed internally into the building's mass. Photograph by Carrie Bernhard.

freestanding Creole cottage are essentially inverted and reconfigured internally in the Creole townhouse as a matrix of interstitial spaces that penetrate the contiguous building mass to provide necessary access and vitally important light, air, and water management.

As a spatial consequence of these relationships, many blocks in the French Quarter, where Creole townhouses are concentrated, read as dense conglomerations of building mass, perforated and aerated by their matrices of interstitial space. As the architect Malcolm Heard so richly describes in the *French Quarter Manual*, "Most of the buildings are hardly perceivable as objects because they cannot be seen in the round. . . . The town blocks and their buildings can be imagined as solids that have been eaten away, like furniture full of worm holes. There is energy in these erosions; they are full of intent. The energy lies in the tension between the clear street grid and the idiosyncratic spaces stacked and wedged and hung in interstices behind the streets."[13]

The idiosyncrasy of these interstitial spaces and their relationships to the street are the very machinery of the Creole townhouse and the reason for its efficacy as a New Orleans house type. The central component of its building strategy is the irregularly shaped, highly informal interstitial space of the courtyard. Shaded for most of the day by the asymmetrically organized, multi-storied buildings and outbuildings that surround and define it, the resulting deep, narrow proportions of the courtyard maximize shade in a way that is functionally specific to the hot, humid climate.[14] The additional shade provided by overhanging balconies, galleries, and loggias further reduces the exposure of surfaces to heat gain. The lush vegetation that has come to be associated with New Orleans courtyards contributes still more shade and additional cooling by transpiration. As a consequence, the interstitial space of the courtyard is significantly cooler than the street. The resulting contrast in air temperature, density and pressure induces the movement of air, as the cooler, heavier air of the courtyard sinks and is drawn through the outlet of the *porte-cochère* or *passage*, where it is caught up in the rising current of the hotter, lighter air of the street.[15] Additionally, high breezes can be captured and drawn through the large openings of the upper floors to wash through the principal rooms and be drawn again into the courtyard by its downward current. The relationships of the street with the idiosyncratic interstices of the Creole townhouse produces a self-generating microclimate within each individual building. Long before the advent of mechanical cooling systems, these interconnected relationships helped to make the reality of a masonry party-wall configuration in a hot, humid climate much more feasible.

As with both the early plantation house and the Creole cottage, the efficacy of the Creole townhouse's systems of interstices is essential to

Figure 3.15. A row of five four-bay shotguns. Many streets in New Orleans are lined with the tight repetition of side-by-side shotguns. Photograph by Carrie Bernhard.

the viability of the type. The same is true of the shotgun, a house type whose development in New Orleans was spurred by the dramatic population increase at the beginning of the nineteenth century, driven in large part by the massive influx of Haitian refugees in need of affordable housing. In order to meet the tremendous demand, lots had to be exploited more fully than could be achieved by the Creole cottage, whose side-gabled roof shape precluded a typical length much greater than two principal rooms.[16] Over the course of the next few decades, a new house type developed that greatly exceeded the Creole cottage in its economy and versatility. By the 1840s, the fully developed and regularized shotgun emerged, and by the conclusion of its production in the early 1900s, it had become the most prolific house type in New Orleans, just as it remains today.[17]

Like the Creole cottage, the shotgun house type is a freestanding wood-frame structure whose variations adjust laterally in bay number, allowing each to maximize its particular lot width. Adjacent buildings typically sit within close proximity and, in many neighborhoods in New Orleans, entire street fronts are lined by the tight and regular cadence of one shotgun followed closely by the next.

In contrast to the side-gabled roof of the Creole cottage, which slopes to the front and rear, however, the gabled roof of the shotgun

Figure 3.16. Floor plan of a four-bay shotgun with front yard, front gallery, side entries, and rear cabinet-like sheds. As the form's most common variation, the four-bay double shotgun typically accommodates two residences. The side entry ensemble of interstitial spaces is a pivot point for moving in a variety of directions and greatly expands the building's spatial flexibility in how it can be accessed, joined, or partitioned. Drawing by Carrie Bernhard.

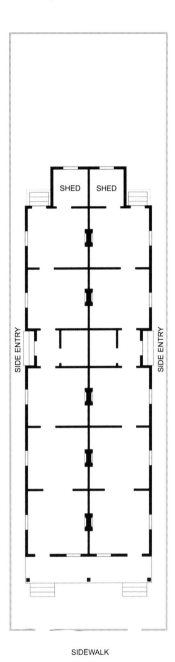

Figure 3.17. Section diagram cutting through the doors along the length of the building. Like the Creole cottage and Creole townhouse, a protective interstitial layer surrounds the principal living spaces, while the side entry ensemble punctuates its attenuated organization. Drawing by Carrie Bernhard.

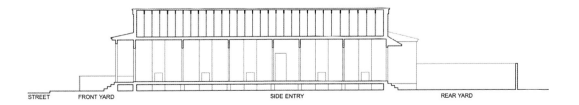

features a ridgeline that runs perpendicular to the street and slopes from side to side. Structurally, this allows the shotgun to stretch longitudinally to maximize the length of its typically long lot, resulting in its linear room organization and distinctly attenuated form.

In contrast to the row house configuration of the Creole townhouse, in which the depth of principal rooms is limited to a maximum of two so that each room has access to vital light and air on at least one side, the tight, side-by-side massing of the shotgun, combined with its typical building depth of five rooms, is made feasible only by means of its system of interstitial side alleys that provides each room with the necessary access to light and air. These long, narrow spaces also facilitate air movement by compressing the air as it moves between buildings, thus forcing its velocity to increase. As an additional benefit, the length of the shotgun's side alleys also increases the distance along which roof runoff can be dispersed and directed, thereby permitting easier rainwater management among such close, slope-facing adjacencies. Finally, the side alleys of many shotguns offer a separate, secondary access to the rear portion, sometimes allowing this unusually long building type to be divided into discrete front and rear occupancies. In these ways, the shotgun's system of interstitial side alleys actually enables the distinct form and organization, multifunctionality, and dense urban disposition that are essential to the economy of the type. This economy is a significant factor in the shotgun's ultimate success and ubiquity in New Orleans, both then and now.

Contributing further to the shotgun's economy is its impressive variability, the many ways in which individual iterations of the shotgun, during the heyday of its production, could adjust to meet the wide-ranging needs of a broad array of people and circumstances. All New Orleans traditional house types have the intrinsic capacity for formal and organizational variation but none so supple as the shotgun. Inherent in the type is its systematic ability to expand and contract, not just laterally by bay number but also longitudinally and sometimes vertically by room number, resulting in a host of building sizes and configurations that fit a multitude of lot conditions and spatial needs. Multiplying its versatility still further is the ease with which it incorporates an impressive array of interstitial spaces: crawlspaces and raised basements; front galleries, inset side galleries, rear galleries, and attached rear sheds; stoops; a range of overhung spaces defined by abat-vents, awnings, and canopies; front yards, side yards, and side alleys; foyers, inset side entries, hallways, and stairways. Depending on the interstitial spaces it employs, individual iterations of the shotgun can be at home either on low ground or high ground, on a narrow lot or wide lot, in a residential context or commercial context, in a modest neighborhood or upscale neighborhood. As the most prolific house type in New Orleans, shotguns appear throughout the city, whether infilling parts of long-established neighborhoods or predominating in the newly-established neighborhoods that developed during the height of their production.[18]

The integration of interstitial spaces expands the usability of a building for different occupants with changing needs over time. They affect the various ways in which principal spaces can relate to one another and their surrounding environment. For example, many shotguns possess a secondary, rear entrance of two to four steps that is usually recessed into the side of the building (see figure 3.16). This entry is accessible by way of the interstitial side alley that serves, in this instance, as a long, exterior hallway. The side entrance itself typically leads into a small interior hallway situated between the forward and rearmost rooms. In the two-story camelback variation, a stairway provides access to the second-floor rooms and, when combined with the separate side entrance, provides the option for a discrete secondary residence. The typical side entry of the shotgun forms an ensemble that, while seemingly insignificant, represents an impressive number of purposeful spaces: a recessed entrance, a covered exterior stoop for sitting, an entry foyer, a hallway between rooms, a stairway, and a landing. Ultimately, this cluster of interstitial spaces works as a junction, as many interstices do—a spatial pivot point for moving in a variety of directions. And whether the doors of the adjoining rooms are open or closed determines whether the building is segmented into multiple parts or connected as one.

As this example illustrates, the spatial relationships within the building are determined to a significant degree by their interstitial spaces. The extent to which principal spaces are connected or separated determines their degrees of openness or privacy, interaction or detachment—qualities that are strongly tied to family life and cultural preference. As with both the Creole cottage and Creole townhouse, variations of the shotgun may or may not possess an interstitial hallway, and the preference for one organization over the other was originally associated with the differing cultural traditions of the French and American residents of New Orleans in the early nineteenth century. The French preferred the more intimate relationship of rooms arranged en suite, with no interior space wasted on circulation, while the Americans preferred to trade a certain amount of interior space for the benefits of privacy.[19] During the era of the shotgun's production, this spatial and experiential flexibility greatly expanded the appeal of the shotgun, satisfying a wide array of living preferences among a demographic that was one of the most ethnically diverse in America.[20]

Figure 3.18. Despite their modesty and the nearly impossible narrowness of their shared side alley, these adjacent "single" shotguns remain protected by an encompassing layer of interstitial space. Photograph by Carrie Bernhard.

Figure 3.19. This five-bay centerhall shotgun demonstrates how an iteration of the same type can vary significantly, depending on its interstitial spaces. This version includes a raised basement, a columned front gallery with an entry stairway, an interior central hallway, and both a front yard and generous side yards. Photograph by Carrie Bernhard.

Expanding the shotgun's appeal still further is the considerable variety in its outward character. Shotgun variations can impart entirely different qualities depending on the interstices they employ. Whether a particular shotgun fronts the sidewalk with a shallow overhang, sitting low to the ground over a tight crawlspace, or perches high above a raised basement with a deep, columned overhang, greatly alters its outward aspect: from simple and modest to stately and grand. Likewise, the shotgun corner store, with the public immediacy of its typically overhung corner entry, contrasts sharply with the private and distinctly residential remove of a shotgun set back from the street by a generous, interstitial front yard. These meaningful differences in the relationship between a building and its surroundings result directly from its particular disposition of interstices.

Figure 3.20. This corner shotgun advertises its commercial nature with its overhung corner entry and wraparound suspended awning. Its operations spill out onto the sidewalk, an overlap of public and private space defined by the protective overhang. Photograph by Carrie Bernhard.

Yet while each shotgun's particular set of surrounding interstices alters its external character, its essential form and organization remain constant, allowing for an enormous range of variability while maintaining its coherence as a building type. That this variability allows for such clear expression of a building's use and status contributes significantly to the shotgun's suitability and historical appeal across a broad economic spectrum.[21] The variability of the type, its simple construction, and the efficiencies of its systematic replication allowed its production to achieve an economy of scale that fueled its proliferation, resulting in the ubiquity that is seen even today. The rich variability of the shotgun, along with its consistent legibility as a type, helps to engender an urban identity that is diverse yet coherent—qualities that are seemingly contradictory but also highly reflective of the city of New Orleans, both historically and presently.

The systems of interstices that are so expressive of their inhabitants over time are also what allow New Orleans's traditional house types to engage their inhabitants in the moment. As in-between spaces, interstices are often ambiguous, hovering between the respective conditions of their associated spaces at a given point in time: public and private, open and enclosed, still and in motion, quiet and noisy, wet and dry, dark and light. They are the spaces where the extreme contrasts in environmental qualities are mediated by their degrees of connection and separation. What Heard calls a "refined negotiation between inside and outside"[22] deeply influences the comfort and mood of a building's inhabitants and thus the way spaces are used or not used. As the environment changes throughout the course of the day, by season and by circumstance, activities can take place in the most amenable space at any given time: sleep in the most secluded room, work in the well-lighted room, coffee on the front gallery overlooking the morning activities of the street, cool drinks in the rear courtyard shaded from the late afternoon sun. If it's raining on a hot afternoon, the protection of interstitial spaces often allows the house to remain open to the rain's cooling effects. In the summer, a south-facing, overhung balcony blocks the infiltration of harsh sunlight, while in the winter, that same balcony permits its welcomed warmth.

That New Orleans's traditional house types can be so finely tuned to their environment is an intrinsic feature of their interstitial systems. Given a wide range of spatial and experiential choices, occupants can mediate their own relationship to the environment. This nuanced way of living, along with most of the interstitial spaces that make it possible, is largely absent in the city's houses of the twentieth and twenty-first centuries. These are generally non-regional house types that populate the low-lying neighborhoods developed after the installation of the massive drainage system at the turn of twentieth century.[23] Houses are sited relatively far apart from one another on spacious lots, and many sit on concrete slabs directly on the ground. Houses are often without crawlspaces or raised basements, galleries, balconies, loggias, side alleys, or other in-between spaces. The increasingly refined technologies of building materials and heating, ventilating, and air-conditioning systems that are highly successful at resisting the elements and precisely controlling the interior environment have largely replaced the necessity of protective interstitial spaces on a habitable scale. What interstitial spaces remain have essentially shrunk to occupy the shallow voids within the building's structure and surrounding skin, where the defense against infiltration now resides in the material performance of insulation and cladding layers. Without a surrounding layer of protective, habitable interstitial space, the point of interface between the building and the environment is effectively returned to the building's surface. The relationship between the building, its occupants, and the environment is harsh and immediate, and the capacity for spatial and experiential nuance is lost, mediated less by the architecture and its adjacencies than by the now-critical operation of its mechanical systems, the durability of its materials, and the all-important integrity of the drainage and levee systems.

Following the disastrous events of Hurricane Katrina, local building ordinances now require new construction in New Orleans to be raised off the ground in accordance with federal guidelines. In addition, many newly-constructed houses, in heightened appreciation of traditional New Orleans architecture, commonly feature certain iconic traditional elements such as balconies and front entry galleries. Their traditional efficacy is rarely achieved, however, when interstices are applied discretely as isolated components rather than comprehensively as part of a whole system. Without a surrounding layer of protection, the doors and windows of buildings are more likely to be kept shut when buildings are situated far apart from one another on wide lots and exposed to the full force of the elements on all sides. The exclusive reliance on efficient mechanical systems and durable surface materials as a single building strategy precludes these buildings from opening to the elements except on the few days of the year when conditions are ideal. More often, these buildings remain tightly sealed, their token interstitial spaces effectively disconnected from the life of the house.

The architectural vitality of traditional New Orleans house types emerges directly from the efficacy of interstitial spaces as part of a comprehensive matrix of working systems with a vast array of spatial and qualitative consequences. They establish the deeply mediated relationships between individual buildings and their surrounding environments. Without these interstitial systems, buildings become spatially and qualitatively fixed, eliminating the richness of all such spatial and experiential possibilities. These systems not only provide essential protection from the elements and access to light and ventilation but also modulate the exchange of sound and view. They not only provide entry and circulation within a building but also affect the ways principal spaces can be used and how they are experienced. Interstitial elements are the interface between the private building and the public street, between a lone building and its neighbors. These systems negotiate the constant interplay between abutting conditions and are consequently charged spaces, continually activated with the ebb and flow of air, moisture, heat, light, sound, and the lives of the occupants who reside among these vibrant systems over time. While new buildings in New Orleans should not replicate this traditional architecture, they might replicate, instead, the efficacy that is achieved, in large part, by these interstitial systems. As humble and overlooked as most interstitial spaces are—the lowly crawlspace, the humble overhang, the insignificant side entry, the shadowy passage—in concert, forming an elegant complex of interconnected systems, these interstices breathe the very life into the traditional architecture of New Orleans.

A Taxonomy of Traditional New Orleans Interstices

Architectural interstices. Intervening spaces that are habitable in scale but subordinate to the primary interior spaces of a building.

Applied interstices. Interstitial spaces created by an additive structural component that is attached to or extended from the primary building volume.

> *balcony.* A narrow exterior platform onto which interior rooms of upper floors open, supported by cantilevers or brackets.
>
> *dormer.* A box-like windowed structure that protrudes from the attic to provide headroom, light, and ventilation.
>
> *gallery.* A long, wide exterior platform onto which upper or lower interior rooms open, supported by columns or piers.
>
> *overhung space* or *shade zone.* The protected space next to a building and defined by an overhanging structure above, such as an abat-vent, canopy, awning, balcony, or gallery.
>
> *stoop.* The area of steps between building and exterior, often flanked by boxes that form a platform to either side (box-steps).

Integrated interstices. Interstitial spaces located within the main volume of the building, oriented to the exterior, and partially open.

> *carriageway* or *porte-cochère.* A wide covered passageway within the volume of a building that connects the street and courtyard, usually gated at the street and open at the rear.
>
> *crawlspace.* The area of limited height between the first floor of a raised building and the ground, typically eighteen to thirty inches.
>
> *inset gallery (side* or *rear).* A long covered space, open or semi-open, cut into the side or rear volume of a building, the opening usually supported by columns. The term *rear gallery* is often interchangeable with *loggia* in a Creole cottage.
>
> *loggia.* A covered space within the main volume of a building, open or semi-open to the courtyard or rear yard, the opening supported by columns or wide arched openings in the exterior wall. In a Creole cottage, it is the same as an inset rear gallery.
>
> *passage.* A narrow passageway within a building that connects the street and the courtyard, often gated at the street and open at the rear.

recessed entry or *open vestibule.* A doorway set back into the volume of a building creating a small entrance hall open to the street.

stairway (exterior). An area of vertical circulation between floors, typically winder stairs within a loggia or cut into a gallery.

Enclosed interstices. Interstitial spaces located within the main volume of the building, fully enclosed.

attic. The space between the ceiling of the top floor and the roof.

cabinet. A small interior service room at the rear corner of a building, next to a principal room and rear gallery, sometimes containing a stairway.

entresol. A low story, often used for storage or service, between principal floors of a building.

hallway. An interior space onto which rooms open, often cutting through the length of the building from front to back.

raised basement. An enclosed ground-floor level under a raised building, lower in height than the principal living floor above and often used for parking or storage.

stairway (interior). An area of vertical circulation between floors, often located in a hallway.

Open interstices. An uncovered interstitial space located outside and adjacent to the main volume of the building.

courtyard. An open space between the main building and surrounding walls and structures.

front yard. An open setback between the main building and the front property line, usually demarcated by a public sidewalk.

rear yard. An open setback between the main building and rear property line, usually demarcated by a fence, wall, rear service structure, or neighboring structure.

side alley. An open setback between the main building and side property line, usually demarcated by a fence, wall, or neighboring structure.

NOTES

1. For more detail, see "Taxonomy of Traditional New Orleans Interstices," above.

2. For early construction efforts and building failures, refer to Samuel Wilson Jr., *The Architecture of Colonial Louisiana: Collected Essays of Samuel Wilson, Jr. F.A.I.A.,*

ed. Jean M. Farnsworth and Ann M. Masson (Lafayette: Center for Louisiana Studies, 1987), 4–23, 52–57, 83–88, 229, 233, 248–53, 262–65, 331–32, 380, 387.

3. Jay D. Edwards, "The Origins of Creole Architecture," *Winterthur Portfolio* 29, no. 2/3 (1994), 164.

4. Wilson, *Architecture of Colonial Louisiana*, 376.

5. Barbara SoRelle Bacot, "The Plantation," in *Louisiana Buildings, 1720–1940: The Historic American Buildings Survey*, ed. Jessie Poesch and Barbara SoRelle Bacot (Baton Rouge: Louisiana State University Press, 1997), 96–97. See also Edwards, "Origins," 162–63.

6. The cabinet-gallery-cabinet assembly is a common room organization characteristic of Creole architecture. A rear-facing gallery (technically a loggia but locally referred to as a gallery) is flanked on one or both sides by a small interior room called a cabinet. See figure 3.7.

7. Edwards, "Origins," 164, 188.

8. For detailed discussion of New Orleans house types and their most common variations, see Malcolm Heard, *French Quarter Manual: An Architectural Guide to New Orleans's Vieux Carré* (Jackson: University Press of Mississippi, 1997), 24–53, hereinafter *FQM*.

9. Jay D. Edwards, "Shotgun: The Most Contested House in America," *Buildings & Landscapes* 16, no. 1 (2009): 68.

10. Wilson, *Architecture of Colonial Louisiana*, 337, 342.

11. Nathaniel Cortlandt Curtis, *New Orleans: Its Old Houses, Shops and Public Buildings* (Philadelphia: J. B. Lippincott, 1933), 55. See also Heard, *FQM*, 25.

12. The thermally massive nature of brick is such that any heat that is accumulated is held very efficiently, and its porosity causes it to wick and hold moisture. The local brick in particular is notoriously weak and erodes easily upon exposure. In order to function in this climate, brick walls have to be aggressively protected to prevent exposure and heat gain. At the same time, ventilation has to be encouraged in order to exhaust any accumulated heat and to facilitate both evaporative cooling and moisture removal. See Edward Jon Cazayoux, AIA, CSI, *A Manual for the Environmental & Climatic Responsive Restoration & Renovation of Older Houses in Louisiana* (Baton Rouge: Energy Section, Technology Assessment Division, Louisiana Department of Natural Resources, 2003), 5–8, 63.

13. Heard, *FQM*, 7.

14. John S. Reynolds, *Courtyards: Aesthetic, Social, and Thermal Delight* (New York: John Wiley & Sons, 2002), 16–17, 77–93.

15. Cazayoux, *Manual*, 8.

16. Edwards, "Shotgun," 65–67.

17. Ibid., 68.

18. See the graphic in Richard Campanella, "Urban Growth Measured by Building Age, Circa 1939," in *Geographies of New Orleans: Urban Fabrics before the Storm* (Lafayette: Center for Louisiana Studies, 2006), 96.

19. Heard, *FQM*, 49.

20. Campanella, *Geographies*, 193–97, 369–72.

21. Edwards, "Shotgun," 85.

22. Heard, *FQM*, 33.

23. Campanella, *Geographies*, 91–97.

CHAPTER FOUR
Harmony Street
An Interstitial House

—John P. Klingman

In architectural discourse, *interstitial* is a term for a spatial, structural, or infrastructural element, often invisible, that enhances a building's accommodative capabilities without disturbing occupation. A famous example is Louis Kahn's sectional strategy at the Salk Institute for Biological Studies, in which there is a hidden floor above each block of laboratories so that services can be reconfigured without compromising the activities in the lab below. A similar example from the Vieux Carré of New Orleans is the *entresol*, a mezzanine, low-ceilinged storage level found in Creole townhouses located above the street-level commercial space and not indicated on the building's facade. This was a clever solution in a city that is not friendly to basements. More familiar perhaps are the steep, winding service stairs often buried in American mansions. Designed to be invisible, they allowed household staff discreet access to all the rooms; Drayton Hall outside of Charleston, South Carolina, is an early example. Later, Monticello, in a strange twist, utilizes the service stairs for the gentry as well. Thomas Jefferson thought that stairs were a waste of space! In contemporary architecture, electrical wiring systems are inherently interstitial. While the electric meter and main panelboard are visible on the exterior of a house, the interior wiring is concealed. Construction drawings conventionally indicate switch and fixture locations; it is assumed that the electrician will find a way to invisibly rout the conductors within the structure. A somewhat bizarre current variation is the smart house, in which there may be no light switches at all; the lighting is controlled from your phone.

In my first years of teaching at the Tulane University School of Architecture beginning in the fall of 1983, my senior colleague Malcolm

Figure 4.1. 1309 Harmony Street, garden facade. Original drawing by Emile Weil (1898) from the collection of John P. Klingman.

Heard befriended me. Mac would invite me to the centerhall Creole cottage on Louisa Street in the Bywater neighborhood, where he and his wife Alicia held intimate dinner parties, the French doors and windows in the dining room and kitchen all wide open to the night air, while overhead the old Hunter ceiling fans were turned up high. The sense of connection between indoors and the garden was powerful, and the pungent scents from the exotic, dimly visible plants outside pervaded the house. It made an indelible impression on me. For this volume inspired by Mac's sensitivity toward interstitiality, I offer a reading of my own house that may similarly open it up, elucidating some of its hidden spaces and in-between elements. What I propose here is a commentary that offers different ways of thinking about how one dwells. One of Mac Heard's favorite quotations was from philosopher Gaston Bachelard: "All really inhabited space bears the essence of the notion of home."[1] Perhaps conditions of domestic interstitiality and even a way of interstitial living can contribute directly to a sense of place and experience of home that many people, not only New Orleanians, can register.

Figure 4.2. Harmony Street house at purchase, 1989. Photograph by John P. Klingman.

Beginning with its location in a nineteenth-century uptown neighborhood, the Harmony Street house exhibits characteristics of interstitiality. The house was built in 1898 within the garden of a larger house next door from the 1880s for the daughter of the original house's owners. This was a common occurrence in the Garden District, which was planned with only four properties per block, one-third the number of lots of the identically-sized French Quarter block. Originally striking in its openness, and even called "the first American suburb," the neighborhood has become, over a century of interstitial development, less recognizably different from others in the city, despite its early novelty.

When I bought the house in 1989, I had already determined that I would live in an open building environment during warm weather, a principle upon which the house had been designed by its skillful twenty-one-year-old architect, Emile Weil. I had also been shocked by the almost bizarre conditions of New Orleans interiors in the summertime, often excruciatingly cold, in startling contrast with the outdoors, because of the invisible but all-pervasive system of mechanical air conditioning. Particularly surreal was the experience of visiting a historic house whose doors, windows, shutters, and draperies were shut tight and temperatures were as cold as a refrigerator, ostensibly to protect the furniture.

Figure 4.3. Upstairs bedroom in summer. Photograph by John P. Klingman.

I had experimented with un-air-conditioned life in the apartment in which I lived since coming to New Orleans in my un-air-conditioned 1974 Honda Civic. I found that it is much easier to live comfortably in a naturally ventilated house than it is to drive an un-air-conditioned car.

Many people think it is impossible to live in New Orleans without air-conditioning. However, what they don't recognize is the immense pleasure of being well-connected to the environment, hearing the birds and the wind in the trees, feeling the nuances of a drop in temperature just before a rain and the change in scent just after. Perhaps it's nutty; maybe it's even a bit subversive. I never think that I'm giving something up. Rather, I feel part of a collective neighborhood organism, attuned to its rhythms. Typically, I get up when my MD neighbor across the street starts his diesel Mercedes, with its sighing, descending octaves of engine noise, signaling his departure around dawn for the West Bank. Even earlier, I can hear the train along the river; and often at night the sounds of the streetcar come through from two and one-half blocks away. More

Figure 4.4. Downstairs living room in winter. Photograph by John P. Klingman.

recently, the sounds of children playing in their nearby courtyard and the clucking of a neighbor's chickens have increased the special ambiance.

In *The Poetics of Space*, Gaston Bachelard posits that the house "is one of the greatest powers of integration for the thoughts, memories and dreams of mankind." Further, he writes, "if I were asked to name the chief benefit of the house I should say: the house shelters daydreaming, the house protects the dreamer, the house allows one to dream in peace. Thought and experience are not the only things that sanction human values. The values that belong to daydreaming mark humanity in its depths."[2] Partially because of New Orleans's semitropical climate, the opportunity to live in between inside and outside richly enhances the phenomenal resonance of which Bachelard speaks. To him the literal embodiment of shelter is less important than the invisible psychological sense of shelter. Surely they are intertwined. I have come to appreciate that the interstitial characteristics of my Harmony Street house enhance a sense of well-being for the dweller.

The Harmony Street house was carefully designed around its systems for winter heating and summer cross ventilation. It has a very unusual plan. The house has a masonry core with back-to-back fireplaces on both the first and second floors. The one-story kitchen adjoins the back of the two-story mass and has its own separate chimney. For light and ventilation, each room has double-hung windows on at least two sides. The living room, master bedroom, and kitchen have windows on three sides. All of the windows and doors originally had operable louvered shutters as well. Most of these were still in operable condition; several I found stored in the crawl space under the house. While there is a strong perceptual difference between cool and warm weather comfort, both conditions are well supported by architectural elements. Originally, the four fireplaces burned coal. What must it have been like when they all were burning! I have enhanced the original condition by having the living room fireplace rebuilt, not an inexpensive change, deepening it to allow for wood burning. Such a deepening is itself interstitial—the fireplace appears unchanged, but its performance is greatly enhanced. In the winter the living room fire and its compelling visual and auditory presence provide a primordial hearth experience. The body is warmed, not so much by air temperature but by the radiant energy emanating from the fireplace. The ambiance of the flickering firelight and the crackling embers add to the transformative sense of shelter.

In the summer the overhead ceiling fan is even more essential, offering profound effects while remaining quiet and unobtrusive enough to often go unnoticed. A power outage, quite common in New Orleans, quickly demonstrates the important of the fans. In a warm humid climate there are two ways for the human body to be comfortable. One is to lower the ambient temperature and humidity, and this is the technique of the increasingly ubiquitous mechanical air conditioning system. The other is to raise the body's comfort zone. This is accomplished by increasing air movement so that moisture can more easily evaporate from the skin, cooling the body. Fans are highly efficient, almost invisible elements of this technology, operating at about a tenth of the cost of air conditioning. To augment the house's original cross ventilation system, I added a ceiling fan in each room so that moving air occurs even when there is no breeze. In the kitchen and study, which now have cathedral ceilings, I initially had the fans installed below the joists that had supported the ceiling to maximize their performance. Eventually, however, I had to have the fans moved above the joists. They had been low enough to be too prominent as objects, making a virtual ceiling and obviating the perception of the larger volume above. After being raised, they disappeared within plain sight. The air movement is only

Figure 4.5. Kitchen with original fan location and posts replacing pantry wall. Photograph by John P. Klingman.

slightly affected, and the interstitial quality of the spatial experience is much improved.

Very much as on a sailboat, adjustments from time to time improve performance as changes in environmental conditions occur. The shutters can be opened at night to encourage airflow and closed in the daytime as the sun strikes their surface. The blades of the louvers can be adjusted from perpendicular, to control midday sun and admit a breeze, to fully closed in a thunderstorm, shutting out rain and blustery wind. The shutters do require maintenance, but the benefits they provide are well worth the expenditure and effort. In warm weather the upstairs windows can remain open. Downstairs, screens are necessary to control mosquitoes. Several years ago, a group of students attempted to monitor the house's performance, using a variety of meters and measuring devices. The house thwarted their efforts rather completely, but they did conclusively establish that the upstairs is always warmer than the downstairs.

Figure 4.6. Bay window shutters on second floor. Photograph by John P. Klingman.

The biggest change in the interior of the house during my renovation also engaged interstitiality, albeit by reduction rather than addition. On the 1898 plan the room directly behind the entry stairhall was labeled "Reception." There was no door into this room; instead, it had a wide-framed opening. Behind the reception room was a long, thin pantry along the full width of the house; and behind that was the kitchen. This plan reflected the logic of nineteenth-century American social convention. Charged with maintaining formal social relationships, women would exchange calling cards noting the day of the week when they were available for visits. The reception room provided an appropriate space to make such visitations without presuming entry into the entire house. The door to the living room could be closed; and of course, the door to the pantry was always shut except for service access. Both the pantry and the kitchen behind were interstitial spaces, denoted as private and invisible to guests. As an indication of this, when I first visited the house, the hot water heater was a prominent object in the kitchen.

In the mid-twentieth century, the US kitchen became a gathering space; today it is frequently the dominant social space within the house. So I took the pantry apart, dissolving that dedicated service space, making some of it a half bath and most of it an enlargement of the kitchen. Two freestanding columns now replace the pantry wall, becoming friendly elements to lean against while having a conversation. I also relocated the

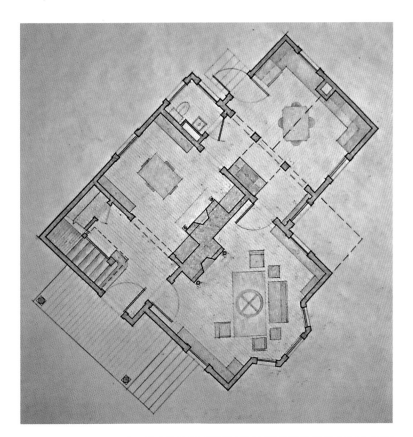

Figure 4.7. Plan for renovation of the first floor; John P. Klingman, architect (1989).

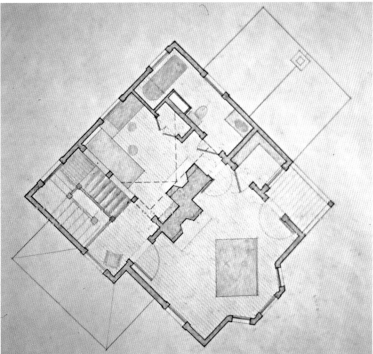

Figure 4.8. Plan for renovation of the second floor; John P. Klingman, architect (1989).

Figure 4.9. Relocation of reception doorway allowing visibility all the way through the house in 1989 renovation. Photograph by John P. Klingman.

Figure 4.10. The unchanged downstairs living room. Photograph by John P. Klingman.

Figure 4.11. Kitchen with reconfigured French doors connecting to deck. Photograph by John P. Klingman.

door between the original "Reception" (now a dining room and library) so that as one enters through the front door, one can see all the way through the house, making the formerly invisible visible. This is also a deliberate evocation of the modernist notion of "flowing space" as opposed to the discrete rooms of earlier times. In contrast, and because they are kind of perfect, I left the living room and the bedroom (its upstairs twin in the plan), as they were originally designed, only modifying the new plaster with paint that emulates the old color palette. Thus the house has a historic side and a contemporary side in counterpoint with one another on both levels. Visitors sense and appreciate the clear dichotomy.

As the renovations have continued, interstitial themes have persisted. One spring, my carpenter friend Jim O'Neil and I removed a downstairs window from the kitchen in order to replace it with French doors made by recutting and glazing an original cypress door, thus providing access to a new deck. While decks are less useful in New Orleans than porches, especially screened porches, I thought the deck would enhance the relationship between the kitchen and its exterior: a subtle

Figure 4.12. Stair hall before renovation, with ladder found under the house. Photograph by John P. Klingman.

perch elevated, partially shaded, and palpably connected to both house and garden yet not invulnerable from the vicissitudes of the weather.

Meanwhile, I had decided to reinstall the kitchen window in the front wall of the stairwell. In order to accomplish this, we constructed a temporary catwalk above the stair. Instantaneously, I realized that there was just enough headroom below that one could use the stairs even with this interstitial element above. So I eventually designed a permanent catwalk. Its deck is a mahogany grillage like that on a boat so that light passes through. Its guardrail is a round wooden pole that was also found under the house; and between the rail and the deck I designed a guard of shattered tempered glass that is visually almost not there. Although I have had three cats (interstitial), I had never had a catwalk before. The catwalk provides access to windows in the stairwell that otherwise must be opened and closed with a tall ladder.

Of course, there is a ladder. It too was under the house; and an early visitor, Bruce Hanson, who was a friend of Mac's, urged me to install it in the stairwell. Like Mac, Bruce found old houses to be fascinating. As soon as he learned I'd purchased this house, he asked if he could walk

Figure 4.13. Catwalk with view of relocated window. Photograph by John P. Klingman.

Figure 4.14. Catwalk from below, with Marigny, the interstitial cat. Photograph by John P. Klingman.

Figure 4.15. Harmony Street front entrance, with new porch ceiling, 2015. Photograph by John P. Klingman.

through it with me. Somehow, the ladder came up. It has been standing on a landing in the stairwell ever since and is invariably commented upon by visitors. Perhaps they are responding to another Bachelardian notion: "The house is imagined as a vertical being. It rises upward. It differentiates itself in terms of its verticality. It is one of the appeals to our consciousness of verticality."[3] The house's verticality is emphasized by the ladder's tall form reaching upward. The vertical sense of the house is rather unusual in New Orleans, where one of the most typical house types is the shotgun, a relentlessly horizontal linear structure.

The most recent Harmony Street house intervention started as a simple front porch repair project. This project also soon developed an element of interstitiality in that, when completed, evidence of the modification would almost be invisible. Recognizing that the porch roof was two inches out of level, in preparation to jacking up the roof, Jim and I removed the beaded board porch ceiling. Old houses carry secrets, and we learned that the wood siding on the front facade extended all the way up above the ceiling. It revealed a much more elegantly proportioned wall, which must have been intended to be visible. So I decided to reat-

Figure 4.16. Harmony Street on a winter evening. Photograph by John P. Klingman.

tach the old beaded boards to the underside of the roof rafters, thus exposing the enlarged volume. You only see it out of your peripheral vision, but it makes the entry feel much more commodious and welcoming. I then designed a built-in bench and a small entrance deck at the base of the porch, further enhancing the sense of hospitality that is an earmark of New Orleans residential architecture. Both of these elements attenuate the transition from the public realm of the street to the intimacy of the interior. In New Orleans dwelling is manifest in many ways; you can't always see it, but you can sense it and breathe it.

In the wake of the destruction of Hurricane Katrina and the influx of many new residents, the debate in New Orleans about the appropriateness of contemporary architecture in the historic city has intensified. In residential areas the focus has too often fallen largely upon exterior appearance—on maintaining or recreating the familiar mix of building types discussed elsewhere in this volume. But too much discussion of appearance yields an incomplete conversation at best, leading at times to a shallow historicism that lacks a true spirit of place. By recognizing and enhancing the connection between architecture and place, by appreciating how architectural conditions, visible and invisible, reflect critical adaptations to this specific city, its climate, and its history, we might better apply new as well as old principles, in a variety of inventive and appropriate ways. Designing and dwelling with the interstitial in mind is certainly one subtle and effective way of intertwining personal and cultural experience, honoring the profound sense of home that marks this particular inhabited place.

NOTES

1. Gaston Bachelard, *The Poetics of Space*, trans. Maria Jolas (Boston: Beacon Press, 1969), 5.
2. Ibid., 6.
3. Ibid., 17.

INTERSPACE THREE ❖ *Representing the In-Between*

Carrie Bernhard's focus on the systems formed by interstitial elements of New Orleans houses opens out in a variety of imaginative directions. While she shows us how a range of features become available for architects to expand, tinker with, or change— as for Klingman—she also suggests that such stylistic elements helped to encourage and to express certain social relations in the city. Making us see how these relations are materially situated, Bernhard prompts scholars in other disciplines to think about how artists and writers have engaged New Orleans's spatial in-betweenness. In this next section, Marilyn R. Brown and Teresa A. Toulouse, one an art historian and the other a literary critic, turn to specific painterly and literary representations of the city that appeared in the mid-nineteenth and early twentieth centuries.

Beginning with Edgar Degas's images of balconies and thresholds in their relation to his Creole family's anxieties about race, gender, and status, Brown broadens her analysis to *A Cotton Office in New Orleans*, reading elements of this famous painting as referencing the artist's ambivalent awareness of his uncle's business as an in-between space in an unstable global economic network dependent on "invisible" black labor. Similarly, in Toulouse's close-reading of novelist John Galsworthy's ghostly sketch, "That Old-Time Place," the interstitial spaces within the rotting St. Louis Hotel—a site of antebellum slave auctions and postbellum conflicts over Reconstruction—evoke not simply the English narrator's increasing horror at on-going Southern intransigence but also Galsworthy's own uncanny complicity in a decadent worldview that he fails to represent as "past." The images in Toulouse's essay begin with tourists' postcards and other idealized representations of the St. Louis and end with period photographs, in order to suggest Galsworthy's narrator's growing awareness of the hotel's dark history.

CHAPTER FIVE
Degas's New Orleanian Spaces

—*Marilyn R. Brown*

When French artist Edgar Degas visited New Orleans during the winter and spring of 1872–73, he found himself positioned in between French and American cultures; between the sequestered spaces of Creole domesticity on Esplanade Avenue, on the one hand, and the privatized public space of his uncle's cotton business on Carondelet Street in the American sector, on the other; and, more than in his previous experience, between white and black races. In Degas's representations of New Orleans, in-between spaces like the veranda of his uncle's rented Esplanade house, where he portrayed his cousin Mathilde Musson Bell, and the back steps, where he painted a scene of a black nanny and white children, not only visualize certain desired relations of race, class, and gender but also indicate the instability at the heart of such fixed categories. His well-known painting *A Cotton Office in New Orleans* also depicts a literal and metaphorical middle space that similarly alludes to and destabilizes social hierarchies of difference.[1] As cotton factors, his relatives served as middlemen of the international trade that extended from the Louisiana fields to the English textile mills. Invisible black labor was not only indexed materially in Degas's scene by the white commodity on display within the office but also implied by the location of the office itself: in between the port, through which the cotton moved, and the slave depots, yards, and pens that had been closed less than a decade before.[2] Degas's New Orleans pictures trouble easy assumptions about distinctions between public and private spaces. As I argue in what follows, they simultaneously expose and mask local anxieties about race and labor as well as the ways social and spatial relations, whether public or private, were linked to broader historical forces of global capitalist exchange.

Figure 5.1. Edgar Degas, *Woman Seated on a Balcony*, 1872, pastel, 24 3/8 x 29 7/8 in. (62.5 x 76.5 cm), Ordrupgaard, Copenhagen, Denmark. Photograph by Pernille Klemp.

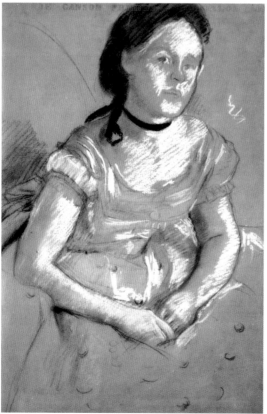

Figure 5.2. Edgar Degas, *Mathilde Musson Bell*, 1872, pastel on beige paper, 25 3/8 x 11 5/8 in. (66 x 49 cm), Göteborgs Konstmuseum, Göteborg, Sweden. Photograph Göteborgs Konstmuseum.

Veranda

The largest proportion of the work produced by Degas in New Orleans depicts women in domestic interiors. Recent interpretations of artistic, literary, and architectural representations of space often frame interiors as physical sites for psychic constructions of subjectivities and for inventions of modern identities.[3] Gail Feigenbaum and others have specifically connected Degas's interactions with and frequent portrayals of his female cousins in New Orleanian domestic interiors with longing for his Creole mother, Célestine Musson, who had died in her early thirties when the artist was barely thirteen[4] (he was thirty-eight when he visited the city of her birth). It can be further argued that the portraits set in the transitional spaces of the balcony or porch could allude to common conceptions of Creole whiteness as well as insecurity about it.

In Degas's lived experience of New Orleans, dwelling was not divided from work. He spent most of his time in the private domestic spaces of the Esplanade house, using an upstairs gallery as his studio even when painting the more public scene of the cotton office.[5] It was here that he created several versions of a portrait of his cousin Mathilde Musson Bell seated on a veranda.

Depictions of figures on balconies as intermediate spaces have the potential of breaking down binary divisions between public and private spheres, traditionally gendered as masculine and feminine.[6] Although potentially visible from the street, Bell does not direct her attention there, as do many sitters in other French Impressionist balcony and window scenes.[7] She instead exchanges an active lateral gaze with the viewer and with the masculine artist himself,[8] who shares with her the extension of "feminine" space beyond the boundaries of the domestic interior, into the in-between, almost public space of the balcony.[9]

When Degas visited New Orleans, Mathilde Musson and her English-speaking husband, William A. Bell, lived in the extended family house on Esplanade with their three children. Although her maternal aspects may have reminded the artist of his own Creole mother (is there a hint of melancholy around the eyes in figure 5.1?), it was mainly his cousin's modern, fashionable, upper middle class demeanor and pale complexion that he featured in the portraits, one of which became the topic of correspondence between Degas and his uncle Michel Musson, Mathilde's father, following her untimely death six years later.[10] In the most definitive of the versions, the Ordrupgaard pastel (figure 5.1), the sitter wears a loose-fitting dress whose short sleeves and décolletage look summery, despite the autumnal or early winter season. The white cotton is faintly highlighted with lavender, which offsets the orange trim, as well as the sketchy suggestion of green leaves beyond the typically New Orleanian cast-iron railing at the rear. The palmetto fan, rather than being deployed for flirtation, adds a tropical note, while the dark green shutter over Mathilde's shoulder and the reflection of her sleeve in a window on the left, along with the placement of the black railing exactly on her eye level at right, help to situate her in the transitional space between indoors and out.[11]

Christopher Benfey has suggested that the working of the silvery pastel on her dress and around her head alludes to moonlight, an effect he sees as enhanced in the drawing in the Metropolitan Museum of Art that focuses on her face, with an aura of light around her dark hair, as well as a doubled, ghostly, disembodied image of the face in whitish cross-hatched pastel.[12] Benfey connects this not only with Creole women's habit of chatting on half-private balconies in the evening as children fell asleep listening to their voices but also with the practice of sheltering highly prized pale complexions from the fierce sun so as to avoid any suggestion of café au lait tinting or tainting.[13] It can be argued that any unwitting allusion by Degas to whiteness as the official, though not actual, Creole ethnicity at the time is emphasized further in the Göteborg variation of the portrait of Bell (figure 5.2).[14] Here the coarsely applied white pastel on Mathilde's face, arms, and neck, which may have been the source of Degas's comment in a letter of November 1872 that he had "just spoiled a large pastel with a certain mortification," proclaims a rather sickly pallor that seems to protest too much in comparison to the somewhat darker shade of the beige paper, from which it is finally not that different.[15] The materialization of this excess of whiteness in the space of a Creole veranda fails to contain insecurity about the possibilities of racial in-betweenness.

Threshold

Degas was more explicit about racial difference in what he wrote from New Orleans than in what he drew and painted there. In letters, he mentioned liking "nothing better than the Negresses of all shades, holding in their arms little white babies, so white, against white houses. . . . And the pretty women of pure blood and the pretty quadroons and the well-built Negresses;" and he described seeing the band of children in the extended family at his uncle's house "watched over by black women of different shades."[16] At the time, there were unspoken racialist assumptions commonly associated with the intimacy between black nursemaids and white children.[17] Yet any subtle implications about race mixture in

Figure 5.3. Edgar Degas, *Children on a Doorstep (New Orleans)*, 1872, oil on canvas, 23 5/8 x 29 1/2 in. (60 x 75 cm), Ordrupgaard, Copenhagen, Denmark. Photograph by Pernille Klemp.

New Orleans and in the artist's own family were fairly abstracted in his only depiction of a person of color in New Orleans, an anonymous nanny shown as a thinly painted (nearly transparent) profile on the left-hand side of a genre scene that is also a signed, if sketchy, family portrait.[18] *Children on a Doorstep (New Orleans)* depicts a transitional zone between portrait and genre, between interior and exterior, between white, sepia, and brown skin tones. Aside from the blond child who gazes at the viewer, the children are not exclusively "so white."

Racial fluidity was commonplace in New Orleans families, including Degas's own. A first cousin of Célestine Musson, the artist's Creole mother, was Norbert Rillieux, a leading chemical engineer, the inventor of a sugar refining process, and a free man of color.[19] Rillieux's white father, Vincent (Degas's maternal granduncle), who had a lifelong relationship with Rillieux's mother, Constance Vivant, a free woman of color, openly acknowledged and supported Norbert and his five siblings. Whether or not the artist actually knew about this (or whether or not it

affected his mother), Creole identity, both then and now, has been characterized by its lack of racial fixity. The fact that the Musson family had
owned African slaves did not make its status any more secure, because
free people of color in New Orleans had done the same thing.[20]

Under the circumstances, the threshold setting that opens onto
Degas's only depiction of an outdoor scene in New Orleans seems an
appropriate middle space for representing the mutability of complexions
and the instability of ethnicities. According to Victoria Rosner, thresholds can embody "in-between states that resist categorization" and can
figure as an "unsettling intermediary" between separate spheres, threatening domestic order as "sites of intersection and difference" where
servants can function as "threshold figures, moving between zones."[21]
Whereas Degas often pointed to racial difference in his letters from New
Orleans, he seemed in the doorstep scene with the nursemaid to paint
instead racial similarities in "different shades."[22] If everyone included in
the scene was at least potentially in between races, the cursory figure
of the nanny failed to reinforce racial hierarchies. Any hesitancy about
class or labor embodied in the threshold figure of the black servant was
likewise occluded, though perhaps not entirely eliminated, within this
locus of "intersection and difference."

Office

In the same letter in which Degas mentioned thoughts about the seductive shades of nannies, he pointedly shifted his tone to describe what he
saw in the American business district as "the contrast of the busy and
so positively appointed offices with this immense black animal force."[23]
In this pregnant phrase, the artist rather nervously offered an opposition of what he saw as positive and negative, of culture and nature, of
white and black, of business and labor. Although he tried to separate the
office from black labor, the two were ultimately imbricated in a global
capitalist system in which Degas's own family was heavily invested. *A
Cotton Office in New Orleans* represents an intermediate space of trade
situated between the cotton fields of Louisiana and the cotton mills of
Great Britain, a space in which African American labor is occluded yet
obliquely indexed. The juxtaposition of a picture of a ship and, below it,
a safe on the right back wall of the painted office alludes, virtually at the
vanishing point of the diagonal perspective system, to transit and the
kind of speculative capitalist trade that engaged the shaky finances of the
artist's family on both sides of the Atlantic Ocean. As we shall see, several family members occupy prominent positions in this depicted spatial

Figure 5.4. Edgar Degas, *A Cotton Office in New Orleans (Portraits in a Cotton Office)*, 1873, 28 3/4 x 36 1/4 in. (73 x 92 cm), Musée des Beaux-Arts, Pau, France. Photograph by Erich Lessing / Art Resource, NY.

network, which extended beyond the painting and beyond Louisiana to Europe and back, and which was predicated upon certain assumptions about race and class.

After the Haitian Revolution, Degas's maternal grandfather, Germain Musson, who was born of French parentage in Port-au-Prince, the capital of the French colony of Saint-Domingue, had, by about 1810, settled in New Orleans, where he exported cotton produced by inland slaves to New England textile mills. When his wife died, he moved to Paris to raise his four New Orleans–born children there, including Degas's mother Célestine. Degas's paternal grandfather, René-Hilaire Degas, became a moneychanger in Naples under the Napoleonic regime in Italy. He ultimately became a successful banker there, sending his eldest son, Auguste Degas, who would become the father of the artist, to Paris to establish a branch of the Neapolitan family bank there.[24]

Degas's maternal uncle, Michel Musson, who is depicted seated in a top hat in the foreground of *Cotton Office* checking the grade of a cotton sample, had been involved in the transatlantic cotton trade since before the American Civil War.[25] In a letter of 1864, the artist's father reported a conversation in Paris with Musson's business partner John Watt, who feared financial ruin was inevitable because of the abolition of black slavery.[26] In fact, Musson never recovered financially from the effects of the Civil War and its aftermath. After the death of his partner Watt in 1867, Musson soon formed the partnership known as Musson, Prestidge, and Company, Cotton Factors and Commission Merchants, which had moved by 1869 to the office in Factor's Row at 63 Carondelet Street subsequently depicted by Degas.[27]

It was in the midst of these changing postwar conditions that Degas's brother René joined Musson and Watt's firm in 1865; he was later to be depicted just off center in *Cotton Office*, leisurely reading the *Daily Picayune*. Letters that René wrote from Europe in the summer of 1866 to Michel Musson in New Orleans reveal the philosophy and practice of speculation that sometimes adversely linked the New Orleans cotton business with the Degas family's banking firm in Paris. Despite acknowledging a disastrous loss from a speculation in cotton futures, René wrote to Musson about an elaborate plan to found an export-import company in collaboration with another uncle in France, Henri Musson, and his brother Achille, who was coming to join him in New Orleans.[28] Achille would appear rather like a top-hatted Parisian flaneur, relaxing casually against the window frame, his "Creole" physiognomy darkened by shadow, on the left of his brother's painting of the cotton office. By 1873, when Edgar Degas visited and admired his brothers' firm, they were listed in local directories as cotton buyers. But their involvement in cotton trading was peripatetic and uneven, and Henri Musson in France worried that they were drawing off too much money to New Orleans.[29] Meanwhile, as I have argued elsewhere, the continuing financial instability of Michel Musson's own firm reached an unforeseen crisis at exactly the time Degas was painting it.[30]

If the various figures in the office suggest the transatlantic family context of the picture, what I want to pursue further here is the way the company's profits, alluded to however uncertainly in the scene, emerged from unstable intersections and unsettling tensions between the work of African Americans, whose labor subtended the global capitalism depicted by Degas, and the fluctuating profits and losses of the British textile industry. Twenty years earlier, in his now-famous memoir of 1853, *Twelve Years a Slave*, Solomon Northup had vividly described what he called the "mournful scene" of the slave depots in New Orleans.[31] The city was, in fact, the largest slave market in North America.[32] Northup described how customers, encouraged by the pen keeper Theophilus Freeman, "would . . . make us open our mouths and show our teeth, precisely as a jockey examines a horse which he is about to barter

A SLAVE-PEN AT NEW ORLEANS—BEFORE THE AUCTION. A SKETCH OF THE PAST.

of vessels before they can be deemed safe or sea-
worthy.

THE MONITOR.

Oh, loyal souls, sunk in a noble ship
  As o'er the waters crossed!
What direful tidings ring from every lip—
  "The *Monitor* is lost!"
Sunk in an instant underneath the wave,
  With half the crew lost in a watery grave.

And yet not lost. Within a higher realm
  We deem they are at rest,
Where a sure Pilot stands beside the helm:
  Surely such peace is best.

There quietly the ship at anchor rides,
  Beyond all fear of adverse winds and tides.

Tenderly, brothers, will we name them o'er,
  Nor think they died in vain,
Who went down with the *Monitor*, no more
  To hoist our flag again.
Their early call has left us more to do;
  But who could falter with their names in view?

OUR "MONITOR"—she earned her title well,
  Though short the race she run;
She left a record, for the world to tell,
  Of "victory nobly won."
Tenderly guard her in thy depths, O sea!
  For never nobler vessel sailed o'er thee.

A SLAVE-PEN AT NEW OR-
LEANS.

IN connection with the gradual downfall of slavery, we publish on this page an illustration of a
gang of negroes in a slave-pen at New Orleans before an auction. The picture is from a sketch
taken by a foreign artist before the war. In describing it the artist wrote:

"The men and women are well clothed, in their
Sunday best—the men in blue cloth of good quality, with beaver hats; and the women in calico
dresses, of more or less brilliancy, with silk ban-
dana handkerchiefs bound round their heads.

Placed in a row in a quiet thoroughfare, where,
without interrupting the traffic, they may com-
mand a good chance of transient custom, they
stand through a great part of the day, subject to
the inspection of the purchasing or non-purchasing
passing crowd. They look heavy, perhaps a little
sad, but not altogether unhappy."

EXODUS OF REBEL WOMEN.

WE illustrate on this page a scene which is frequently renewed at Washington, viz., THE DE-
PARTURE OF SECESH WOMEN FOR RICHMOND.

Figure 5.5. "A Slave-Pen at New Orleans— Before the Auction," *Harper's Weekly*, January 24, 1863, 61. Special Collections, Norlin Library, University of Colorado, Boulder.

for or purchase."[33] Northup was describing not the public auction markets at the St. Louis Hotel in the French Quarter or the St. Charles Hotel in the American sector but rather one of the numerous private pens that were scattered throughout the Central Business District in New Orleans, where hundreds of thousands of slaves were sold to walk-in customers by dealers, brokers, and traders dealing not in cotton but in human beings.

Edgar Degas was probably familiar with the presence of enslaved human beings in his New Orleans family: his mother's dowry had come from the sale of a female slave given to her by her father in New Orleans, and her brother, the artist's uncle, had owned seven slaves.[34] When Degas visited his uncle's cotton firm, he would have been surrounded by physical remnants and reminders of slave markets that had closed less than a decade previously. (Emancipation had come in 1863, but the Thirteenth Amendment to the US Constitution did not go into effect until 1865.) Even more than today, New Orleans was a palimpsest whose buildings retained traces of earlier uses.

Since the late 1850s, the Central Business District had teemed with slave depots, yards, pens, and booths. Some twenty-five had been located on Baronne, Gravier, Common, and Magazine Streets in the vicinity of the St. Charles Hotel, which was located on St. Charles Avenue between Gravier and Common Streets. The site of Degas's uncle's cotton firm at the corner of Carondelet and Perdido Streets had literally been encircled by vestiges of these smaller slave markets. Another dozen were situated across Canal Street in the French Quarter on Exchange Place, St. Louis and Chartres Streets, and Esplanade Avenue—which extends out to Mid-City, where Degas's uncle's house was located.[35]

The complicit spatial and historical positioning that Degas point- edly avoided acknowledging is confirmed by an earlier *Harper's Weekly* illustration of a slave pen in New Orleans, probably in the vicinity of the St. Charles Hotel. It depicts the practice described by Solomon Northup of pen keepers parading temporarily well-fed slaves in new clothes and exhorting them to "look smart": here, top-hatted black men, who can- not relax like the white men in the Degas. The text below states they must stand there all day for inspection.[36] Despite the fashionable attire, they are not flaneurs or even idlers, like the portly, top-hatted white bystander (*badaud*) who ogles the enslaved black women. As extensively documented by historian Walter Johnson, people became products sold for profit, graded for sale by skin color, height, weight, gender, and age.[37] Just as cotton was graded for sale ("fair to middling"), so were human beings. Slaves sold in New Orleans thus represented "a congealed form of the capital upon which the commercial development of the [Missis- sippi] Valley depended." The separation between labor and capital in conventional political economy was here collapsed.[38]

By the time Degas visited New Orleans, despite the political facts of emancipation and Reconstruction, despite the changed market for cot- ton and the supplanting of the old planter-slave system with the share- cropping system of newly freed black tenant farmers, the economic subjugation of black laborers in the fields had not ended. Both political and economic oppression were exacerbated by the emergence of Jim Crow as well as the rise of supremacist paramilitary groups like the New Orleans White League, whose members included René Degas, Michel Musson, and his son-in-law William Bell, who shows a handful of cot- ton to a customer at the center of Degas's picture.[39] Despite occasional resistance, the vast majority of former slaves remained disfranchised in their old homes, working under the surveillance of the same overseers who had driven them before, in what amounted to wage slavery. Oppres- sive workloads, whether for indentured freedmen or slaves, remained a

Figure 5.6. Janet-Lange, "La Culture du coton aux Etats-Unis," *L'Illustration* XXXIX (March 22, 1862), 180. [Public domain]. Photograph provided by Marilyn R. Brown.

Figure 5.7. Winslow Homer, *The Cotton Pickers*, 1876, oil on canvas, 24 1/16 x 38 1/8 in. (61.12 x 96.84 cm), Los Angeles County Museum of Art, Los Angeles. Photograph www.lacma.org.

Figure 5.8. Leonardo Drew, *Untitled # 25*, 1992, cotton and wax, 102 x 158 x 33 in. (259 x 401.3 x 83.8 cm), Rubell Family Collection, Miami. Artwork © Leonardo Drew, courtesy Sikkema Jenkins & Co., New York.

constant.[40] The new system of wage labor was founded upon institutions and networks that had been created by slavery.

Both before and after Reconstruction, visual representations of labor in the cotton fields suppressed this social reality by rendering bales, huge bags, and baskets as near weightless, as lifted with ease.

In what Johnson would term a "carceral landscape,"[41] whose discipline spatially transforms nature and human beings into capitalist profit, a French illustration of "La Culture du coton aux Etats-Unis" from 1862 depicts planters and equestrian overseers enforcing the black labor that produces cotton as a raw material. The subdivided vignette format likewise enforces the separated and mechanical tasks of planting, picking, carding, grading, pressing, baling, and draying that comprised the systemic production of cotton that, with few changes, would continue after emancipation. However anodyne its depiction, this illustration can serve as a reminder of the various kinds of black labor absent from, yet implied by, Degas's painting.[42] In a different way, Winslow Homer, inspired by a visit to Virginia in 1875–76 at a time when radical black Republican Reconstruction was being suppressed, completely eschewed the grueling work of both male and female field hands in his painting of *Cotton Pickers*, which was bought by an English cotton merchant. Idealizing the two unthreatening and picturesque black women for an industrialist patron, the painting gently suggests, even as it dematerializes African American labor, that picking cotton was to be the eternal lot of blacks, despite emancipation.[43]

A corrective to this kind of imagery, as well as to Degas's, can be found in an untitled sculpture from 1992 by African American artist Leonardo Drew.[44] This impenetrable wall of raw cotton bales and wax, over thirteen feet long, eight feet tall, and three feet thick, embodies cotton's enormous weight and materiality. As a monument of oppressive whiteness that threatens to crush the viewer in a return of the repressed, this deceptively minimalist sculpture can be fruitfully paired with Johnson's observations about the transformation of "lashes into labor into bales into dollars into pounds sterling" in the global economy of the nineteenth century; workers who came up short received the lash, as Northup attests.[45] Records from one Louisiana plantation reveal how during the week of September 6, 1852, a cotton picker named John picked 280 pounds on Monday, 135 on Tuesday, 320 on Wednesday, 330 on Thursday, 315 on Friday, and 325 on Saturday, making his weekly total 1,705 pounds. Another picker named Letty picked 320 pounds on Monday, 325 on Tuesday, 385 on Wednesday, 365 on Thursday, 365 on Friday, and 350 on Saturday, making her weekly total 2,110 pounds. Notations such as these in plantation record books translated finger-bleeding, back-breaking labor into the abstract terms of commerce.[46] Leonardo Drew's sculpture speaks both of forced labor in the fields and of the abstraction of that labor into compressed units of exchange.

Unlike the dense material in Drew's sculpture, the fluffy cotton in Degas's painting does not speak to the conditions of its production.

Figure 5.9. Edgar Degas, *The Cotton Merchants*, 1873, oil on linen, (23 1/8 x 38 3/16 in.; 58.7 x 71.8 cm), Fogg Museum, Harvard Art Museums, Cambridge, MA, gift of Herbert N. Straus, 1929.90. Photograph Imaging Department © President and Fellows of Harvard College.

Absent black labor may be indexed inversely in the painting by the white commodity for sale by black-suited white men, in what Degas referred to in a letter as "the precious material." Yet the labor of the artist himself, what he mentioned in a letter as "a better hand than many others," is likewise present in the picture, most tangibly in the painterly representation of that same cotton.[47] Tactile traces of the literal work of the artist's hand thus disavow and supplant reference to more latent forms of manual labor in the free-floating white sign of the product of that labor. The ostensible effortlessness of the artist's brushstroke meanwhile denies the notion of mere work. This aestheticizing displacement is magnified by the close visual analogy between the painted cotton and the painting on the wall, in what Degas called in his letter the "better art" of the sketch version, which is today in the Fogg Museum.

The only depicted labor admitted to Degas's scene is the quiet recording of figures by the three men, including Musson's partner John Livaudais, who have shed their jackets in the right foreground and center background (figure 5.4). Their white collars are as close as we come to *cotonniers*, or cotton workers, a term Degas curiously employed in occasional later references to the painting.[48] Yet, according to Johnson, as well as historians Edward E. Baptist and Sven Beckert, the Atlantic market for cotton was intricately tethered to labor in the fields, just as the economic fabric of capitalism itself had been based on a long complicity with slavery.[49] The metric rule of "bales per hand per acre"[50] was linked in the global capitalist economy to the record keeping of factors in the markets of New Orleans as well as to merchant houses in New York, brokerage firms and exchanges in Liverpool, and textile mills in Manchester. Cotton factors used notations in account books, invoices, graphs, and charts to calculate the hard work of African Americans in terms of profit that was registered in credit as "fictional capital."[51] They were middlemen, occupying an intermediate position in the precarious capitalist trade between Louisiana and Lancashire. Across the Atlantic, the circuit of exchange of labor to credit to labor to profit was dependent upon the wage slavery of textile factory workers in Manchester cotton mills.[52]

The cotton factors' practice of keeping a set of books for the planter—recording income, expenditures, debts, and surpluses—is depicted on the right-hand side of Degas's picture. This "hurry-up-and-wait rhythm" of activity[53] is counterweighted, in the center and at the left, by the relaxed exchange among factors, brokers, and buyers, including René and Achille Degas.[54] Degas's cotton factors' account books and invoices, jettisoned into a wastebasket that figures prominently in the right foreground, can be seen to reduce to abstract ciphers the social relations of the global cotton industry. Degas's cotton, compared to Leonardo Drew's, has no weight because, as Anna Arabindan-Kesson has astutely observed, it is depicted at the moment of its dematerialization into purely monetary value in an unstable global market.[55] As visualized by Degas, the exhausting labor of human beings in cotton fields becomes transformed into commodity fetishism, through which the marketability of, and speculation upon, finely graded cotton obscures its oppressive production.[56]

The failure of Degas's uncle's cotton business at precisely the time the artist was painting it can be linked to the altered market conditions of Reconstruction, the shift to cotton exchanges, and the international stock market crash of 1873. It can likewise be connected to the social instability of life on the Mississippi River, as well as the risks, jolts, and unsettling shifts of the Atlantic market for cotton, which earlier had constituted such a large sector of the global economy.[57] Such instabilities were foundational for the wider modern world. Given the uncertainty about whether the middlemen might actually profit from the commodity produced by black field hands, Degas can in many respects be seen to represent the beleaguered status of what Johnson terms "global whitemanism,"[58] here engaged in a misleadlingly relaxed performance of anxious white masculinity beset by the crises of capitalism.

In view of the British-dominated world market for cotton, it is not surprising that Degas formulated a plan in a letter written from New Orleans to artist James Tissot in London to sell the picture of raw cotton

in his uncle's office to a Manchester cotton spinner (Manchester being
known at the time as a "cottonopolis") and to do so through the British dealer Agnew.[59] Given the subject matter and style of paintings that
Agnew typically sold and that the industrialist "millocrat" William Cottrill typically collected, Degas's idea was seemingly fueled more by ambition and abstract cotton marketing logic than by pragmatic art market
sense. Perhaps the artist was too caught up in the middle position occupied by his relatives in the cotton trade. The final nail in the coffin was
that Cottrill was forced to sell his palatial home and art collection in
April, 1873, to keep his business afloat in dire financial times. So the venture in transatlantic artistic futures plotted by Degas from New Orleans
did not prove to be immediately successful. Like any business speculation, including his uncle's, it involved unforeseen risks and shifting circumstances that destabilized the artist's attempt to produce a painted
product for a changing market.[60]

Conclusion

While Degas's representations of in-between domestic spaces in New
Orleans suggest that differences of race and class were not as clear-cut as
white Creoles might have desired, his picture of the cotton office opens
up larger questions of the risks, contradictions, tensions, instabilities, and
injustices of the system of global capitalist exchange on which such bina-
ries depended.[61] Although the room painted by Degas has a shutter and a
window[62] that open to the unseen outside world, as well as interior windows opening onto an inner office where a seated figure stifles a sneeze,
this privatized public space is not particularly represented as in between in
the physical sense of the built environment. Yet within the local geography
and infrastructure of New Orleans, the actual site of the office *was* located
in between labor and commodity, in between the pens and the port, the
latter pointing to the larger world. The picture can be read as representing an unstable interstitial zone of intersection in the broader network
of transatlantic capitalism and the risky marketing of cotton. It depicts a
deceptively leisurely yet contested space of speculation, positioned precariously within the circuits of cotton capitalism, in between the dehumaniz-
ing labor of picking raw cotton in Louisiana and the unsteady economics
of the manufacturing of fine cotton textiles in Britain.

Degas's *Cotton Office* ultimately represses, disavows, and dematerializes the oppression of black labor by transforming its white product into
a commodity sold by anxious white men in a space whose complex relation to the outer world it simultaneously reveals and occludes. Indeed,

the picture itself aspires to be a similar commodity, however unstable. Despite depicting a middle space, this painted office in New Orleans is not a sweet spot. Like the Creole spaces of the domestic veranda or threshold, it alludes in spite of itself to interrelated uncertainties about family, race, labor, and commerce in an unsettled transatlantic world.

NOTES

1. Žižek's thinking about intermediate architectural spaces as imaginary solutions to social antagonism is useful here: Slavoj Žižek, "Architectural Parallax: Spandrel and Other Phenomena of Class Struggle," lecture delivered at Jack Tilton Gallery, New York City, April 23, 2009, as discussed by Lahiji Nadir, "In Interstitial Space: Žižek on 'Architectural Parallax,'" *International Journal of Žižek Studies* 3, no. 3 (2009), 1–19. My thanks to Prof. Teresa Toulouse for this reference, as well as other editorial suggestions.

2. I am inspired here by the discussion of the visible and invisible overlapping and intersecting cultural landscapes of black and white Americans in Craig Evan Barton, ed., *Sites of Memory: Perspectives on Architecture and Race* (New York: Princeton Architectural Press, 2001).

3. The ideas of Sigmund Freud and Walter Benjamin are often invoked. See Susan Sidlauskas, *Body, Place, and Self in Nineteenth-Century Painting* (Cambridge: Cambridge University Press, 2000); Diana Fuss, *The Sense of an Interior: Four Writers and the Rooms That Shaped Them* (London: Routledge, 2004); and Charles Rice, *The Emergence of the Interior: Architecture, Modernity, Domesticity* (London: Routledge, 2007).

4. Gail Feigenbaum, "Edgar Degas, Almost a Son of Louisiana," in Gail Feigenbaum et al., *Degas and New Orleans: A French Impressionist in America* (New York: Rizzoli, distributed for the New Orleans Museum of Art and Ordrupgaard, Copenhagen, 1999), 15–16.

5. Marilyn R. Brown, *Degas and the Business of Art: A Cotton Office in New Orleans* (University Park: Pennsylvania State University Press for College Art Association, 1994; reissued in 2010 as an ACLS Humanities E-Book: https://quod.lib.umich.edu/cgi/t/text/text-idx?c=acls;idno=heb04023), 21, note 22, quoting undated letter [1933] from Odile Musson to P. A. Lemoisne, DeGas-Musson archive, box V, folder 3, Special Collections, Tulane University, New Orleans.

6. Feminist critiques of the gendered opposition of public and private include Hilde Heynen, "Modernity and Domesticity: Tensions and Contradictions," in *Negotiating Domesticity: Spatial Productions of Gender in Modern Architecture*, ed. Hilde Heynen and Gülsüm Baydar (London: Routledge, 2005), 1–29.

7. For balcony and window scenes by the likes of Caillebotte, Cassatt, Manet, Monet, and Morisot, see, among others, Griselda Pollock, "Modernity and the Spaces of Femininity," *Vision and Difference: Femininity, Feminism, and the Histories of Art* (London: Routledge, 1988), especially 56–61; Hollis Clayson, "Threshold Space: Parisian Modernism Betwixt and Between (1869 to 1891)," in *Impressionist Interiors* (Dublin: National Gallery of Ireland, 2008), 14–29.

8. On her gaze, see Walters Art Museum, *The Age of Impressionism: European Paintings from Ordrupgaard, Copenhagen* (Baltimore: Walters Art Museum, 2002), 108–10.

9. Given Degas's express complaint about the brilliant light in New Orleans, it

makes sense that he would have preferred the balcony (letter to James Tissot, November 19, 1872, in Feigenbaum et al., *Degas and New Orleans*, 291). On balconies as transitional zones between interior and exterior, private and public, see François Loyer, *Paris Nineteenth Century: Architecture and Urbanism* (New York: Abbeville Press, 1988), 138–39, 354; and Malcolm Heard, *French Quarter Manual: An Architectural Guide to New Orleans's Vieux Carré* (Jackson: University Press of Mississippi, 1997), 82–87, hereinafter *FQM*.

10. See Jean Sutherland Boggs's discussion of the portraits and citations of the correspondence in "New Orleans and the Work of Degas," in Feigenbaum et al., *Degas and New Orleans*, 200–206.

11. On shutters, see Heard, *FQM*, 72–75.

12. Christopher Benfey, *Degas in New Orleans: Encounters in the Creole World of Kate Chopin and George Washington Cable* (New York: Alfred A. Knopf, 1997), 92–93; Edgar Degas, *The Artist's Cousin, Probably Mrs. William Bell*, 1872–73, charcoal and pastel on cardboard, 25 x 22 7/8 in., Metropolitan Museum of Art, H. O. Havemeyer Collection.

13. Benfey, *Degas in New Orleans*, 93, 96, drawing upon the writings of Edward King, Grace King, and Robert Tallant. Benfey, ibid., 192, mentions Mathilde Musson Bell's relief efforts in caring for families of the dead and wounded of the New Orleans White League, of which her husband was treasurer, after the Battle of Liberty Place in 1874.

14. See Virginia R. Dominguez, *White by Definition: Social Classification in Creole Louisiana* (New Brunswick: Rutgers University Press, 1986); Arnold R. Hirsch and Joseph Logsdon, eds., *Creole New Orleans: Race and Americanization* (Baton Rouge: Louisiana State University Press, 1992).

15. While it is likely the paper has darkened over time, it is less likely, for reasons of visibility, that Degas would have loaded white pastel onto pure white paper; he is known to have used tinted paper in other drawings. Boggs, from whom my interpretation differs, cites Degas's letter to James Tissot, November 27, 1872; see Boggs, "New Orleans," 204. On the artist's depictions of women as invalids in New Orleans, also see ibid., 186–97. These pictures may allude unconsciously to Degas's mother.

16. Degas to Lorenz Frölich, November 27, 1872, and to Désiré Dihau, November 11, 1872, in *Degas Letters*, ed. Marcel Guérin, trans. Marguerite Kay (Oxford: Bruno Cassirer, 1947), quoted in Feigenbaum et al., *Degas and New Orleans*, 292, 290; and Marcel Guérin, ed., *Lettres de Degas* (Paris: Bernard Grasset, 1945), 22, 19.

17. See Pierre Larousse, *Grand dictionnaire universel du XIXe siècle* (Paris: Larousse, 1866–76), vol. 11, 904; C. Vann Woodward, *The Strange Career of Jim Crow*, 3rd revised ed. (New York: Oxford University Press, 1974), 42–43; Ann Laura Stoler, *Race and the Education of Desire: Foucault's History of Sexuality and the Colonial Order of Things* (Durham: Duke University Press, 1995), 149–83.

18. On this painting, see Boggs, "New Orleans," 214–16, and Jean Sutherland Boggs et al., *Degas, 1834–1917* (New York: Metropolitan Museum of Art, 1988), 180–81.

19. Benfey, *Degas*, ch. 7; on the two branches of the New Orleans family, also see James B. Byrnes and Victoria Cooke, "Appendix I: Degas's Family in New Orleans: A Who's Who," in Feigenbaum et al., *Degas and New Orleans*, 275–88. Norbert Rillieux (1806–94) was educated in Paris and became a professor of engineering at the École Centrale at the age of twenty years.

20. See note 14 above. Henri Loyrette reveals that part of Degas's mother's dowry came from the sale of a female slave given to her by her father in New Orleans, *Degas* (Paris: Fayard, 1991), 18. Brown points out that Michel Musson had owned seven slaves

before the Civil War (28). On the racial attitudes of the New Orleans family, see Marilyn R. Brown, "Documentation: The DeGas-Musson Papers at Tulane University," *Art Bulletin* 72, no. 1 (1990), 124–25.

21. Victoria Rosner, *Modernism and the Architecture of Private Life* (New York: Columbia University Press, 2005), 61–62, 65, 68. Also see Clayson, "Threshold Space," on the visual representations of thresholds; and on the related setting of courtyards, see Heard, *FQM*, 104–9.

22. For interpretations of the picture's "in-between states" of a more temporal nature, see Walters Art Museum, *Age of Impressionism*, on the image of "unfinished" children in the process of growing up (112). On Boggs's suggestion of an unwitting temporal interregnum between current childhood happiness and the destruction six years later of the equilibrium of the family on Esplanade by Degas's brother René's elopement with America Durrive Olivier, who lived in the house over the fence in the background of the doorstep scene, beyond the faithful dog whom Degas had dubbed Vasco da Gama, see Boggs, "New Orleans," 218.

23. Degas to Frölich, as in note 16: "cette immense force animale noire." See Brown, *Degas and the Business*, 37, note 77, on that point that not all of the black population of New Orleans at the time was engaged exclusively in physical labor: free people of color, for instance, were often involved in retail, and there were, in fact, a few black-owned commission houses that catered to black planters.

24. Roy McMullen states that Germain Musson's family belonged to Saint-Domingue's population of some thirty thousand whites, mostly French or Creole, who lived by exporting the sugar, cotton, coffee, cocoa, and indigo produced by half a million slaves shipped from Africa" (5); *Degas: His Life, Times, and Work* (London: Secker & Warburg, 1985), 2–7.

25. Brown, *Degas and the Business*, 28.

26. DeGas-Musson archive, box II, folder 13; Brown, "Documentation," 125.

27. Brown, *Degas and the Business*, 29; today 407 Carondelet Street.

28. DeGas-Musson archive, box II, folder 24. Brown, "Documentation," 126.

29. DeGas-Musson archive, box II, folder 48; Brown, *Degas and the Business*, 31.

30. Brown, *Degas and the Business*, 31–36.

31. Solomon Northup, *Twelve Years a Slave* (1853; Mineola, NY: Dover Publications, 2000), 82.

32. Walter Johnson, *River of Dark Dreams: Slavery and Empire in the Cotton Kingdom* (Cambridge, MA: Belknap Press of Harvard University Press, 2013), 2.

33. Northup, 79–80. He does not comment on the irony of the pen owner's name.

34. See above, note 20. Also see Brown, *Degas and the Business*, 28, note 39, on a pro-slavery tract written and published in London in 1862 by Degas's Paris-based uncle Eugène Musson (brother of Michel and Célestine).

35. Richard Campanella, "On the Structural Basis of Social Memory: Cityscapes of the New Orleans Slave Trade, Part II," *Preservation in Print*, April 2013, 19.

36. "A Slave Pen at New Orleans—Before the Auction," *Harper's Weekly*, January 24, 1863, 61. On the image's previous appearance in the *London Daily News* (April 6, 1861), see Maurie D. McInnis, *Slaves Waiting for Sale: Abolitionist Art and the American Slave Trade* (Chicago: University of Chicago Press, 2011), 162–63. McInnis suggests that the illustration depicts one of the numerous slave pens near the St. Charles Hotel, perhaps that operated by J. M. Wilson, since the name "Wilson" appears over the central doorway. If so, the site would have been approximately two blocks from Factor's Row, where Musson's cotton office was located by 1869. See the map, ibid., 158. Walter

Johnson suggests that identical suits worn by enslaved men masked differences among the slaves, including individual pasts and potential problems; *Soul by Soul: Life inside the Antebellum Slave Market* (Cambridge, MA: Harvard University Press, 1999), 121. See also Northup, *Twelve Years*, 78–79.

37. Johnson, *Soul by Soul*, passim, and *River*, 162.

38. Johnson, *River*, 86; also see 249, 279. Among recent histories of global cotton capitalism, I draw more extensively upon Johnson because of the depth and detail of his focus on the Mississippi River valley and specifically Louisiana and New Orleans. But see also Edward E. Baptist, *The Half Has Never Been Told: Slavery and the Making of American Capitalism* (New York: Basic Books, 2014) and Sven Beckert, *Empire of Cotton: A Global History* (New York: Alfred A. Knopf, 2014).

39. Brown, "Documentation," 125; Benfey, *Degas*, chs. 9 and 10. See note 13 above on Mathilde Musson Bell's activities with the White League.

40. Susan Eva O'Donovan, *Becoming Free in the Cotton South* (Cambridge, MA: Harvard University Press, 2007), especially ch. 3; Brown, *Degas and the Business*, 34–36.

41. Johnson, *River*, ch. 8.

42. Brown, *Degas and the Business*, 38–40. Compare Alfred R. Wand, "Scenes of a Cotton Plantation," wood engraving, *Harper's Weekly*, February 2, 1867, 72–73, reproduced as fig. 3.7 in an excellent study I was able to access only after I had completed a substantial draft of this essay: Anna Arabindan-Kesson, "Threads of Empire: The Visual Economy of the Cotton Trade in the Indian and Atlantic Ocean Worlds, 1840–1900," PhD diss., Yale University, 2014, ch. 3, "Cotton, Industry and Landscape in Britain and the United States, 1865–1880."

43. Brown, *Degas and the Business*, 39–41. See Arabindan-Kesson's discussion for a rather different reading of this picture and its dialogue with Degas's painting, 18–42.

44. Robert Hobbs et al., *30 Americans: Rubell Family Collection* (New York: Distributed Art Publishers, 2011), 62–63; Huey Copeland, *Bound to Appear: Art, Slavery, and the Site of Blackness in Multicultural America* (Chicago: University of Chicago Press, 2013), 14; see also the television episode featuring Leonardo Drew, "Investigation," *Art 21*, PBS, 2014. Arabindan-Kesson, "Threads of Empire," 4–5, argues that Drew embeds and compresses history in his bales, whose abstract formal arrangement she sees as evoking the industrial labor of cotton production.

45. Johnson, *River*, 224, 248. See also Northup, *Twelve Years*.

46. Johnson, *River*, 245–46.

47. Letter from Degas, no. 6, to Tissot, February 18, 1873, in Guérin, *Degas Letters*, 29–30.

48. Brown, *Degas and the Business*, 42.

49. Whereas earlier historians like Eugene Genovese saw the South as noncapitalistic compared to the industrial North, Johnson and other recent historians of global cotton capitalism insist on the interdependency of the capitalist market economy and black southern labor. See Eugene D. Genovese, *The Political Economy of Slavery: Studies in the Economy and Society of the Slave South*, 2nd ed. (1965; repr. Middletown, CT: Wesleyan University Press, 1989). See also Baptist, *Half*, and Beckert, *Empire of Cotton*.

50. Johnson, *River*, 13, 153, 246, 254.

51. Ibid., 261; on factors' "creative accounting," see 275.

52. Brown, *Degas and the Business*, 51–54. Contemporary observers linked the "enslavement" of textile workers in Lancashire factories with the servitude of black cotton pickers in the American South. Yet English painters like Eyre Crowe (*The Dinner Hour, Wigan*, 1874, Manchester City Art Galleries) typically presented rather benign images of

clean and well-nourished female cotton workers relaxing from their labors. In the guise of documentary realism, not unlike that of Homer's scenes of cotton pickers in America, such pictures personified residual capital as much as labor and did so in picturesque and unthreatening ways—with workers, for example, gendered as submissive—that were acceptable to the manufacturing classes. For a more extensive discussion of the Crowe painting, see Arabindan-Kesson, 42–61.

53. Johnson, *River*, 270.

54. Brown, *Degas and the Business*, 29–30.

55. Arabindan-Kesson, 12–15.

56. See Johnson, *River*, 261, 265–66, though he does not mention Degas. The simultaneous masking and revealing of the oppressive production of fine cotton, namely the connection between cotton capitalism, slavery, and the textile industry, has been brilliantly addressed by contemporary African American artist Renée Green, who, for her installation *Mise-en-scène* (1992, Fabric Workshop and Museum, Philadelphia and subsequent iterations), produced white cotton sateen fabric silkscreened with eighteenth- and nineteenth-century prints of slavery, including scenes of violence; the fabric was then upholstered on period domestic furniture and arranged as a genteel parlor, with the iconography of enslavement hidden in plain sight. See Copeland, *Bound to Appear*, 174–93.

57. Brown, *Degas and the Business*, 31–36; Johnson, *River*, 10.

58. Johnson, *River*, 418, referring in particular to the southerners' supremacist, expansionist ideology and attendant insecurities.

59. See Brown, *Degas and the Business*, 17: "I have set to work on a fairly vigorous picture which is destined for Agnew and which he should place in Manchester; for if a spinner ever wished to find his painter, he really ought to snap me up."

60. Brown, *Degas and the Business*, 43–58.

61. In light of economist Thomas Piketty's recent arguments about the inequality of capital in our own century, we can look at the past through the lens of the present: Thomas Piketty, *Capital in the Twenty-First Century* (Cambridge, MA: Belknap Press of Harvard University Press, 2014), especially part 3. Piketty is cited in a different light by Marnin Young, "Capital in the Nineteenth Century: Edgar Degas's Portraits at the Stock Exchange in 1879," *Nonsite* 14 (December 15, 2014), http://nonsite.org/article/capital-in-the-nineteenth-century.

62. That window, along with the whole back wall of the original room, unfortunately collapsed in March 2013, probably due to a heavy steel fire escape added later to the exterior of the circa 1858 structure. It was reported soon to be rebuilt in "Wall Down," *Preservation in Print*, May 2013, 16.

CHAPTER SIX
John Galsworthy's "That Old-Time Place"
Nostalgia, Repetition, and Interstitial Space in the St. Louis "Exchange" Hotel

—Teresa A. Toulouse

In 1912, English novelist John Galsworthy and his wife, Ada, visited New Orleans on part of a long tour across the United States. One of their more memorable moments as tourists involved a visit to the decaying St. Louis Hotel, a well-known city landmark that had been abandoned to pigeons and bats, and was then serving as a stable. Partially destroyed by a hurricane three years later, the hotel was finally torn down in 1917. Lamenting its destruction, but skipping over its complicated history, Lyle Saxon, the early twentieth-century New Orleans preservationist, noted, "It had been the center of society once, but, in time, it became outmoded." His contemporary, architectural historian Nathaniel Cortlandt Curtis, equally mourning its demise, praised the soaring dome of the destroyed hotel as "one of the outstanding achievements in the annals of American architecture."[1]

Designed by Jacques Nicholas Bussière de Pouilly, the French-born architect who also designed a new St. Louis Cathedral in 1849 and built a number of famous Creole family tombs, the St. Louis Hotel was originally completed in 1838 at the then-staggering cost of $500,000 and rebuilt two years later, after a fire. The massive structure, modeled on the neoclassical buildings along the Rue de Rivoli in Paris, became etched into the memories of generations of New Orleanians for a wide range of reasons. Historians point out that the banking speculators who constructed it wished to lure the city's business patrons to stay in the Creole French Quarter and to compete with the St. Charles Hotel built across Canal Street in the American sector.[2] The "Exchange" Hotel, as the first building had been commonly known, thus became the hotel of choice for wealthy Creole plantation owners. Saxon nostalgically points out in

Figure 6.1. St. Louis Hotel, an illustration from Edwin Jewell, *Crescent City Illustrated* (New Orleans, 1873), 179. The Historic New Orleans Collection, Gift of Mr. Edmund Leet Jr., acc. no. 2001-115-RL.

Fabulous New Orleans (1928): "It was to the old St. Louis Hotel that the rich planters came when they shipped their cotton to New Orleans in the fall. It was here that magnificent balls were given in the Great Hall."[3] But not only did people involved in the interrelated exchanges of cotton and rice and enslaved people in the opulent years before the Civil War patronize the St. Louis. Local and even national politicians were among its guests, most famously Henry Clay at one grand ball. During the Civil War, it came to serve as a hospital for soldiers of both sides. After the war, however, despite intermittent grand renovations and reopenings, the St. Louis gradually foundered. Newly purchased by the State of Louisiana, with its famous rotunda room divided to create a top and lower floor, the hotel became the seat of Louisiana's Reconstruction government from 1874 to 1882. The St. Louis not only witnessed the heated debates and controversies surrounding that government, but as the statehouse, it was the object of an armed insurgency by members of the city's White League on September 14, 1874. The league was composed of powerful city elites and others who, in the lingering white mythology of the city, "saved" it from the "carpetbaggers" in the Battle of Liberty Place of September 1874.[4] Most pertinently for the sketch that Galsworthy would write, the St. Louis Hotel was, from its beginning until the Civil War, one of the prominent sites in New Orleans for slave auctions.[5]

Galsworthy's sketch, "That Old-Time Place," appears in the first section—"Concerning Life"—of his 1912 collection of sketches and essays, *The Inn of Tranquility*. Since the sketch deals, if somewhat inaccurately,

Figure 6.2. "The Lobby, Old St. Louis Hotel, New Orleans, LA," postcard, collection of Teresa A. Toulouse.

with the structure of the St. Louis, it is useful to describe briefly three of the hotel's more significant features. While it was a massive structure, originally stretching from Royal Street to Chartres Street along St. Louis Street and rising to eighty-six feet in the central rotunda, in the beginning it had only two hundred rooms for guests. (In later incarnations, its ballrooms demolished, it would sport nearly six hundred rooms.) Rooms for travelers and ballrooms were accessed from a smaller entrance on Royal Street, while the hotel's most famous space was its dome room, approached through an imposing granite and marble portico on St. Louis Street, which opened onto a foyer that gave into the rotunda with its dome.

A vast overarching structure, the dome was ornamented with patriotic frescoes and circled with sixteen portrait heads of American and Southern statesmen, most of whom had been slaveholders.[6] The heads were so cleverly painted that they appeared to be sculpted. Like many hotels of that period, when there were no commercial exchanges, the rotunda of the St. Louis served as the site of all varieties of commerce, including exchanges in bondsmen. Galsworthy, visiting in 1912, and conceivably unaware that a floor had been laid in the 1870s that cut the rotunda into two rooms, differentiates the upper section of the rotunda with the dome, where the embattled state legislature had met, from the lower section, where many exchanges, but for him chiefly the slave auctions, had originally taken place.

"That Old-Time Place," originally the fifteenth of eighteen sketches, makes use of particular features of these three spaces—the upper halls and rooms, the dome room, and the covered-over lower portion of the dome room—-to develop a ghost story about what Galsworthy represents as the "Old South." What follows is a brief summary. The narrator and his companion arrive at the decaying hotel to take a house tour. In a nod to Dante, their aged female guide, almost totally deaf, leads the tourists through the hotel's halls, rotunda, and auction sites, as Galsworthy's prose becomes increasingly gothic.[7] Approaching the lower level beneath the dome, the level where the auctions were held, they encounter a gaunt, beaten live horse wandering the halls, whose image gives way to a vision of ghosts, both black and white, and the sound of a slight laugh. These odd conjunctions lead the narrator to exclaim, "Who laughed in there? The Old South itself—that incredible, fine, lost soul! That 'old-time' thing of old ideals, blindfolded by its own history! That queer proud blend of simple chivalry and tyranny, of piety and the abhorrent thing!" The narrator and his companion then flee that "old-time place," accompanied by a melancholy and evocative "drip, drip, drip of water down the walls."[8]

While the sketch's ghostly, sorrowful qualities are often remarked, those who mention it seem most often drawn to its depiction of the old horse wandering the ruin.[9] In what follows, I want to examine more closely the ways in which Galsworthy uses descriptions of a number of differing interstitial spaces in the hotel to comment on Southern history. In the course of this commentary, not only the South but also the narrator becomes implicated in a fantasy of historical stasis. In its exploration of the powerful, invisible, yet palpable space between nature and culture, between death and life, and between violence and pleasure, "That Old-Time Place" raises uncomfortable questions about the uncanny space between history as nostalgia and history as a threatening repetition that not only permeates New Orleans but also threatens to spill over into and haunt the more properly English sketches with which Galsworthy surrounds it.

Nature and Culture

As the guide takes her charges up a spiral staircase to view hallways and rooms, she moves creepily, "touching this fungused wall, that rusting stairway." The air is pervaded with the smell of rot, and as the tourists walk "along the mouldering corridors and rooms," they observe how "the black peeling papers hung like stalactites." These images of natural processes, including fungus, rust, damp, water, and "stalactites," suggest initially that nature—the outside world—is entering and covering over the hotel's inside spaces of culture and history.[10] One could interpret this

Figure 6.3. "Stairway, Old St. Louis Hotel, New Orleans, LA," postcard, collection of Teresa A. Toulouse.

process as simply a temporal and even a necessary one—a Southern slave culture has become overtaken by an ahistorical nature that will blessedly consign it to oblivion. Then, perhaps, history might begin anew. But the narrator's and his companion's experience of the relation of culture and nature at the St. Louis apprizes them not of natural or historical change, but of an ongoing repetition, a relation between nature and culture, the sense of a something between that binds outside and inside together and refuses change.

As they experience these moldering, peeling, yet fecund spaces and breathe in the smell of decay, "the dominance of [their] senses gradually dropped from [them], and with [their] souls [they] saw its soul—the soul of *this old-time place*; this mustering house of the old South."[11] These images of moldering beauty are not about renewal, but about continuity in time. They seem to serve—as the hotel becomes a "mustering house"—an endlessly repeated call to arms, not an admission of historical defeat.

"Fluttering" in the Dome Room

Questions about a something that links nature and culture but refuses change are raised on another level by the fluttering death-in-life figures that the tourists conjure out of the bats and pigeons in the famous decaying dome room. Here, quite explicitly, the narrator is struck with the architectural beauty of the space even as he marks its decomposition: "A fine—yea, even a splendid room, of great height, and carved grandeur, with hand-wrought bronze scones and a band of metal bordering, all blackened with oblivion."[12] In contrast to the earlier descriptions of a nature-culture relation in the halls and rooms, the narrator and his friend here remark the human figures painted into the architecture. The guide gestures to the heads of the "heroes" encircling the dome—figures from American political and economic and increasingly Southern and Confederate history—"Washington, Hamilton, Jefferson, Davis, and Lee." The narrator notes how their rotting faces are "blackened too, and scarred with damp, beyond recognition."[13] As in the case of the fungused walls and peeling papers, this description might also suggest historical distance from the ideas of the "fathers" who participated in the construction of a Southern ideology. The guide notes, "All gone—now." The narrator's own meditation on the space begins in this vein—"Here, beneath their gaze, men had banqueted and danced and ruled"—but then suddenly swerves as he and his companion begin to sense ghostly presences in the hall. "The pride and the might and the vivid strength of things still fluttered their uneasy flags of spirit, moved disherited wings! Those old-time feasts and grave discussions—we seemed to see them printed on the thick air, imprisoned in this great chamber built above their dark foundation."[14] In the temple-like dome room, once the seat of social, commercial, political and legal life, the living dead whose blackened, rotting political and financial fathers still gaze downward, themselves continue to "flutter" in "pride" and "might" and "vivid strength."

The motion of the lively interstitial "fluttering" of the undead becomes stilled for an instant as the tourists imagine their vanished pleasures and their politics—"printed on the thick air." As the narrator fantasizes these airy imprints, he moves to seeing the undead "imprisoned" in their dome above "their dark foundations." Repeating his initial comment about pride, might, and strength, he concludes by echoing the old guide's own language, "gone, all gone!" The image of fixing their fluttering—seeing them "printed"—seems here to invoke their absence, the fact that they are now "all gone." But is this so? Almost immediately following the narrator's invocation of their "printed" imprisonment, the

Figure 6.4. "Rotunda, Old St. Louis Hotel, New Orleans, LA," postcard, collection of Teresa A. Toulouse.

Rotunda, Old St. Louis Hotel, New Orleans, La.

old guide, as if reading his mind, remarks, "Not hearing very well, suh, I have it all *printed*, lady—beautifully told here—yes, indeed!"[15] Here, in the guide's printed version of the hotel's history, the ghosts, rather than being imprisoned by their printing "on the air," emerge in a form through which the present reader can purportedly see into an undead past. Like the sketch itself, the print on the cards, instead of relegating the ghosts to the past, becomes another space between that ensures the ghosts' "fluttering" in the imaginations of the living who read them.

Seeing through Water, Shadow, and Arch

In the sketch's first section, the relation of nature and culture, or outside and inside, is presented as a repetition—a repetition of an ongoing *condition* of rot, not change; in the second section, a similar moldering informs the historical figures painted on the dome, under whose blackened gaze their adherents continue their vivid display of social and political might, fluttering between death and life, absence and presence. The third section ostensibly reveals what lies beneath the ideology of the dome and concludes with the narrator's passionate depiction of what he presents as the ineluctable paradox of the Old South.

As elsewhere, the deaf guide remarks "what any can see": the dome room stands directly above the auction space to which they next descend. In this spatial movement downwards towards darkness, the narrator quite clearly points out the relation between the Southern political, social, and commercial ideology of the dome above and the slave exchange below. The moment they enter the auction room, he notes the marble pillars ringed with iron that serve as the hotel's "foundation." This rather obvious image of bondage does not, however, address the terrors aroused by the tourists' gradual encounter with the spaces below, as they are described in a whole range of images of in-betweenness. If these images at once corroborate the relation of slavery's ideology to practice, they also point to a far more disturbing fantasy that links the ideology above with the market below.

From the vertical spaces of the high dome, the sketch moves to the horizontal spaces of the hotel's lower reaches. The first space that the tourists encounter upon their descent is a long hallway comprised of black and white tiles. Strikingly, the tiles are covered by flowing water welling up from beneath—clearly the source of the building's pervasive rot. Literally as well as metaphorically, this upheaving water flowing intermittently along the hallway serves as the medium through which the tourists observe the tiles, suggesting that what is to come will be less seen than seen through.

Moving down the hallway, they encounter the much-remarked live horse. Literally, perhaps, the poor creature has come from its stable to drink the water, but for the tourists whom it startles, its presence physically highlights the space between the actual life of the present and the ruin through which they are traveling. We will return to a slightly different reading of the horse's function in this hall in a moment.

As the sound of the horse's hooves die out, the tourists reach the space of the auction. In the chiaroscuro flickering of a newspaper torch that the guide lights to display the "shadowy room," they come to experience the "slow uncanny feeling of someone standing there."[16] Beneath the name of the auctioneer still printed on the wall, the man himself seems to appear, along with the "forms and faces" of the teeming buyers and sellers in front of him.

Here in the space below, the auctioneer, in an eerie parallel to the "heroes" circling the wall above, is called into shape beneath his printed

SALE OF ESTATES, PICTURES AND SLAVES IN THE ROTUNDA, NEW ORLEANS.

Figure 6.5. "Sale of Estates, Pictures and Slaves in the Rotunda, New Orleans." The Historic New Orleans Collection, acc. no. 1974.25.23.4.

name. The auctioneer's ghost enacts at the commercial level the ideology of exchange expressed at the social and political levels in the dome above. Curiously, it is his feeling for the auctioneer's presence that elicits the narrator's use of the term *uncanny*. From simply observing the rotting hallways or marking the feelings of the spirits in the dome room above, the narrator and friend in the auction room experience their own feeling: a feeling of the uncanny.

While the concept of the uncanny has long been generally associated with the terror evoked by ghost stories, it was explicitly and famously interpreted by Sigmund Freud in his 1919 essay, "The Uncanny," which appeared just two years after the destruction of the old St Louis. As Freud describes it, "The uncanny is that species of the frightening that goes back to what was once well known and had long been familiar."[17] Viewed in these terms, the figure of the Creole auctioneer, the *encanteur* who mediates "exchanges" of flesh into money, evokes a feeling about "what was once well known and . . . familiar" in the narrator and his friend. What is "known" is terrifyingly revealed at a hallucinatory level in the tourists' horrific encounter with the "abhorrent" thing.

Figure 6.6. Old slave block in the St. Louis Hotel, New Orleans. The Historic New Orleans Collection, acc. no. 1974.25.29.131.

Peering into a "long and low vault," the narrator becomes "conscious, as it seemed, of innumerable eyes gazing, not at us, but through the archway where we stood; innumerable white eyeballs gleaming out of blackness."[18] The narrator does not meditate on the terrifyingly surrealistic "eyes," as he had done earlier with the fluttering ghosts in the dome; instead, he sets them, "gleaming" and "glaring," in a *relation*: "From behind us came a little laugh. It floated through the archway toward those eyes."[19] If here, at last, is a representation of the "abhorrent thing" of slavery, the system is not evoked in the "innumerable eyeballs" of the imprisoned slaves alone, but in their charged encounter with the laugh through the arch in which the tourists themselves stand. The sense of the uncanny represented in the figure of the auctioneer who orchestrates the exchanges moves here to reveal at a deeper level the intimate relation which grounds such exchanges in the first place—the power relation between slaves and masters.

While the glare of the "innumerable" eyeballs surely suggests the bondsmen's own ongoing fear and rage at this abhorrent connection, the narrator instead focuses on the "little laugh" that "floated through the archway" towards those eyes. "Who was that?" he says. "Who laughed in there?" The question at once reveals and conceals. If the answer that the question demands is most generally the Old South, and more particularly, the old guide, who "with her sweet smile" literally stands behind them, this evasive response does not confront what the laughter itself suggests. Does not the "little laugh" figure some kind of pleasure in meeting the gazing eyes of the enslaved? Is it not a fantasy of seeing and being seen by them and maintaining power over them that elicits such pleasure? The true horror of the Exchange Hotel is not its rot as such, nor its ideology, nor even its auction block; it is the unremitting pleasure in the control of the bondsmen that is figured in the meeting of the laugh with the eyeballs in the arch.

At this moment, the representation of upwelling water covering the black and white tiles of the hallway below stands revealed as an image of the unquenched desire through which black-white relations are perceived by the masters in the dome room above; a desire, surely, for the joys of exchange itself, but more intimately and familiarly, as the image of the gazing eyes and laughter in the auction room indicates, a sadistic pleasure in power over others. It is the pleasure involved in this unequal and unholy connection that invisibly binds nature and culture, outside and inside, death and life, and even up and down, within the St. Louis Exchange Hotel.

Rather Quickly We Passed Away

Were we to stop here, we might have already solved the question of what binds the apparent oppositions found elsewhere in the hotel, but we would also have missed out on the ways in which the narrator both approaches and avoids the fact of his own participation in the obscene pleasure he has not simply experienced but also used the hotel's various interstitial spaces to evoke. The narrator's knowledge of his complicity in what he only seems to describe is revealed in several ways: first, by his admission that *he* is the meeting point in the arch where the gazing and the laugh encounter one another; then, by the series of antinomies through which he describes the Old South; and finally, as we now return to it, the "strangest thing that ever wandered through deserted grandeur," the figure of the beaten horse, which the tourists first meet in the hall on their way to the auction block.[20]

In contrast to other areas of the hotel (where the narrator and friend observe its rot or its fluttering ghosts from a distance), in the "crypt-like chamber," they are overtaken by an "uncanny" sense of familiarity, such that, rather than merely "oozing" into the "cattle car" of the slave pens, they become the medium through which the gazing and laugh meet. As much as the narrator denies that the slaves gazed "not at us," it is his peering into the darkness and his hearing of the laugh "behind" that evokes the terrifying hallucination of their presence and their meeting in the first place. As Freud and later commentators have observed in further teasing out the anxiety aroused in the experience of the uncanny, the specific apprehension involves coming too close to an "object cause" of both fear and desire, of something known that one wishes not to acknowledge—here the narrator's participation in the pleasure of mastery that must be transformed into terror lest he know it.[21]

The narrator immediately moves from that meeting "through the arch" to ascribe the laugh to the Old South. His description falls into another series of apparent oppositions, this time not to describe specific hotel features, but to make generalizing, more distanced claims about the South as a whole. In the narrator's view, the South becomes "that 'old-time' thing of old ideals, blindfolded by its own history! That queer proud blend of simple chivalry and tyranny, of piety and the abhorrent thing."[22] While ideals may indeed blind one to history, here the relationship is reversed: it is history that blindfolds ideals. And what are these ideals? As the narrator presents them, they are "chivalry" and "piety"—the fantasized ideals of a precapitalist, integrated, and aesthetically beautiful medieval world in which social hierarchy and social roles, whether gendered or raced, seemed both natural and moral. What then is the "history" that blindfolds such ideals, so that chivalry becomes "tyranny" and "piety" defends the morality of the "abhorrent thing"? Clearly, it is the history of a system of exchange dependent on slave labor that, as historians have recently argued, is far from medieval but in fact very modern, a part of the industrialized transformation of relations of labor and capital.[23] Rather than acknowledging the modernity of slavery, the narrator persists in stressing the disparity between the past and present, suggesting that there is nothing wrong with the South's traditional ideals—what is wrong is that they have been somehow waylaid, blindfolded by a modern historical process before which their proponents are oddly represented as passive.

What the narrator seems to separate, however—"old ideals" and history—become intimately related in his own phrasing. Rather than being done in by history, Southern ideals are in fact "blended" with it—chivalry "blends" with tyranny, piety "blends" with the "abhorrent thing." Beginning with a claim about ideals "blindfolded" by history, the narrator's own meditation thus ends with the inextricable *relation* between Southern ideals and Southern practice in actual time. Once again, in a sketch filled with repetitions, the narrator is compelled to ask, "Who was it laughed there in the old slave-market—laughed at these white eyeballs glaring out of the darkness of their dark cattle-pen?"[24] The narrator's meditation on the "paradox" of the Old South is set between this twice-asked question, referencing again the intransigent pleasure in "the power, the might, and the vivid strength" that enables, rather than separates, the distinctive Southern "blend" of "old" ideals and modernity.

Clearly, from the narrator's point of view, the deaf old guide, the "guardian of the Old South," who cannot or will not hear or respond to outside questions, is intended to represent the perverse pleasure permeating the high culture of the "old Southern families" who come to "the finest hotel—before the war-time; . . . buyin' and sellin' their property."[25] Hers is the unspoken yet almost audible "voice" inhabiting the broken bells "to all the rooms" that called and, in her own mind, still call that "property" to toil for the families of the "exchange hotel" in the sketch's penultimate image. And it is perhaps her use of the term *broken*, not *gone*, that drives the narrator and his companion to "quickly pass away" out of that "old-time place."[26]

In contrast to the phrase *all gone*, the word *broken* suggests the possibility of fixing something that is, in fact, not gone but somehow still sounding, resonating in the hotel's thick atmosphere. The narrator's own discomfort with this knowledge of something that continues leads to a curious shift in his reading of the water with which the sketch concludes. Fleeing the "old-time place," he is left, on the one hand, with an image of the laugh and, on the other, with "the drip, drip, drip of water down the walls" that was, as he now rewrites it, "the sound of a spirit grieving."[27] Here, the water, rather than serving to reflect the upwelling and ongoing pleasure in mastery, becomes transformed into tears for the loss of this power and the entire culture that expressed it. But, of course, this image is again accompanied by the laugh—which does not grieve but, as in other images of water that accompany it, persists.

Why the transformation in the image of the water? The narrator seems attempting here to again evoke the pastness of the past, the grief for what is "gone . . . all gone." At the same time, as the word "broken" also reminds us, the burden of the sketch has fallen not on what is gone, exactly, but on what repeats itself. The sketch has not only gradually demonstrated that the desire permeating the hotel is also related to the narrator's own desire, it has in a variety of ways suggested that this fantasy of control over bodies is present, not only in the hotel, not only in the South, but also in the actual life to which the narrator ostensibly flees.

And thus we return to the moment of the descent into the "long hall" below the dome room where the tourists encounter "the strangest thing that ever strayed through deserted grandeur—a brown, broken horse, lean, with a sore flank and a head of tremendous age." While for the narrator the contrast between the living horse and the rotting building highlights the "strangeness" of the whole experience, its presence in the hallway, drinking the water covering the black and white tiles, also strikingly suggests that it belongs in, indeed depends on, the "deserted grandeur" it inhabits. Two features are compelling here: the horse's "tremendous age" and its brokenness.[28] The narrator attempts to differentiate the horse's condition from its "grand" surroundings, just as he attempts, at the end, to differentiate between history and ideals and to counter the ongoing laugh with a spirit's grieving the past. But the ancient, sore, and very much alive brown horse in the lower hall-way implies the continuation of an actual coerced labor that is not at all dead or gone. In this knowing and unknowing of the violence involved in slavery's "ancient" past as well as in his evocation of the brokenness of beaten bodies in the present, Galsworthy's narrator moves us out of the sketch proper and into a consideration of the nostalgia at work in other sketches, particularly in such nostalgia's relation to the decadent order, now "gone," in his sketch of the South.

La Nostalgie de la Boue

The final evidence of the narrator's complicity with the world he seems to flee is apparent in other sketches in *The Inn of Tranquility*. One of the central motifs running through the section of the original collection, entitled "Concerning Life," is the narrator's languid nostalgia over, as well as his outright lament for, how a beautiful world of artisanal and pas-toral labor, supported by the benevolent paternalism of a quasi-aristo-cratic upper-middle class, is passing or has already passed as a result of the crass and seemingly inevitable commercial "progress" of a bourgeois exchange culture. At the same time that he laments the old and criticizes the new, however, the narrator also very candidly shows "rot" in the older institutions, especially in the law, that does not equally treat those "oth-ers," whether immigrant Jew, working-class man, or lower-class prosti-tute, under its purview. Instead, as the narrator demonstrates in his own feelings and behaviors, the law is complicit in desiring the illicit services, here often represented as sexual, of those it excludes from its "fairness."[29]

Seeking to move out of the distressing moral complexities of human history, the narrator dreams in some sketches of an escape to an untainted "nature" only to experience in others nature's utter indifference to human suffering and grief. In the sketch following "That Old-Time Place," he pos-its an immense desire for an indeterminate, lasting space of "romance" between which human "ideals" and natural "reality" can somehow be mediated. While this desire is thwarted, another sentimental sketch about a beloved dead dog with "dark brown eyes" reveals the narrator's fantasy of a servile creature that goes to its death demonstrating an unde-manding and always-loyal love for his master. The sketches end with a paean to a day and night in a dense English nature that is utterly divorced from any other consciousness than that of the narrator himself.

Figure 6.7. Demolition of the dome of the St. Louis Hotel, 1917. Photograph by George Francois Mugnier, from the George Francois Mugnier Photograph Collection, Louisiana Division/City Archives, New Orleans Public Library.

As his biography reveals, the real John Galsworthy, winner of the 1932 Nobel Prize in Literature, did, in many respects, cast off his own in-between birthright as the scion of an aristocratic mother on one side, and an upper-middle class solicitor and industrialist on the other. He became not only a fellow traveler of liberal, socialist, and emergent workers' movements but also a vocal proponent of women's and even animal rights in the years just before and following World War I. While not often recognized as one himself, he emotionally and financially supported great early modernists like Ford Maddox Ford and especially Joseph Conrad in their scathing explorations of the British class system and British imperialism more generally.[30] Read in the best light, perhaps, Galsworthy's shifting presentation of himself as narrator in these Edwardian prewar sketches may have functioned as a filter through which he could explore his own yearnings for a space of romance between history and nature that might replace a current fraught reality. At the same time, his use of this in-between space reveals something less innocent in such dreams of romance. Attempting at the end of "That Old-Time Place" to keep the uncanny pleasure in mastery experienced in the in-between spaces of the St. Louis Hotel *contained* in the Southern past, the narrator's depiction of the upwelling desire linking nature and culture, outside and inside, and violence and pleasure instead reveals a repetitive and ongoing historical "rot" that threatens all the English sketches between which stands his Southern tale.

NOTES

1. Lyle Saxon, *Fabulous New Orleans* (1928; repr. New Orleans: Pelican, 1989), 173; Nathaniel Cortlandt Curtis, *New Orleans: Its Old Houses, Shops, and Public Buildings* (Philadelphia: J. P. Lippincott, 1933), 185.

2. The most complete history of the hotel remains Curtis, *New Orleans*, 171–85. For a more extended discussion of de Pouilly's work in New Orleans, including the hotel and the cathedral, see the important recent discussion by Ann Masson, "J. N. B. de Pouilly," *KnowLA: The Digital Encyclopedia of Louisiana History and Culture*, ed. David Johnson, June 4, 2013, http://www.knowla.org/entry/473.

Masson points out how imposing the vista of the hotel and dome must have been as viewed down the three-block long Exchange Alley, which opened on to it from Canal Street. For more commentary on the architectural history of the hotel in its historical context, see Gary Van Zante, *New Orleans, 1867: Photographs by Theodore Lilienthal* (London: Merrell, 2008), 83–86. I am grateful to architectural historians Ann Masson, Gary Van Zante, and Ellen Weiss for referring me to Curtis and for helping to correct some earlier misconstructions about its style and structure. For an anecdotal history of the St. Louis Hotel, see also the Omni Hotel website, "Royal Orleans History," Omni Hotels and Resorts, http://www.omnihotels.com/hotels/new-orleans-royal-orleans/property-details/history. I have also benefited from John Kendall, *History of New Orleans* (Chicago: Lewis, 1922), ch. 43, on Bill Thayer's Website, n.d., http://penelope.uchicago.edu/Thayer/E/Gazetteer/Places/America/United_States/Louisiana/New_Orleans/_Texts/KENHNO/home.html.

3. Saxon, *Fabulous New Orleans*, 273.

4. For an extended discussion of the White Leagues that demonstrates the local, state, and federal importance of political and military struggles within, around, and over the hotel turned statehouse, see James Hogue, *The Uncivil War: Five New Orleans Street Battles and the Rise and Fall of Radical Reconstruction* (Baton Rouge: Louisiana State University Press, 2006). Thanks to Prof. Lawrence Powell for this reference.

5. For a recent discussion of the multiple sites of slave auctions in New Orleans, including those at the St. Louis Hotel, see Richard Campanella, "On the Structural Basis of Social Memory: Cityscapes of the New Orleans Slave Trade, Part I," *Preservation in Print*, March 2013, https://prcno.org/preservation-in-print/archive/2013/. See also Walter Johnson, *Soul by Soul: Life inside the Antebellum Slave Market* (Cambridge, MA: Harvard University Press, 1999). As Gary Van Zante points out, earlier commentators in both the nineteenth and twentieth centuries noted the discrepancy between the hotel's grandeur, its display of the Founding Fathers, and its slave auctions. See Gary A. Van Zante, *New Orleans, 1867: Photographs by Theodore Lilienthal* (London: Merrell, 2008), 83–86.

6. Curtis has a list that differs slightly from that of Galsworthy, who obviously wished to stress the slaveholding connection. Curtis does not include Davis or Lee, for example, but notes two faces that were entirely unrecognizable and perhaps reputed to be theirs. See Curtis, *New Orleans*, 180.

7. Curtis points out that there was an actual Creole "grand dame," who had rooms in the ruined hotel and charged "two-bits" for people to wander through it. See Curtis, *New Orleans*, 183.

8. John Galsworthy, "That Old-Time Place," in *The Works of John Galsworthy*, vol. 15, *The Inn of Tranquility and Other Impressions, Poems* (New York: Charles Scribner's Sons, 1923), 119.

9. See, for example, Saxon, *Fabulous New Orleans*, 273. There are no detailed close readings of "That Old-Time Place" that I could locate. The *New Orleans City Guide*, overseen by Lyle Saxon and published by the Works Progress Administration in 1938, notes that Galsworthy was impressed by the hotel's "melancholy grandeur" and that it evoked one of his "haunting 'prose poems.'" See the recent reprint of the guide, *New Orleans City Guide*, introduction by Lawrence N. Powell (New Orleans: Garrett County Press, 2009), 122. In a recent study, Paul Oswell quotes Ada Galsworthy's response to the St. Louis: "For gruesome, unfaked melancholy, I've never seen anything like it." See Oswell's *New Orleans Historic Hotels* (Charleston, SC: History Press, 2014), 82. Deirdre Sanforth incorrectly notes that Galsworthy wrote a *poem* about the St. Louis, specifically noting his encounter with a "white horse wandering through the interior of the once grand hotel." See her *Romantic New Orleans* (New Orleans: Pelican, 1979), 65. Scott Ellis also calls the novelist a "poet" and notes how the meeting with the "gaunt horse shuffling from room to room" is the "apotheosis of this (the hotel's) decadence." Galsworthy did write poems, but was primarily known as a novelist and playwright. See Scott Ellis, *Madame Vieux Carré: The French Quarter in the Twentieth Century* (Jackson: University Press of Mississippi, 2010), 134. It is important for this analysis that the horse is brown.

10. Galsworthy, "That Old-Time Place," 116.

11. Ibid. Rather than simply referring to the Civil War, Galsworthy's use of the term "mustering" suggests his knowledge of the more recent armed conflicts in New Orleans in which the hotel had played a role. See Hogue, *Uncivil War*.

12. Ibid.

13. Ibid.

14. Ibid., 117.

15. Ibid. My emphasis.

16. Ibid., 118.

17. Sigmund Freud, "The Uncanny," in *The Uncanny*, ed. David McLintock and Hugh Haughton (London: Penguin Books, 2003), 124.

18. Galsworthy, "That Old-Time Place," 119.

19. Ibid.

20. Ibid., 117.

21. See Freud, "The Uncanny," especially part 2, 131–151. If, using Freud's analysis, one reads the disembodied eyes as images for a kind of castration—in this case, the enforced powerlessness of slavery—then the laugh seems to represent the white desire involved in such castrating. The narrator, as the site where they meet, seems to be acknowledging both his own fear of such castration and his concomitant desire to associate himself with the power of the old woman's laugh. The charged encounter surely marks the complex emotion that would come to be known as the "return of the repressed." If "every affect arising from an emotional impulse of whatever kind—is converted into fear by being repressed, it follows that from those things that are felt to be frightening, there must be one group in which it can be shown that the frightening element is something that has been repressed and now returns." Freud, "The Uncanny," 147.

22. Galsworthy, "That Old-Time Place," 119.

23. For a recent discussion of the modernity of Southern slavery, see Edward E. Baptist, *The Half Has Never Been Told: Slavery and the Making of American Capitalism* (New York: Basic Books, 2014). See also Walter Johnson, *Soul by Soul*. See also Marilyn Brown's astute comments in this volume about the continuities of labor practices developed under slavery well into the late nineteenth and early twentieth centuries.

24. Galsworthy, "That Old-Time Pace," 119.

25. Ibid.

26. Ibid.

27. Ibid.

28. Ibid., 117.

29. I am particularly referring to the following sketches in the 1912 edition of *The Inn of Tranquility*: "Quality," "The Grand Jury," "Gone," "Threshing," "That Old-Time Place," "Romance—Three Gleams," "Memories," and "Felicity." Many had been originally published in small journals. For sketches concerned with artisanal and pastoral labor, see "Quality," "Gone," and "Threshing." For the sketch on a Jewish immigrant woman and a young prostitute, see "The Grand Jury." For the narrator's sketch about his loyal dog, see "Memories." On his yearning for "romance" and his dreams of natural "felicity," see "Romance—Three Gleams," and "Felicity." For this interpretation, it is striking that "That Old-Time Place" was originally placed between "Threshing" and "Romance—Three Gleams." For this ordering of the sketches, I am referencing a 1919 reprint of the 1912 edition. See John Galsworthy, *The Inn of Tranquility, Studies and Essays* (New York: Charles Scribner's Sons, 1919).

30. For Galsworthy's biography and for useful analysis of his novels and plays, see, for example, James Gindin, *John Galsworthy's Life and Art: An Alien's Fortress* (Ann Arbor: University of Michigan Press, 1987).

INTERSPACE FOUR   ❧   *Constituting and Contesting the Interstitial*

While Brown and Toulouse address what is revealed by in-between elements of individual structures, pursuing the questions raised by Carrie and Scott Bernhard's essays also leads to stories associated with, and lived in, broader areas of the city's "interstitial system." In this section, cultural geographer Richard Campanella and sociologists Beth Willinger and Angel Adams Parham examine how the "edges" of New Orleans, both literal and imagined, take on a range of contrasting meanings for those seeking to produce and to sell the city's salaciousness, on the one hand, and those wishing to reject, reform, or transform this gendered, classed, and raced narrative, on the other.

Campanella examines the city's shifting geographies in the nineteenth and early twentieth centuries to account for the continuing reputation of Bourbon Street in the civic imaginary for locals and tourists alike. Beth Willinger, similarly interested in how and why different areas of New Orleans become constituted as moral or immoral spaces, focuses on the role played by assumptions about gender and the public sphere in the organization and construction of "homes" for single women at the turn of the nineteenth century. Angel Parham then traces significant features of the history of Congo Square, that meeting ground between the city walls and the surrounding swamps that from the colonial era has functioned as a crucial space for cultural production by people of color, enslaved and free. Parham parallels the effort to fix racial possession of the Square during the post–Civil War period with growing local and national assumptions about the fixity of racial identity. She argues that Congo Square, historically and culturally, should instead be read as an interstitial "place of memory" where variants of Blackness have been performed, celebrated, and reinvented.

CHAPTER SEVEN

"Seeing the Elephant" in New Orleans's Interstitial Spaces
A Look behind Modern-Day Bourbon Street to the Origins of Civic Repute

—*Richard Campanella*

Americans in the nineteenth century used an enigmatic phrase for the inflection points of their humdrum lives. To "see the elephant" meant to witness the utmost, to see everything you expected and more, to complete a journey and experience life to the fullest. The expression probably originated from traveling carnivals that held out as a climax their most sensational exhibit, a live elephant. Later usage leaned toward adversity, implying that one had had enough of an overbearing experience, and it eventually transformed into a euphemism for near-death experiences. The literal-to-figurative shift in meaning had occurred by the early 1840s; a New Orleans newspaper in the steamy summer of 1844, for example, reported that an "'Anxious Enquirer' wishes to know something about the phrase 'I've seen the elephant,'" to which the editor jestingly suggested he take a walk "any of these hot days about noon . . . and if you don't 'see the elephant' before you get to the Lower Cotton Press, we are a little out in our calculation."[1] Usage peaked in the late 1850s and 1860s, often in reference to death and dying on the frontier or Civil War battlefields. In its original sentiment, however, to "see the elephant" was usually salacious, to the point of inviting trouble. An 1848 article, for instance, spoke of a traveler to New Orleans "having but lately arrived from the upper country [with] a strong desire to see the 'elephant.'" Like his counterparts today, the chap ended up getting drunk—and robbed.[2]

Rural westerners, almost always men, sought the elephant in New Orleans. In that distant and isolated metropolis, they encountered an exotic and worldly society where, liberated by their anonymity, they could find plenty of opportunities to satisfy curiosities and desires and return home no worse for the wear. New Orleanians made money on this

Figure 7.1. High-grain urban granularity: New Orleans cityscape, ca. 1900. Courtesy of the Library of Congress, Prints and Photographs Division, Detroit Publishing Company Collection, LC-DIG-det-4a19018.

sub rosa economy, and made space for it usually at the city's fringes and interstices, where such activities benefited from a high urban granularity.

I use *urban granularity* to refer to the structural texture of a cityscape. A city with a coarse grain has few constituent elements with little diversity and a minimum of intricacies, interfaces, and interstices. It is spatially homogenous, visually quiet and unbusy. A superblock of big boxy identical buildings, for example, would have a low or coarse urban granularity, as would a typical suburban subdivision with spacious lawns and tract housing. A vast empty parking lot would be maximally coarse-grain.

High granularity, on the other hand, is crowded, busy, noisy, finely textured, sliced and diced, and loaded with interstices and pockets. Paris, Venice, and Jerusalem have high urban granularity, as do most older cities in their nucleated cores. Constituent elements include narrow, winding streets with minimum setback distances; passageways and alleyways; serrated roofs; ziggurat walls; street furniture and fire escapes; porches and balconies; and dormers, gables, chimneys, and water towers punctuating jumbled roofscapes. Urban granularity is essentially three-dimensional interstitiality.

It would be overly deterministic to suggest that urban granularity causes human behavior. It does not; people and their conditions and choices ultimately account for their activities. Cityscapes do, however, inform and affect behavior. High urban granularity can abet that which is permitted or encouraged through other more explicit means. A convoluted, multifaceted, spatially heterogeneous, and walkable urban geography increases the likelihood of chance encounters and lends itself to capricious experimentation, particularly if opportunities to so indulge are liberally provided, and the social restraints discouraging them are relaxed or nonexistent. High urban granularity fosters a liberating sense of anonymity and leverages the historical imaginary (that is, internalized mental imagery of a romanticized past) to animate the passions of the present.

In this chapter, I explore the origins and development of New Orleans's sybaritic reputation, with special attention to how and where the quest to see the elephant spatially manifested itself, how urban granularity and interstitiality lent it a hand and gave it an architecture, how social and legislative marginalization gave it soft (de facto) and hard (de jure) spaces to take root, and how much of the modern-day tourism economy rests on these historical spatialities. Drawing from my research on the cultural history and geography of modern-day Bourbon Street, the investigation spans the full three centuries of the city's history, with an emphasis on the late antebellum and Victorian eras.[3]

Structurally Based Social Memory

Collective memory benefits from an associated structural framework—that is, a public place or object that evokes a mental image. As individuals cherish mementos to commemorate times past and loved ones lost, societies collectively save old buildings, erect monuments, name and rename streets, and designate hallowed grounds so that citizens may synchronize their narratives of who they are as a people, where they came from, and where they should be going. As a city with a colorful past—and a modern-day economy based on marketing it—New Orleans proliferates in structurally based social memory. It uses the French Quarter, for example, to preserve the social memory of antebellum Creole society; it points to the Garden District to recall wealthy nineteenth-century Anglophone society; and it upholds Tremé to remind us about the *gens de couleur libre* (free people of color).

Preservation is intrinsic to this arrangement. Without a preserved historical built environment, we would forget, or fail to convince newcomers, of these past narratives. Cases in point: the burning of the Old French Opera House on Bourbon Street in 1919 helped bring an end to the French Quarter's old Francophone Creole society.[4] The destruction of the South Rampart Street commercial corridor, Louis Armstrong's neighborhood, and Storyville so impaired the social memory of jazz that tourists regularly come away disappointed when they learn the "birthplace of jazz" is not visitable. Similarly, the near-total disappearance of slavery sites—nearly all structural vestiges of slave pens and auction

Figure 7.2. High-grain urban granularity: Bourbon Street, ca. 1900. Courtesy of the Library of Congress, Prints and Photographs Division, Detroit Publishing Company Collection, LC-DIG-det-4a19018.

blocks are gone—occludes the remembrance of bondage and its impacts. Out of sight, out of mind—and conversely, in sight, in mind. Hence the power of preservation.

The power goes beyond specific sites. The collective perception of New Orleans as unique and exceptional—which is an article of faith among residents and a cornerstone of civic pride—may be largely traced, I believe, to historic preservation. Had the decaying old neighborhood known colloquially as "the French quarters" been demolished, as was regularly suggested a hundred years ago, the tourism industry never would have germinated; the sense of exoticism and romance never would have been instilled by writers and playwrights; culinary and musical traditions would have lacked a space for paying customers; and photographs of iconic iron-lace galleries never would have been taken. It's not the only factor—Mardi Gras plays a major role—but without the preserved French Quarter, the cherished mantra of uniqueness would have gone unsung, and New Orleans might have ended up with a collective memory and a nationwide reputation little different than that of Mobile or Galveston.

Instead, the French Quarter was saved, and wisely so, because its preservation inspired the same for other historical neighborhoods. Today, locals and visitors alike utilize that structural substratum—thousands of nineteenth-century buildings bearing a magnificent Euro-Caribbean-American aesthetic—to substantiate and justify a collective memory that strums many melodious chords: Frenchness. Creoleness. Joie de vivre. An air of mystery and a sense that something different happened here; a certain subtropical brand of eccentricity; a whiff of Caribbean escapism; an indulgence in the pleasures of the moment. It is appealing stuff, but it is only convincing when it rests on a tactile, visible structural foundation. Try selling this in Peoria and see what happens.

High urban granularity seals the deal. Its armature in New Orleans includes narrow streets crowded with columned galleries and cantilevered balconies, articulated hip and gable roofs complicated with dormers and chimneys, French doors and shutters with wrought-iron straps, dark alleys and *portes-cochères* disappearing into hidden courtyards, protruding store signs none too domineering, quaint streetlamps and cast-iron filigree galore. "The general effect is very pleasing," wrote Lafcadio Hearn in 1881; "no one with an artistic eye can avoid loving the zigzag outline of peaked roofs with the pretty dormers; the iron arabesques of graceful balconies, the solid doors and . . . shutters, so brightly green."[5] Replete with nooks and crannies, this pointillistic urban texture fosters a sense of intrigue and piques curiosity to seek what's behind those closed doors, what lurks down that dark alley. Walkability is key because it facilitates social interaction with strangers while maintaining anonymity and, if one chooses to imbibe, enabling ambulatory inebriety. Walt Whitman recognized, in the words of one modern writer, the "continually tantalizing, pullulating field of sexual potential" of walking among crowds of strangers. In "City of Orgies," Whitman rhapsodized, "as I pass O Manhattan, your frequent and swift flash of eyes offering me love . . ."[6] Recalling his visit to New Orleans, he wrote,

> Once I pass'd though a populous city imprinting my brain for
>   future use with its shows, architecture, customs, traditions,
> Yet now of all that city I remember only a woman I casually met
>   there who detain'd me for love of me.[7]

It's worth noting that while the lover Whitman "casually met" in New Orleans was long thought to be a woman of color, handwritten drafts

suggest it was in fact a man. Both relationships would have been ver-
boten at the time, yet possible in the social and spatial milieu of the
crowded city. And whoever it was, there's a good chance the tryst (Whitman was a tad too urbane to say he "saw the elephant," though it sounds
like he did) took place in the intimacy of the French Quarter.[8]

What Whitman sensed in the 1840s emanates still in the 2010s. Per-
ambulating aimlessly and namelessly in that cozy, insulating old cityscape
invites the bending of rules and the pushing of envelopes—drinking in
public, slipping into an exotic show, hooking up with a stranger, crossing
a Rubicon—in ways that a coarse-grain suburban environment does not.
A walk down a boulevard in Phoenix or Salt Lake City, for example, is
an exposed experience under a dome of blue sky, with few pedestrians
and great distance between social spaces. It's more alienating than anonymous, more mundane than mysterious, and anything but scintillating.

Bourbon Street represents an extreme case of structurally based
social memory. It is the modern-day space in which New Orleans's cen-
turies-old reputation for the bacchanal is concentrated, exaggerated,
and sold—noisily, constantly, for a tidy profit. It is participatory street
theater in perpetual motion, pounded by music, teased by sexuality, and
dazed by alcohol. It is a carefully crafted sociological "backspace" within
which newcomers, tutored by T-shirt slogans and patronizing signage,
are induced to view deviance as acceptable and restraint as deviant.[9]
What completes the picture is the same structural corroboration that
supports New Orleans's broader social memory and validates its claim
to exceptionalism: the finely textured edifices, the iron-lace balconies,
the old-time gas lamps, the *tout ensemble* of subtropical urbanism—all
nestled tightly, yours to explore, on foot, anonymously.

Which all raises the question, where did this piquant reputation
come from?

Origins of Civic Repute

Great ports regularly developed sectors catering to pleasure because
steady streams of transients made such enterprises economically lucrative. In New Orleans, "strangers," overwhelmingly male, would settle
into exchange hotels, rented rooms, or cheap "caravanserai," flop houses
operating in interstitial spaces. Some newcomers were northern businessmen; others were foreign sailors, upcountry flatboatmen, soldiers,
traders, opportunity-seekers "on the make," immigrants in transit, or
vagrants. Their numbers were substantial: in 1831, when New Orleans
had roughly 55,000 permanent residents, one journalist estimated "there

are frequently from 25 to 50,000 strangers in the place" during the winter.[10] Flush with cash and released from the responsibilities and restraints of home, men disembarked with pent-up demand for immediate gratification. Exploiting the crossroads of anonymity, desire, and opportunity, New Orleans catered to the itinerant male seeking the elephant by creating innumerable outlets, wedged into marginal spaces, for liquor, sex, games of chance, entertainment, and victuals. Bars and brothels were geographically widespread, and because transients arrived at all hours, pleasure outlets made themselves available around the clock, the Sabbath be damned. (To this day New Orleans has no legislated closing times on alcohol outlets.) From these circumstances arose the Crescent City's enduring civic reputation.

The geography of tolerance abetted that repute. Unlike interior communities, port societies must make peace with the varied hordes disembarking at their docks, and the larger their hinterlands and forelands, the greater the hordes' diversity. Thus international ports were, and remain, typically more cosmopolitan and tolerant than interior cities. By no means was New Orleans unusual in this regard; the "lax" standards reported in hundreds of historical sources on New Orleans may also be found in literature about the Liverpools and New Yorks and San Franciscos of the world, although not necessarily in the same form or proportion.

Ports of the South Atlantic and Caribbean basins were additionally influenced by the Latin Catholic cultures of the Mediterranean world, which lacked the judgmental tone of Anglo-American societies and viewed alcohol as part of the daily bread rather than an escapist's vice. Ergo, New Orleans gained roughly the same laissez-faire reputation as Havana, San Juan, Veracruz, Cartagena, Salvador, Rio de Janeiro, and other nodes of the Creole Atlantic. Many of those sister cities today celebrate some form of carnival, romanticize their histories, take pride in their roguish reputations, nurture tourist industries, designate spaces for Bourbon Street–like activity, and boast high urban granularities. New Orleans's brand of pleasure seeking did not form independently or internally but rather orbited throughout the Atlantic Caribbean system. What distinguished it was its situation at the northernmost apogee in that realm, and, after 1803, its situation within the expanding borders of the United States—the southern United States, a region of traditionalism against which the hedonism of New Orleans stood out like, well, an elephant in the room.

Finally, New Orleans gained a sporting reputation because it earned one, deserved one, and wasted no time in developing one. The city did not merely import outside influences, but actively produced, molded, and exported its own ethos. Eyewitnesses by the score attest to this, and while their testimonies are not without nationalistic biases and epistemological shortcomings, they evidence that New Orleans offered a range of raucous, sexualized, and oftentimes hellacious spaces fueled by copious quantities of alcohol—all provenances of the core ingredients of today's Bourbon Street.

Earning a Reputation

The reports start in the colonial era, and through them we see urban interstitiality and granularity playing an underlying or abetting role. As early as 1720, as John Law's Mississippi Bubble burst and ruined investors, depictions of Louisiana as a debauched society circulated in European presses. It did not help that much of the colony's white population comprised *forçats*, immigrants forced out of the mother country for, among other reasons, depravity and vice. Nor did it help that the colony's economy, particularly after 1730, increasingly broke loose of sanctioned mercantilism and resorted to smuggling. Contraband was regularly fenced in in-between spaces such as taverns, grog shops, and saloons or along isolated ingresses and egresses, away from official eyes.

Where there were rogues making money, there was indulgence. Alcohol of various origins—wine, brandy, the local rum tafia, beer made from corn—flowed plentifully.[11] An anonymous critic noted in 1744 that even men of little means "are seldom without wine in their cellars; the tradesman is seldom a week without drinking it beyond moderation; but that is nothing in comparison with the soldier."[12] Later in the colonial era, wine and liquor comprised fully one-third of Louisiana imports.[13] The geographies of transshipment and transience coincided in New Orleans with the geographies of hedonism and indulgence—the perfect petri dish to spawn a rambunctious reputation.

And that is exactly what it did. One indignant visitor, Pierre-Louis Berquin-Duvallon, writing during the 1800–1803 interregnum, excoriated New Orleanians not only as bibulous but libidinous, loquacious, mendacious, narcissistic, vulgar, cruel, "rude, envious . . . avaricious, and presumptuous. . . . Their ignorance exceeds all human credibility." He viewed local women as stupid, illiterate, frivolous, bawdy, and vain, and slaves as "lazy, libertine, and given to lying, but not incorrigibly wicked," that last judgment intended more as a stab at whites than a compliment to blacks.[14] Many themes in Berquin-Duvallon's diatribe—of depravity and debauchery, of lavish living amidst poverty, of ostentation over austerity and indulgence over discipline—persist today in criticism of New Orleans and particularly of Bourbon Street.

New Orleans's infamy grew as the population and economy expanded. "This place is one of the worst I ever witnessed," wrote a newcomer in 1817; "the chief amusements are gambling and drinking[;] quarrels and even murders are very frequent here."[15] John H. B. Latrobe, who visited in 1834, critiqued that "cafés and barrooms were open" on the Sabbath, and that "rum and gin . . . here live in palaces [with a] whole army of bottles . . . lin[ing] the shelves."[16] Such appraisals were frequent throughout the nineteenth century, one complaining in 1847 about the proliferation of eateries, from which "the profit is on the liquor," and whose spatial density sounds Bourbonesque: "they monopolize the corners of every square; whole rows of them may be found in some localities, and new ones are springing up every day."[17] An exposé written in 1850 likewise excoriated the local embrace of spirits and, alluding to urban granularity, reported that "grog shops . . . are found in whole blocks—on three of every four corners . . . from street to street, every door leading into a drinking house."[18]

Local officials, fearing economic repercussions, took offense at these characterizations. The city fought back with ordinances regulating alcohol sales, curtailing the behavior of "lewd and abandoned women" in public space, and forbidding "cries, songs, noise or otherwise . . . from disturbing . . . the peace and tranquility of the neighbourhood." It stipulated $50 annual license fees for all inns, boarding houses, and billiard halls, and $150 for all "coffee houses" as well as taverns, grog-shops, and cabarets, the last three defined as "where liquors are retailed by the glass."[19]

Another factor forming New Orleans's reputation may seem to undercut these eyewitness accounts but actually bolsters them. Most of these testimonies were produced by visitors, not locals. Like tourists today, newcomers' attentions gravitated to that which deviated from perceived norms. They scribbled in their journals that which startled, offended, thrilled, or intrigued them, and ignored that which seemed familiar and quotidian. No surprise, then, that the "elephants" they saw—tippling bons vivants, brawling boatmen, quadroon balls, carnival revelry, "continental Sabbaths"—got plenty of coverage, while caring parents, diligent laborers, and responsible authorities went unrecorded. Thus the danger of over-relying on historical travel writers: their warped lenses may create an inverted reality in which the exceptional seems normal and normal exceptional. For our purposes, however, visitor representations are fair game because we are investigating the origin of a reputation—a perception, not a material truth. Testimonies about New Orleans did not have to be accurate or valid to justify the formation of an urban image; like gossip, they just had to be believed. And they were. Whatever reality existed in the streets and hidden parlors of historic New Orleans, visiting writers represented them in ways that constructed a metropolitan imaginary that resonated with readers and produced a subsequent generation of notepad-toting visitors—who in turn further reified the received reputation when their preconceived expectations were inevitably confirmed.

What resulted was a meta-belief in New Orleans's social deviancy, diffused through the printed word and reinforced through confirmation bias. Add to this the widely read genre of local color in the late 1800s; the rise of the tourism industry in the early 1900s; cinema, television and modern telecommunications; and finally the nightly Bourbon Street bacchanals, and the reputation of New Orleans becomes gospel believed worldwide. It is even embraced locally: New Orleanians love to be viewed as carpe diem epicureans with a devilish flair, regardless that they may be bus drivers or tax accountants when the sun is up.

So formed the perceptual backstory that legitimizes Bourbon Street's success, and while the average reveler might not articulate it as such, most feel their indulgence is socially sanctioned. After all, they've heard all their lives this is what people have always done here. They've sought the elephant.

Seeing the Elephant in Soft Spaces

Bourbon Street has more than historical memory and urban granularity to justify its existence. It also has geographical antecedents, comparable nineteenth-century spaces that laid the groundwork upon which the modern tourism industry would, in the twentieth century, erect a credible replicate with a Bourbon Street address. In a survey of New Orleans's historical geography of sin to find these proto-Bourbons, two geographical histories emerge: an era of soft concentrations from the 1700s to 1857, during which vice occurred at the city's edges, and an era of hard districts, from 1857 to 1917, when city authorities corralled vice within specified spaces.

Vice, abundant as it was, generally scattered itself throughout colonial and antebellum New Orleans. Grog shops and tippling houses, caravansaries, music and dance halls, gambling dens, and brothels popped up interstitially wherever demand and supply worked out a deal, and that meant in most neighborhoods, if not on most blocks. Yet concentrations did occur, and they tended to be in the premier interstitial spaces of the city: the areas in between the urban core and the rural periphery, spe-

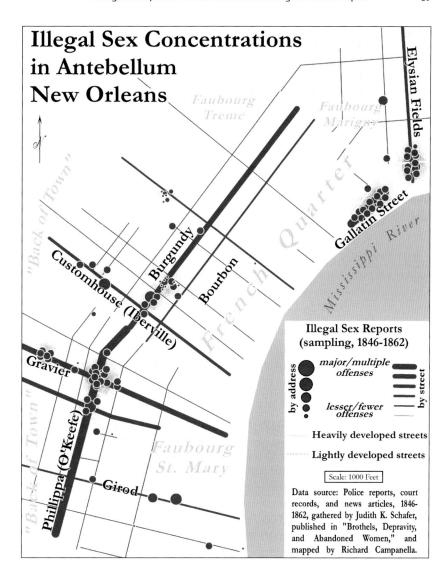

Figure 7.3. Soft concentrations of vice in antebellum New Orleans, based on data collected by Judith K. Shafer and mapped by Richard Campanella.

cifically in the back of town between the higher-elevation city and the lower-elevation swamp, and in the upper and lower *banlieues* (outskirts) between the city and the plantations.

Police reports, court records, and news articles about illegal sex activity (1846–62), gathered by the late historian Judith Kelleher Schafer and mapped by me, show that most prostitution—which was usually accompanied by drinking and gambling—occurred in three principal zones: the rear edge of town, the upper edge, and along the lower riverfront. All were between the core and the periphery. In the first district—that is, the French Quarter and Faubourg Tremé—the vice zone lay around the intersection of Customhouse (renamed Iberville in 1901) and Burgundy Streets, where Schafer unearthed at least seventy-five illegal

sex reports from court records and other sources, many of them involv-
ing scores of arrests. Why here? This was the rear of the old city—none
too elegant, none too pricey, yet convenient. It was a between world, and
it had the foot traffic of a high-grain city, what with the nearby Old Basin
(Carondelet) Canal turning basin and its working-class laborers as well
as the popular Globe Ballroom.[20]

In the second district (today's Warehouse District, Central Business
District, Superdome area, and Lower Garden District), a crescent-shaped
geography of sin spanned from the rears of Gravier and Perdido Streets,
up Phillippa Street (now O'Keefe Avenue) and down Girod and Julia
Streets to the Mississippi River. Therein could be found the hardscrabble
back of town near Charity Hospital, the turning basin of the New Basin
Canal and its leatherneck workforce, heavy-labor industries along the
semirural periphery, and above all, the uptown flatboat wharf along the
Mississippi. Venues gratifying flatboatmen's wants opened along the flatboat wharf itself (present-day South Peters Street), in part because the
unruly lads utilized their docked vessels as illegal rent-free basecamps.
One visitor reported seeing flatboats "used as huckster shops, dwellings,
pigpens . . . ." Others disdained the mile-long "line of gambling-shops"
formed by the flatboats on Sundays, not to mention the boatmen themselves, who, by one 1830 account, numbered "5000 or 6000," or ten percent of the entire city's population.[21] Curious visitors made a point of
seeing the flatboat wharf; it was a space that was, at once, interstitial,
ephemeral, and high-grain.

The most adventurous males debauched in a sketchy precinct known
as the Swamp. Located a dozen blocks inland from the flatboat wharf,
where Julia and Girod Streets petered out into damp thickets, this area
took in all that civilized society shoved out: the eerie Girod Street Ceme-
tery (1822); the smelly New Basin Canal (1832); and Charity Hospital and
its pestilential patients (1835), not to mention gas works, garbage dumps,
shantytowns, and city stables. Girod Street, the artery connecting the
riverfront wharves and New Basin Canal dock, hosted a disproportion-
ate share of vice venues and crime. Detailed descriptions of Girod's high-
grain, lowbrow streetscape come from an 1852 *Daily Picayune* article.
"Rows of low tenements . . . leaning against one another, [their] fronts
shattered and broken, [with] a few crazy, creaky steps lead[ing] to each
door," lined the infamous corridor. Each "tenement generally consists
of three apartments, the drinking shop, about four feet deep and eight
feet long, a larger or rather deeper room in the rear . . . and a loft [used]
as common sleeping apartments." A closer look revealed the activities
inside: "There is a red curtain in every window, and drunkenness and
vice seem to peep through. . . . Each of those rickety sheds brings to

the owner a monthly payment of $25 or $30 . . . raised by the sale of poisonous liquors . . . a bottle [visible in every] open door." The woman of the house—such enterprises were usually run by women, likely mad-ams—"enlarges her business by accommodating boarders and lodgers." Upstairs, strangers paid a picayune for a rude bunk, and endured "men in a beastly state of intoxication, with bloody clothes . . . a broken jaw, a stab in the body; while slovenly bloated women hang around them. . . . This is not a fancy picture," the article concluded.[22]

Last but not least of the soft concentrations of antebellum vice was Gallatin Street. Only two blocks long, Gallatin probably comes closest to an antebellum proto-Bourbon, except that it was incomparably more violent and unrestrained. Newspapers described the strip as "filled with low groggeries[,] the resort of the worst and most abandoned of both sexes."[23] The raucous space achieved metaphoric status, such that if one spoke of a woman having a "career on Gallatin Street," or of "the frail daughters of Gallatin Street," everyone knew what that meant. It also earned the rhetorical flares of sarcasm and irony, through such refer-ences as "that classic thoroughfare," "the numerous and chaste nymphs of that poetic region," and "that quiet, respectable thoroughfare."[24] Few New Orleanians would have challenged the journalist who, in inventory-ing the city's geography of sin in 1855, wrote that "worst among the worse is Gallatin street . . . sons of fraud, treachery and blood meet there the daughters of the night, and with them hold high wassail and unhal-lowed revelry. There is no redeeming feature to this street of streets."[25] Yet more wickedness lay a short distance downriver, around the dog-leg-shaped intersection of Elysian Fields Street (now Avenue): here operated the Sign of the Lion, the Stadt Amsterdam, The Mobile, Pon-tchartrain House, The Whitehall, and Tivoli Gardens, known together as Sanctity Row. Why here? Gallatin Street and Sanctity Row lay at the lower edge of the French (or Creole) Market, the city's largest munici-pal emporium, which buzzed with stalls, conveyances, errand-runners, day-hires, cheap food, running water, distractions, amusements, shel-ter, and a steady stream of customers. Such activity attracted loiterers, transients, curiosity-seekers, and adventurers to whom the sin sector catered. The adjacent streets also ranked fairly low socioeconomically; one visitor called this area "the St. Gilles of New Orleans . . . where poverty and vice run races with want and passion." It attracted trou-blemakers with its cheap rents and lacked the civic clout to keep them out.[26] And on Elysian Fields was the Pontchartrain Railroad Station, which landed visitors from Mobile via Lake Pontchartrain. For many disoriented coastwise travelers, this spot formed the back-end gateway to New Orleans. Railroads, ships, markets, low rents, cheap eats, day jobs, strangers coming and going at all hours: a perfect in-between spot to see the elephant.

Seeing the Elephant in Hard Spaces

Laws had been on the books for years targeting prostitution, but they mainly prohibited "occasion[ing] scandal or disturb[ing] the tranquility of the neighborhood" rather than paid sex per se.[27] The spatial ubiquity of brothels, however, impelled city authorities to step up their intervention. In March 1857, the City Council passed "An Ordinance concerning Lewd and Abandoned Women," a sixteen-act, thrice-amended piece of legislation said to be the first of its kind in the United States. Dubbed the Lorette Law, the ordinance restricted the sex trade by taxing, in certain areas, prostitutes $100 and brothel keepers $250 annually.[28] The law thus reworked the geography of prostitution and, by not banning it outright, routed industry profits into city coffers. The spatial restrictions aimed to make the sex trade invisible, not illegal. That is, it aimed to hide it in the dense interstices of the cityscape: harlots could not occupy any one-story building, or the lower floor of any structure, nor could they "stand upon the sidewalk . . . or at the alley way, door or gate . . . nor sit upon the steps [with] an indecent posture [nor] stroll about the streets of the city indecently attired."[29] The Lorette Law also segregated white and free colored prostitutes and banned solicitation in cabarets or coffeehouses. Most significantly, it ascribed these restrictions to certain hard-defined spaces, curtailing prostitution in the front of town and pushing it to the outskirts of the city.[30] The Lorette Law marked the beginning of the end of the old soft Phillippa-Girod and Gallatin-Elysian Fields vice concentrations, not to mention the scores of dispersed brothels. However, one old concentration evaded the new delimitations. Because the Lorette Law did not restrict prostitution on the swamp (lake) side of Basin Street between Canal Street and Toulouse, the old Customhouse Street concentration around the Franklin Street intersection managed to persist—with great consequence forty years later.[31]

The Lorette Law came under legal attack immediately from public women, brothel keepers, and the landlords who rented to them. In 1859, the Louisiana Supreme Court ruled the ordinance unconstitutional on licensing technicalities, and authorities fought back with adjustments. "For the next forty years," wrote historian Schafer, "city leaders passed eight new versions of the Lorette Law, all of which attempted unsuccessfully to control, regulate, or just make money on prostitution."[32] Licensing fees and penalties were tweaked variously, but the spatial limits of the law generally remained the same as in 1857. This meant that, by default, the one place in the city where sex workers could ply their trade with no costs, minimal police interference, and maximum proximity to johns, was around the old Customhouse Street concentration. That space would form an opportunity for the city to attempt its next and greatest corralling of vice, one that would cinch New Orleans's notorious national reputation and lay the groundwork for today's Bourbon Street.

In early 1897, a newly elected councilman named Sidney Story came forth to present a spatial solution to the geography of sin. In the felicitous words of historian Alecia Long, Alderman Story and his allies in city hall, "acknowledging their belief that sins of the flesh were inevitable, looked Satan in the eye, cut a deal, and gave him his own address."[33] Story proposed spatially isolating prostitution to a compact area bounded by Basin, Customhouse, Robertson, and St. Louis Streets—the very heart of the pre-1857 soft vice zone around Customhouse and Franklin, and the same area excluded from the Lorette Law in 1857. Although spanning barely sixteen blocks, a fraction of the Lorette footprint, Story's ordinance differed in that it banned prostitution outright throughout the rest of the city. By default, prostitution became legal therein, without licenses or taxes for sex services. The Lorette laws, by contrast, curbed (but did not ban) prostitution within a large delimited area, and left it unmolested beyond.

Story's prostitution solution was radical, and subsequent amendments made it unique in the nation for its rigor and clarity. One modification stipulated that public women not only had to ply their avocation exclusively in the designated area, but also had to establish their permanent residency there. This led to concerns that those sixteen blocks (already home to two thousand people) could not accommodate a vast throng of migrating harlots. A later proviso made it "unlawful for any prostitute of the colored or black race to occupy any house outside the limits of Perdido, Gravier, Franklin, and Locust streets," creating a so-called Uptown District that also matched an earlier antebellum vice concentration.[34] Another called for opaque windows on all houses of ill repute. Significantly from the perspective of Bourbon Street, yet another addendum to Story's ordinance made his district—"Storyville," as the whores called it—a depot for "any concert-saloon or place where can-can, clodoche or similar female dancing or sensational performance are shown." Starting January 1, 1898, Storyville alone became "the only physical space in the city where concert saloons and other sexually oriented entertainment establishments could be legally established."[35] The amendment shifted the full suite of risqué entertainment businesses out of the upper French Quarter and into Storyville.

In the opening years of the 1900s, Storyville formed what all of New Orleans's earlier vice concentrations had not: a legally delineated high-grain district for sex, drinking, dancing, music, and wagering. Business boomed, and in the process, the vice industry invented and christened its own neighborhood. It created a signature streetscape in the form of Basin Street (dubbed "the Line," the same moniker given to Broadway in Manhattan's Tenderloin District), where magnificent mansions became gaudy "sporting houses" and prostitutes called down from balconies to men walking "down the Line." Storyville mastered the interstitial geography of high urban granularity. It produced an iconic gateway to "the District" in the form of Tom Anderson's famous Basin Street saloon. It had accessibility, being minutes from urban core and steps from a new passenger train station. It boasted, only three years into its existence, 230 brothels, sixty houses of assignation, and scores of cribs, concert saloons, bars, cafés, and restaurants—this despite a steep $5000 licensing fee for concert saloons mandated by a 1903 ordinance.[36] Storyville also generated employment for pianists and other musicians, nurturing the development of what would later be called "jass" or jazz.

The phrase "seeing the elephant," by the 1900s, had disappeared from American English, and the Great War would eventually bring an end to Storyville in 1917. But by that time, the space had garnered national fame and infamy, and, to the chagrin of reformers, breathed new twentieth-century life into New Orleans's eighteenth- and nineteenth-century reputation for sin. After a few years in the Tango Belt—the North Rampart–Burgundy–Dauphine–Iberville Street area that lay precisely between the heart of the original city and Storyville—the fulcrum of the indulgence industry would find a new home amid the galleries, balconies, steep-pitched roofs, dark alleys, *portes-cochères*, and hidden courtyards of Bourbon Street.

Inevitable, Interstitial Bourbon Street

The Bourbon Street we love or hate today—there are no in-between emotions on this matter—happened when New Orleanians realized their city's historical reputation for sin could be repackaged as pleasure and sold to the modern-day leisure class. Bourbon Street was forged into the marvelously lucrative perpetual-gratification machine it is today through an ongoing civic wrestling match between enterprising plebian proprietors who figured out how to monetize merriment, and educated professionals and patricians who wanted peace, order, and preservation. It succeeded because it supplied the demanded expectations and indul-

Figure 7.4. Alcohol outlet in interstitial space on Bourbon Street (2012). Photograph by Richard Campanella.

gences within a walkable space and within a high-grain historic setting, making it maximally appealing and consumable by pleasure pilgrims from places like Peoria.

Which begs the question, why did that spatial concentration of bars, nightclubs, and restaurants end up on Bourbon and not some other street? After all, its predecessors were located as far down as Gallatin Street, as far up as Girod, and as far back as the Swamp, Franklin Street, and Storyville, all between the city and the periphery. Bourbon Street is very much in the city's core.

Process of elimination helps answer this question. Why did Bourbon the phenomenon not end up on, for example, St. Charles Avenue, Camp, Carondelet, Baronne, or Magazine Street, or another Central Business District street? A handful of nighttime entertainment venues did exist here, and do to this day, but high-priced office space, white-collar jobs, and incompatible zoning would have prevented a critical mass from forming, let alone along a single street. Additionally, the district's arteries are multilaned, its buildings scrape the sky, and it urban granularity is hardly intimate.

Returning to the Quarter, why not Decatur or North Peters? These streets were simply too commercial, industrial, or arterial and lacked the texture to exude the optimal twilight aura. Call it bad interstitial: fronting the river, these thoroughfares bustled with industry, retail, and up to four lanes of traffic along the region's premier sugar and rice shipping district. It was similar for Rampart Street, which, from colonial times to today, always had a dangerous edge, not to mention four vehicular lanes and poverty on its other side. If Decatur and North Peters were too close to the river and its industrial nuisances, Rampart was too close to the urban and demographic echoes of the old back of town, neither of which would have been conducive to the commodification of pleasure for risk-averse tourists.

What about Dauphine or Burgundy? These were, after, the Tango Belt, Storyville's successor and Bourbon Street's predecessor. Could they have snared Bourbon's trade? Not likely, because beyond the first block, these streets are mostly residential. Cottages and shotgun houses are tough spaces to reprogram for nightclubs and restaurants. Dauphine and Burgundy simply did not have the right architecture to host the Bourbon phenomenon, and subsequent land-use zoning made sure of that.

Chartres and Royal Streets are different stories. Replete with storehouses and townhouses and as high-grain as any of the French Quarter's cityscapes, these elegant streets, famous in their own right, had since the 1860s laid claim to their share of nighttime entertainment, much like Bourbon. Why they did not draw the nightclub economy may well be because they actively rejected it. The highbrow antiquarian trade had since the 1890s come to characterize Royal and Chartres, and both streets cultivated an aristocratic, ladies' club air. Their proprietors were less inclined to emulate Bourbon Street and more inclined to hold their noses to it.

This leaves Iberville as the best contender for the Bourbon phenomenon. This street had ill repute going back to antebellum times. It had concert saloons as early as the 1860s; it penetrated into Storyville during 1897–1917; it intersected the extraordinarily wild Franklin Street; it ran through the Tango Belt in the 1910s and 1920s; and even today, it rates as the closest surviving example of those edgy spaces. And perhaps that's the reason why Iberville never succeeded in attracting Bourbon-like nightclubs: it was a little too edgy.

So then, why Bourbon Street? The thoroughfare benefited from its in-between spatial and (relatedly) social position. It was far enough from the riverfront to be buffered from its industrial nuisances, and equally far from the back of town to be insulated from its déclassé denizens. Bourbon avoided both the pricey real estate and patrician antiquarians

Figure 7.5. High-grain urban granularity: Mardi Gras on Bourbon Street. Photograph by Richard Campanella, 2012.

of Royal and Chartres, as well as the humble cottages of Dauphine and Burgundy. It benefitted from a rather good mix of architectural typologies available at reasonable prices, and it possessed many old commercial storehouses with alleyways and courtyards, all of which fostered that key blend of antiquity and mystery. Most importantly, much of Bourbon Street was owned by creative working-class immigrants who monopolized the entertainment and tourism niche eschewed by old-money bluebloods. It had a streetcar line connecting it with all points uptown, where many patrons lived, and with all points downtown, where many employees lived. Bourbon Street, in sum, comprised fertile interstitial ground. It had a good urban geography for an entertainment industry to flourish, proximate to favorable factors and distant from detrimental ones.

Tonight and every night, 365 days a year, revelers liberated by their anonymity find opportunities in these spaces to let their guard down and indulge in the moment. The spectacle earns the condemnations of conservatives and the sneers of progressives, but in its behavioral and spatial essence, it differs little from the times when flatboatmen and smugglers sought the elephant in the streets of New Orleans.

NOTES

1. "To Correspondents," *Daily Picayune*, July 23, 1844, 2.

2. "City Intelligence—Highway Robbery," *Daily Picayune*, November 11, 1848, 2.

3. Material in this chapter is adapted from my recent book, *Bourbon Street: A History* (Baton Rouge: Louisiana State University Press, 2014).

4. Richard Campanella, "Remembering the Old French Opera House: The Bourbon Street Landmark (1859–1919) Testifies to the Cultural Power of Old Buildings, and the Significance of Their Loss," *Preservation in Print*, February 2013, 16–18.

5. Lafcadio Hearn, "Old-Fashioned Houses," January 12, 1881, in S. Frederick Starr, *Inventing New Orleans: Writings of Lafcadio Hearn* (Jackson: University Press of Mississippi, 2001), 177.

6. Phillip Lopate, *Waterfront: A Walk Around Manhattan* (New York: Anchor Books, 2004), 203–4.

7. Walt Whitman, "Once I Pass'd through a Populous City," *Leaves of Grass* (London: G. P. Putnam's Sons, 1897), 94.

8. David Metzer, "Reclaiming Walt: Marc Blitzstein's Whitman Settings," *Journal of the American Musicological Society* 48, no. 2 (Summer 1995): 242.

9. Erving Goffman, *Stigma* (Englewood Cliffs, NJ: Prentice Hall, 1963); David Redmon, "Playful Deviance as an Urban Leisure Activity: Secret Selves, Self-Validation, and Entertaining Performances," *Deviant Behavior* 24, no. 1 (2003), 27–51.

10. "New-Orleans," *New-Bedford (MA) Courier*, August 16, 1831, 1.

11. Lawrence N. Powell, *The Accidental City: Improvising New Orleans* (Cambridge, MA: Harvard University Press, 2011), 92–105.

12. "The Present State of the Country . . . of Louisiana . . . by an Officer at New Orleans to his Friend at Paris," in *Narratives of Colonial America, 1704–1765*, ed. Howard H. Peckham (Chicago: Lakeside Press, 1971), 61–62.

13. As quoted by Shannon Lee Dawdy, *Madame John's Legacy (16OR51) Revisited: A Closer Look at the Archeology of Colonial New Orleans* (New Orleans: Greater New Orleans Archaeology Project, 1998), 122.

14. Pierre-Louis Berquin-Duvallon, *Travels in Louisiana and the Floridas in the Year 1802, Giving a Correct Picture of Those Countries*, trans. John Davis (New York, 1806), 59.

15. "Extract of a Letter from an Emigrant in New-Orleans," *Newburyport (MA) Herald*, October 17, 1817, 3.

16. John H. B. Latrobe, *Southern Travels: Journal of John H. B. Latrobe, 1834*, ed. Samuel Wilson Jr. (New Orleans, 1986), 42.

17. "Life in New Orleans," *Ohio Statesman (Columbus, OH)*, May 7, 1847, 3. The French geographer Elisée Réclus noted in 1853 that "the city's more than twenty-five hundred taverns are always filled with drinkers . . . especially during election time." *A Voyage to New Orleans*, trans. John Clark and Camille Martin (Thetford, VT: Glad Day Books, 2004), 56–57.

18. *New Orleans As It Is: Its Manners and Customs* ([New Orleans?]: printed for the publisher, 1850), 52–55.

19. "An Ordinance concerning Inns, Boarding-Houses, Coffee-Houses, Billiards-Houses, Taverns, Grog-Shops, and Other Houses with the City of New-Orleans," March 8, 1831, *A General Digest of the Ordinances and Resolutions of the Corporation of New-Orleans* (New Orleans: Jerome Bayon, 1831), 63–70. Evidence suggests sporad-

ic enforcement, but license fees were taken more seriously. Grog shops alone, by one estimate, numbered well over six hundred and brought in over $100,000 to city coffers annually in the late 1830s. See the *Journal of the American Temperance Union* (Philadelphia, Pennsylvania) 3, no. 1 (January 1839): 15.

20. Spatial analysis by author based on police reports, court records, and news articles of illegal sex arrests and related activities collected and interpreted by Judith Kelleher Schafer in *Brothels, Depravity, and Abandoned Women: Illegal Sex in Antebellum New Orleans* (Baton Rouge: Louisiana State University Press, 2009).

21. Journal of Welcome A. Greene, reproduced in "Being the Journal of a Quaker Merchant Who Visited N.O. in 1823," *Times-Picayune*, October 16, 1921, Section 4, 1–6; James Stuart, *Three Years in North America*, vol. 2 (Edinburgh and London: Robert Cadell and Whittaker and Company, 1833), 232.

22. "Girod Street," *Daily Picayune*, July 25, 1852, 1.

23. As quoted by Schafer, *Brothels, Depravity, and Abandoned Women*, 6.

24. Gleaned from articles quoted by Schafer in *Brothels, Depravity, and Abandoned Women*; emphases added.

25. *Daily Picayune*, December 1 and 29, 1855, as referenced by Schafer.

26. A. Oakey Hall, *The Manhattaner in New Orleans; or, Phases of "Crescent City" Life* (New York: J. S. Redfield, Clinton Hall, 1851), 102.

27. These particular restrictions come from John Calhoun, *Digest of the Ordinances and Resolutions of the Second Municipality of New-Orleans* (New Orleans: F. Cook & A. Levy, 1840), which were typical of many other city laws.

28. Prostitutes in Paris loitered near the Church of Notre Dame de Lorette, and thus became known as Lorettes throughout the Francophone world, including in New Orleans. Schafer, *Brothels, Depravity, and Abandoned Women*, 145.

29. "No Lewd Women—An Ordinance concerning Lewd and Abandoned Women," in *The Laws and General Ordinances of the City of New Orleans*, ed. Henry J. Leovy (New Orleans: E. C. Wharton, 1857), 376.

30. The restricted zone stretched from the Mississippi River to the upper limits of the city (Toledano Street at that time), along the Carrollton railroad (present-day streetcar line) on St. Charles Avenue, lakeward on Felicity, then downriver along Hercules, Circus, Rampart, and Basin Streets (roughly today's Loyola Avenue–Elk Place–Basin Street corridor) until Toulouse Street, which aligned with the Old Basin Canal. All areas from that canal straight back to Bayou St. John and over to Esplanade Street (now Avenue) were also included in the restricted zone, as were all areas from Esplanade down Broad Street and along Elysian Fields back to the Mississippi River.

31. Act Nos. 1084 and 1102 of "No Lewd Women—An Ordinance concerning Lewd and Abandoned Women," *The Laws and General Ordinances of the City of New Orleans*, 376–80.

32. Schafer, *Brothels, Depravity, and Abandoned Women*, 153.

33. Alecia P. Long, *The Great Southern Babylon: Sex, Race, and Respectability in New Orleans, 1865–1920* (Baton Rouge: Louisiana State University Press, 2004), 106.

34. Ordinance 4118 C.C.S. City of New Orleans, February [illegible], 1917.

35. The first quotation comes from Mayoralty of New Orleans, City Hall, Ordinance 13,604, September 1, 1897; the second quotation comes from Long, *Great Southern Babylon*, 121.

36. Ordinance No. 2155, New Council Series (N.C.S.), Mayoralty of New Orleans, City Hall, December 3, 1903; Long, *Great Southern Babylon*, 158.

CHAPTER EIGHT

Where Women Live

Creating and Regulating the Spaces of Women's Lives, 1880–1950

—Beth Willinger

One woman stood against the backdrop of a lush southern garden, another against a wall decorated with college pennants, and still another woman alongside a bedroom dresser adorned with photos. Some of the women were "dressed to the nines, some erotically naked," all were photographed by E. J. Bellocq "in homely circumstances that affirm[ed] both sensuality and domestic ease."[1] The display of "domestic ease" was achievable quite possibly because the Storyville brothel *was* home to Bellocq's subjects—by order of the Common Council of the City of New Orleans.

In 1897, the city council made it "unlawful for any public prostitute or woman notoriously abandoned to lewdness to occupy, inhabit, live, or sleep in any house, room, or closet" situated outside a sixteen-block district. The ordinance created Storyville, the only neighborhood devoted to prostitution in the United States. The District, as the area came to be called, was an effort to control corruption and tame a more than century-old image of the city as Louisiana's Babylon or the Devil's Empire by geographically containing prostitution.[2] A lesser known district was created uptown by the same 1897 city ordinance but was not approved until 1917, just months before Storyville was officially closed by the United States Department of the Navy. However, several historians contend the so-called Uptown District operated illegally all along, mainly as a district where African American women catered to a largely African American clientele.[3] In the Jim Crow era, legalization of the Uptown District was considered a deliberate act by the city council to control prostitution across the color line by forcing women of color out and making Storyville an all-white district.[4]

151

The requirement that prostitutes live within the boundaries of Storyville and its uptown African American counterpart meant home was a brothel or a crib for several thousand "immoral" women.[5] Consequently, the seemingly personal and private matter of where a woman lives, and with whom, became the purview of government, law enforcement agencies, and reform-minded citizens.

The reform-minded women of New Orleans, working for the "encouragement, improvement and reclamation of their own sex," created their own organizations and institutions to save women from prostitution.[6] In doing so, they helped to shape civil society in New Orleans—the space between the public sphere where men exercise their political and economic power, and the private sphere with its normative ideal of women's work and place within the home.[7] This essay focuses on a moment in history when New Orleans women moved outside the gendered constraints of the private sphere to bring their own perspectives to the problem of prostitution. Organizing on behalf of women, they promoted women's economic security and founded respectable and affordable residences for single working women as settings situated in-between the geographically defined private household and the public commercial boarding houses and brothels of Storyville.

The ideology of separate spheres for men and women has been the subject of long debate. The point here is not to formalize a theory of difference but to use that ideology as an analytical tool for exploring the spaces in between. While feminist critiques of the dichotomy challenge the rigidity of separate spheres, as well as the gender assignment, most researchers view women's activism outside the domestic realm as either an expansion of their domestic role or as a crack in the boundary of the public.[8] This essay considers women's organizing and institution building as creating an unchartered spatial territory in between the public and private. That is, studying women's activism outside the private household as merely an extension of women's domestic duties disaffirms women's full capabilities. At the same time, women's activities outside the private sphere do not necessarily make those undertakings entirely or even recognizably public.

Historically concurrent with the ideology of separate spheres was the concept of True Womanhood, or the "cult of domesticity." The True Woman was defined by the appearance of piety, purity, submissiveness, and domesticity; in essence, she was the antithesis of the prostitute.[9] In the narrative developed by cultural historians, the duty of the wife and other female dependents was to provide a refuge for the "man of the house" who, in return for women's loyalty and service, was to offer support and protection. For the white upper- or middle-class southern

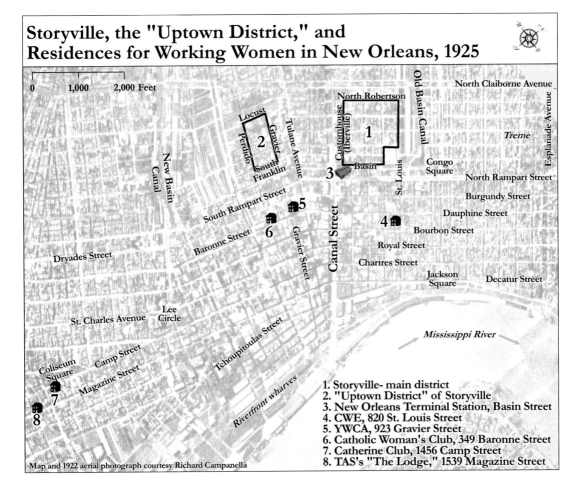

Storyville, the "Uptown District," and Residences for Working Women in New Orleans, 1925

0   1,000   2,000 Feet

1. Storyville- main district
2. "Uptown District" of Storyville
3. New Orleans Terminal Station, Basin Street
4. CWE, 820 St. Louis Street
5. YWCA, 923 Gravier Street
6. Catholic Woman's Club, 349 Baronne Street
7. Catherine Club, 1456 Camp Street
8. TAS's "The Lodge," 1539 Magazine Street

Map and 1922 aerial photograph courtesy Richard Campanella.

Figure 8.1. Storyville, the Uptown District, and residences for working women in New Orleans (1925). Map and 1922 aerial photograph courtesy of Richard Campanella.

woman, such comforts included food, clothing, shelter and the protection of her "honorable" reputation.

In New Orleans, the ideology of the True Woman was heightened by the decision of city officials to confine prostitution to the geographical areas of Storyville and its African American equivalent. The presumed spatial segregation endorsed a fictional dichotomy of women as recognizably "moral" or "immoral," "virgin" or "whore," based on where they lived. The geographic segregation of virtue was attended by racial segregation and regulation within each space. In this way, a bifurcated map of the city, delineating neighborhoods as good or bad, black or white, could emerge for residents who sought to ensure the respectability of their own neighborhoods and the women and girls who resided therein.[10] The residential restrictions also likely controlled the behaviors of "good" women by establishing what constituted "bad," not solely with respect to governing sexual desire, but also with respect to marital status and behaviors ranging from appropriate dress and manners to prohibitions against alcohol, dancing, smoking, boisterous behavior, interracial interactions, and choices about where and with whom to live.

Geography thus functioned as an instrument of social control, operating to contain women according to patriarchal interests. Purity and domesticity, markers of the True Woman, remained safely confined in the private homes and neighborhoods of the white elite. However, as this volume argues, there was an in-between. The borders of Storyville bled. Its boundaries were always more legally mandated than assiduously maintained. Prostitution was rampant in the city's hotels as well as in the French Quarter, where a clandestine movement out of Storyville to the Quarter began around 1913.[11] In 1917, the commissioner of public safety and other city officials led a crackdown to force prostitutes who lived outside Storyville to relocate within its boundaries or face fines or jail time. The ruling pertained mainly to cribs, requiring "that the women must actually live in the houses they occupy instead of renting them at exorbitant rentals from night to night."[12] Rose quotes Louis Armstrong as saying that some of the women lived elsewhere and "would come down to Storyville just like they had a job."[13] Long gives the example of the well-known Storyville madam, Josie Arlington, who, as Mrs. J. T. Brady, moved rather freely about the city and traveled abroad and, as Mary Deubler, bought a house on Esplanade Avenue where she, her paramour, brother, sister-in-law, and their three children lived.[14]

Sundays on Canal Street, the city's grand shopping and commercial thoroughfare, created a particular challenge to maintaining Storyville's borders and distinguishing between good and fallen women. In 1911, the rules of the H. Sophie Newcomb Memorial College for Women (founded in 1886) prohibited students from walking on Canal Street on Sundays. Historians initially thought the prohibition to be a means of restricting the young women's social activities on a day intended for quiet devotion. However, the city's Sunday closing laws also gave the women of Storyville an afternoon of rest, and strolling along Canal Street, just a block away, was a popular way to spend the day. College administrators were thus apparently not so much concerned about encouraging piety as they were fearful of the students' loss of purity should they be mistaken for Storyville residents, witness inappropriate behaviors, or be seduced into a life of crime. The ruling was lifted in 1918, the year after Storyville was officially closed.[15]

Such measures suggest that moral ruin was an ever-present possibility for a young single woman in New Orleans. Her respectability depended on having a home where she was properly chaperoned, a suitable job, and, in the not-too-distant future, a husband. However, single women faced a range of obstacles in their quest. First, the skewed population of women in Orleans Parish, averaging between 52 and 53 percent in the years from 1880 to 1940, meant marriage and male protection was not an option for a sizeable number of white and African American women.[16] Second, finding respectable housing was especially problematic for single women because of their requirements for protection, their limited resources owing to their lower wages, and their desire for the amenities of a home. Given these prerequisites, it was nearly impossible for a woman to live alone in her own home, whether rented or owned. In fact, it was rare for anyone, male or female, to live alone. Until the 1950s, single-person households accounted for only one in twenty in the United States, while only one in five families owned their own home.[17] Moreover, in New Orleans, as in other large American cities, an already tight housing market was severely tested by the influx of immigrants. As a result, regardless of age, most single adults lived with family members in a rented house or apartment.

What then became of the never-married, the orphaned, the widowed, separated, or divorced, the woman whose rural family depended on her urban wages, or the independent woman who sought respectable housing? Anxieties about single women, amplified by race, class, status, and sometimes religion, as well as concerns by women themselves directly contributed to the construction of a range of interstitial settings where respectable women could live in New Orleans in a space of their own.

The first group of reform-minded citizens to address the challenges presented by "these difficult and troubled times" met in April of 1881 and promptly established themselves as the Christian Woman's Exchange (CWE), an "efficient organization of ladies, ready and willing to do whatever their hearts and hands may find to do for the . . . reclamation of their own sex."[18]

The CWE's approach to social problems differed markedly from the methods of the city fathers. While city officials sought to spatially contain and regulate prostitution by requiring prostitutes to live in the same dwelling where they worked, the CWE sought to suppress prostitution itself by creating an alternative living space that was neither fully public and commercial nor private and determined. Ignoring the boundaries separating public and private, the CWE and other women's groups (as will be discussed later) organized to construct an in-between space where their collective actions on behalf of single working women could be realized.

The initial aim of the CWE was to help women achieve economic security by establishing a consignment shop for the sale of homemade food products and traditional handiwork in the decorative and domestic arts. This primary objective was firmly rooted in the exchange movement that originated with the Philadelphia (PA) Ladies' Depository in 1832, and drew upon both the Arts and Crafts movement of Great Britain and the European philosophy of self-help and self-improvement.[19]

However, unlike some seventy-two woman's exchanges nationally, the New Orleans CWE was the only exchange to specifically include in its charter a duty to counteract the implied, but unnamed, problem of prostitution. Their second objective spoke to their "earnest effort to reclaim the Lord's own from the pernicious amusements and allurement of the world and to cultivate . . . the Christian grace of compassion, as shown by our Lord's example when He kindly said to that guilty woman, 'Go and sin no more.'"[20]

The CWE also was the only exchange to insert "Christian" or indeed any religious suggestion in the name of the organization. Perhaps the respectable women of New Orleans thought it necessary to emphasize the piety and purity of their endeavors. Yet despite the strong rhetoric, there is little to suggest the CWE restricted their membership, or their services, to Christian women. They did, however, limit both to white women.

In 1887, the CWE began renting furnished rooms "for ladies (*en suite* or single) with access to Drawing Room" and "all the refinements and protection of homelife at reasonable rates." CWE's ability to provide safe, affordable, and respectable housing for single working women was made possible by the purchase of a twenty-six-room building at the corner of Camp and South Streets on Lafayette Square. Two prominent New Orleanians and board members, Mrs. Charles L. (Florestile) Howard and Mrs. Charles A. (Marie Louise) Whitney, both of whom were widows, together donated $28,000 for the purchase. The building also allowed the CWE to operate a day care facility for the children of working mothers. Both services, day care and rooming house, are thought to have been the first of their kind in the city.[21]

The expansion of the CWE's services to include a residence alongside the exchange shop—unusual though not unique among exchanges nationally—served as a way for the CWE to fulfill its mission of saving women from prostitution. Commercial, for-profit boarding or rooming houses were largely unaffordable for single women, and the absence of a chaperone as well as rules governing (sexual) behaviors meant they generally were unacceptable as respectable dwellings. After all, a brothel was a boarding house![22] CWE attempted to counter these problems by providing a form of single-sex "sheltered" housing that included monitoring visitors and a curfew; making the rent of a furnished room affordable and the premises homelike; and assuring that the residents, who were interviewed by a committee of the board and required to provide written character references, were themselves beyond reproach.

The CWE also served as the first headquarters of another reform-minded group of women who, identifying an unmet need among young women arriving in the city, similarly disrupted the geographic border of the private sphere to create a new organization in the space between the public and private. In 1908, a "mass meeting of the women of New Orleans" led to the creation of the Travelers' Aid Society (TAS), whose primary objective was suppressing "the fearful barter in women's bodies known under the title of 'The White Slave Traffic,' . . . which . . . had grown more heinous than usual."[23] Their plan was designed to "provide protection to women and girls arriving in the city, who, through ignorance or inexperience," might be influenced by "the representatives of organized vice; to suppress . . . the decoying of young women to the city, under guise of remunerative employment; [and] to provide a temporary home for such unfortunate women until permanent protection" could be secured.[24]

The likely impetus for the TAS was the completion of the New Orleans Terminal station in 1908, which directly abutted the bordellos along Basin Street. TAS began by hiring female "agents" to meet incoming trains and to "care for girls under suspicion or in need of protection." The CWE kept a room available to the TAS for white girls who, arriving "penniless or without a means of support," were "rescued" from prostitution. However, the demands on the TAS became "immensely complicated" as a consequence of World War I, and they too found it necessary to provide additional, short-term lodging for women and girls. In 1918, they rented a house at 1539 Magazine Street, called it "the Lodge," and maintained it until 1934 as a place where white women and girls, under any number of circumstances, could find temporary shelter, and where they might occasionally be housed "instead of being sent to jails and precinct stations."[25]

Newspaper reports and TAS minutes are filled with melodramatic tales of TAS's successful efforts to return runaway girls to their families. A common scenario pits the naïveté of a young girl against urban vice or an older man's depravity, as in the example of the "young girl of 14 years, who eloped from Texas with a married man three times her age." Like her—finally "induced to return home by her distressed father"—nearly all these narratives conclude with the TAS reuniting the girl with her family or returning her home. Thus, while the women volunteers and staff of the TAS were working outside the restraints of conventional domesticity, they nevertheless perpetuated the ideology of the True Woman and the sanctity of the home for young women and girls."[26] That young women should join the labor force seems never to have altered their minds.

Figure 8.2. The residence of the Christian Woman's Exchange, 820 St. Louis Street, between 1925 and 1950. The Collins C. Diboll Vieux Carré Digital Survey, Historic New Orleans Collection, N-193.

About the same time, efforts "to take the homeless and runaway negro girls off the streets" were begun by the "colored Volunteers of America." Designed to do "much the same work as the Travelers' Aid society now does among the white girls," they called upon the "negro preachers" of the city to join hands in suppressing "immorality. . . . and waging a successful fight against social disease among the negroes of the city." In contrast to reform efforts in the white community, which were led by women, within the African American community, it was the all-male Volunteers of America who called upon preachers (presumably fellow males) to lead the reform. Since only one article and no records can be found about this project, we are left to ponder whether women of color also took part in organizing this rescue mission, and even whether the Volunteers of America had any success in raising the funds to provide the service.[27]

In the early 1920s, the CWE sold their Lafayette Square property for a handsome profit and purchased what was known as the Grima house at 820 St. Louis Street in the French Quarter. A major concern expressed by CWE members in acquiring this property was "the questionable character of the surrounding neighborhood" and providing a safe home for women in the French Quarter.[28] Storyville had been located just across Basin Street with St. Louis Street as an outer boundary. Norma Wallace, the French Quarter madam, maintained a bordello at 328 Burgundy Street, and later at 410 Dauphine Street, both just a few blocks away. Wallace later claimed that "between Iberville and St. Louis Streets and from Bourbon to Rampart, every door had a girl hustling in it." In the 1920s, this corner of the Quarter became known as the Tango Belt, an area filled with dance halls and cabarets where couples would dance in sensuous close embrace.[29]

To address these neighborhood concerns and to ensure that the CWE's new home was anchored in respectability, the board strengthened its admitting requirements. CWE members proposed that if no women under thirty years of age were accepted for permanent residency, objections to buying the house could be waived. CWE members also expressed other reasons for choosing to serve the "older woman":

> It has been forcibly brought home to the members of the board of the Christian Woman's Exchange that there is no place in the city provided for the older woman who is thrown upon her own resources for support. The younger woman is provided for by more than one splendid organization, but the older woman, whose earning powers are not so great as that of her younger sister, is forced to seek her lodging in out of the way rooming-houses, or with reluctant relatives and her lot is far from enviable. She is a tragic figure.[30]

The "tragic figure" of the older working woman reveals the normative ideals of the organization's middle- and upper-class board. It may not have been an identity that CWE residents, as independent, semiprofessional, and skilled workers, claimed for themselves.[31]

Still, the CWE board's conventional view of the older single woman highlights the diversity of women in need of housing. Writing in 1898, Mary Ferguson observed that there were two "classes" of women who were served by the rooming or boarding house. The first was "the young, the inexperienced, the morally weak, the stranger within our city doors, the discouraged, and perhaps, the tempted." For them, the rooming house was both protection and prevention, "a powerful social as well as economic factor in the life of the working girl." The other class of "self-supporting women," wrote Ferguson, was "self-reliant, self respecting, and perfectly able, from a moral and social point of view, to stand alone."[32]

All evidence suggests that the residents of the CWE were "self-sup-porting women." When, for example, the CWE hung its sign on the Grima mansion reading "Home of the Christian Woman's Exchange," the residents protested. Although the board minutes do not explain the reasons for the protests, several may be proposed. First, Ferguson reports that the word *home* is "suggestive of an institution and has about it the odor of charity." In New Orleans, *home* was frequently applied to establishments serving the "deserving poor" or institutionalized popula-tions, as in the Home for Incurables, Home for the Aged, and Widow's Faith Home for Negro Women. Self-supporting women might well have wished to avoid "the shape or appearance of the so-called 'charitable' home" and the attendant paternalism of charity. Or, perhaps the resi-dents themselves recognized their interstitial place, preferring the new sign reading "Residence of the Christian Woman's Exchange."[33]

Factually, however, the CWE had served the "older woman" even before relocating to St. Louis Street. According to the 1920 US census, the average age of the thirty-seven residents of the CWE was 39.2 years. What then of the younger woman and the "more than one splendid orga-nization" serving her? Between 1910 and 1920, the lack of safe and suit-able housing for "familyless young women" concerned several women's organizations, including the New Orleans Young Women's Christian Association, the Catherine Club, and the Catholic Woman's Club. These three, as the *Times-Picayune* reported in 1919, housed "several hundred girls . . . in the sort of surroundings girls like."[34]

Founded in 1911, the New Orleans Young Women's Christian Associa-tion (YWCA) first provided housing for single working girls in 1919. Their initial residence, located in a former home at 1729 Coliseum Street, accom-modated up to fifty women. In 1922, the YWCA moved to 923 Gravier Street in a purpose-built structure designed to serve as its headquarters and as a residence. While the CWE board had reasoned that their French Quarter location was actually "better than that surrounding the YWCA," it might have been a toss-up as to which neighborhood would have been more respectable. The YWCA was just two to three blocks southeast from what had been the Uptown District. But any apprehensions the YWCA board might have had concerning the neighborhood went unmentioned as they contracted with the architectural firm of Favrot and Livaudais, Limited, to construct a three-story building with twenty bedrooms, suf-ficient for sixty-five single white women. Residents were required to be from outside the city and sixteen years of age or older, and they were per-mitted to remain in residence for no more than two years.[35]

Despite the desire for safe and respectable neighborhoods, resi-dences for single working women were often established in transitional,

Figure 8.3. The Catherine Club, 1456 Camp Street, between 1925 and 1930. Historic New Orleans Collection, donated in memory of John Code, acc. no. 1993.50.16

in-between neighborhoods, where property was more affordable than in more desirable neighborhoods.[36] The YWCA, like the CWE, appears to have curbed any questions about the environs with heightened efforts to make the homes themselves—and the residents therein—models of respectability. In addition to a careful review of applicants by the residence director, the YWCA required a medical examination including a Wassermann test (an antibody test for syphilis) and a vaginal smear, requirements that today would be considered a severe violation of privacy.[37]

Like the Woman's Club, out of which it grew, the Catherine Club, founded in 1913, was another organization of women familiar with crossing into spaces well outside the traditional definitions of home.[38] By 1919, the nonsectarian Catherine Club had purchased a home at 700 St. Charles Avenue, advertising as "one of the distinctive features" its aid to "ambitious girls who are seeking an education." Often called simply "the Catherine" and adopting the motto "the city's big sister to the working girl," the residence offered housing to forty-six white working girls and students for three to six dollars per week. The organization later purchased a home at 1456 Camp Street on Coliseum Square.[39] Similarly, the Catholic Woman's Club, founded in 1914, was located initially at 349 Baronne Street to serve thirty white girls and later moved to 207 Camp Street.[40] The choice of *club* rather than *home* by both organizations represented a common practice among residences for the "business girl" that avoided the appearance of both charity and strict religious governance while introducing the image of female friendship among residents.[41]

Whether or not the young women who took up residence at these homes were the inexperienced, morally weak, "stranger within our city doors" that Ferguson described, the boards of directors perceived them as such and assumed a corresponding responsibility. Perhaps they had reason. Compared to all gainfully employed women in New Orleans in 1920, the 155 white residents at the four homes for single working women identified here were more likely to be younger (63.9 percent between the ages of sixteen and twenty-four versus 44.3 percent) and unmarried (85.8 percent versus 52.3 percent). Table 1 shows the residence of the CWE to be unusual in serving the "older woman," who was, on average, fifteen years older than women at the other three residences. Even so, all the homes had residents over fifty years of age, which was not uncommon for most rooming houses. Mature women set a tone of stability and gentility, removing any suspicion that the rooming house was anything other than a highly respectable domicile for ladies—a particularly important desideratum in New Orleans, where public spaces remained notoriously suspect.

In creating new spaces and conditions for women to live, these organizations also fashioned new purposes. Embracing the Progressive Era's emphasis on the health, morals, and, strikingly, the insufficient pay of the young unmarried woman away from home, the organizations shifted their efforts from rescuing women from prostitution to preventing prostitution altogether by stressing self-improvement and self-sufficiency.[42]

The occupations available to women in this era largely involved skills learned on-the-job; all four residences sought to assist women in preparing for employment and advancement by offering evening classes in stenography, telegraph operation, bookkeeping, English, and math, for "the present day needs in the business world." They also offered classes in the domestic arts, such as cooking, dressmaking, managing money, and millinery.[43] Having first constructed residences for single working women in the interstitial spaces between private households and public boarding houses and brothels, these organizations proceeded to widen this space to include opportunities for domestic training—skills young women typically acquired beside their mothers or grandmothers—as

Table 1. Residents living at the Catherine Club, the Catholic Woman's Club, the Christian Woman's Exchange, and the Young Women's Christian Association. *Source*: US Census of 1920.

Residence and address	# of residents	Age range	Average age	% single	Most common occupations
Catherine Club 709 St. Charles Ave.	43	16–60	23.0	90.7	Stenographer, billing clerk, student
Catholic Woman's 349 Baronne St.	34	16–60	22.3	97	Stenographer, saleslady, clerk
CWE 602 South St.	36	15–76	39.2	75.7	Seamstress, clerk, none
YWCA 1729 Coliseum St.	42	17–56	24.0	78.6	Stenographer, operator, clerk

well as education of the kind offered in public schools and colleges. Neither fully public nor private but in between, these residences sought to improve the young women's earnings—and marriage potential—through education and training.

An additional service provided by the boards to address the residents' limited and unsuitable choices of eating establishments was the creation of lunchrooms where working girls could eat "cheaply and wholesomely." The "well-balanced menu" offered by the YWCA included "Creole gumbo with rice at 9 cents; meat and potatoes at 15 cents; salads with real mayonnaise at 10 cents." Both the Catholic Woman's Club and the Catherine estimated serving five hundred persons a day, while the YWCA fed more than seven hundred girls daily.[44] Although the lunchrooms were open to the public and obviously much needed, they were not public in the same way as the commercial restaurants and clubs frequented by businessmen, and neither were they the private, homemade lunch of wage workers. Rather, the lunchrooms, like the homes in which they operated, took shape in the interstices.

In 1920, the 155 residents of these four homes represented just a fraction of some 13.3 percent of the unmarried, widowed, or divorced population of women "gainfully occupied" in New Orleans who were reported to be living in a boarding or lodging house, with more than half classified as "Negro." While the primary occupations of boarding women generally were as dressmakers and seamstresses, laundresses (not in a laundry), and semiskilled operatives (mainly in cigar and tobacco factories), the rooming houses for single working women encouraged their residents to emulate the upward national trend toward clerical employment.[45] Most younger residents held jobs as stenographers, clerks, and telephone or telegraph operators.

Apart from the efforts of the male Volunteers of America to rescue young women arriving at the train station, there is only one instance of early endeavors to provide safe and affordable housing for working women of color. The 1920 *New Orleans City Directory* lists the Colored Working Girls Home at 223 South Liberty Street. The US census of that year shows there to be just six residents of the home: the matron and her daughter, a teacher, who were both classified as mulatto; and four boarders, three classified as black and one as mulatto, three of whom were "maids."[46] Not until the mid-1930s was there any record of a substantive attempt to provide housing for working women of color. In 1936, a "Negro Branch" of the YWCA was established; Straight College, a historically black institution, offered the rent-free use of their girls' dormitory at 2436 Canal Street—until the college's founders and the property's owners, the American Missionary Association, sold the building. The residence remained in existence until at least 1942, and possibly longer.[47] In contrast to the many lodging choices available to New Orleans's white citizens and tourists, the YWCA, the YMCA, the Page Hotel and the Patterson Hotel were the only four options listed under "Accommodations for Negroes" in the 1938 *WPA Guide to New Orleans.*

Like their white counterparts, the Canal Street branch of the YWCA offered classes in the domestic sciences as well as academic classes in child psychology, current literature, and dramatics. But in significant contrast to those offered by the white residences, all classes were "free and open to the women and girls of New Orleans."[48]

However, by the time the YWCA branch opened in the late 1930s, respectability and domesticity were no longer the national obsession.[49] The TAS had closed its residence for stranded young women and girls and refocused its mission to provide "casework service to the traveler and nonresident."[50] Moreover, New Orleans reformers, like women elsewhere, redirected their concerns to prohibition, which, to varying degrees, encompassed many of the same issues of corruption, segregation, and prostitution, just under a different name. Prior to 1920, single women had comprised the vast majority of the female labor force, and during the Progressive Era their morals, health, and training were of great social concern. But with the advent of World War I, employment opportunities for women opened and the labor force participation of married as well as single women increased considerably.[51] By 1940, residency at the white homes had declined by 40 percent to 94 women; the average age of residents had increased by more than 10 years to 38.9; and the number of single women dropped from an average of 85.5 percent in 1920 to 59.8 percent in 1940.[52] The decline in the number of single women, or the rise in married women, might well have been a consequence of the Great Depression, when wives, abandoned by husbands in search of work, were required to fend for themselves. More likely, however, the overall changes in the characteristics of the women living at the homes occurred as a result of women's labor market experiences.

The offer of "homelike" surroundings at the Catherine Club, the Catholic Woman's Club, the Christian Woman's Exchange, and the YWCA makes visible a decidedly in-between space. Certainly the boards sought to fashion a "home away from home." All of the residences, except the later YWCAs, occupied former family homes, with drawing rooms tastefully emulating a middle-class living room, including overstuffed sofas and chairs, a piano, abundant plants, and vases of flowers on the fireplace mantel. Unlike the public/private spaces of lobbies and reception rooms in most boarding houses, the drawing room was intended to foster a "family" of residents. Family roles within the residence were constructed around "sisterhood," with the matron often referred to as "mother." At the Catherine, it was "'Mother O'Hara'—that is what the girls call her . . . [for] it is [she] who is mother, friend, and helper."[53] The matron's duties included teaching lunch-room manners and supervising social events in order to promote the behaviors expected of respectable women.[54] In these residences without a family patriarch, it was the matron who assumed the role of "protector." Housekeeping services provided the residents with models of cleanliness and evidence of the work that goes into maintaining such a home.[55] While ideas about women's roles as wife and mother were changing—partly as a result of their own activities—the boards promoted a venerable image of "homelife" and paradoxically perpetuated women's traditional functions within the family. For the young women at the Catherine, the Catholic Woman's Club, and the YWCA, the residence was designed to serve as a transitory period between the family and home of their birth to the family and home of their creation. Various accounts of nameless residents describe the happy fate of previously vulnerable young women: "to marriage all the stories flow and finish there."[56]

Despite such noble intentions, might not one still expect that a number of young women came to New Orleans precisely to circumvent the constraints, drudgery, violence, or poverty of their own not-so-happy or respectable "home-life"? Certainly the TAS documents the allure of the city to many women. And surely for some, marriage was not their ultimate goal. Research indicates that young women who boarded earned more on average than those who lived at home, presumably because they were freed from household chores, and quite possibly because they possessed greater abilities and ambition than those remaining with their parents.[57] Perhaps, like the more mature residents at the CWE, they simply wanted a room of their own, independent of familial obligations, or even of "sisterhood." For many CWE residents, some of whom remained in residency for over twenty years, their room was not "a home away from home": it was their home.

Regardless of whether the residents considered their accommodations a mere space or house, rather than a place and home to which they formed an emotional bond, these instances of *home* functioned to codify who in society might be considered a family member. Through formal and informal policies concerning appropriate activities and behaviors, as well as who was allowed entry, the boards imposed their own moral codes and exercised their power to regulate these in-between spaces. Their power involved inclusion and exclusion based on age, employment, respectability, and—as was the case throughout the United States, the South, and New Orleans—distinctions based on race. Although the reformers' creation of organizations by and for women represented a radical departure from their roles as wives and mothers, they did not altogether reject the ideal of the True Woman or the ideology of separate spheres.[58] Women reformers like those featured here have often been described as "municipal housekeepers": women who expanded their domestic duties into the public sphere to organize for better sanitation, water quality, and public services. Yet despite their traditional beliefs, the reformers here could more aptly be called early feminists or grassroots organizers, committed to working on behalf of women in neither fully public nor fully private enterprises.

While a central focus of this essay is the work of the women reformers who created new spaces—and new institutions within those spaces—they themselves remained in between. More than housewives and mothers, yet neither politically nor historically notable, they tackled important issues that were invisible or considered unimportant to male city leaders. They proved themselves to be independent and powerful, even as they believed young women needed their paternalistic protection. Yet little more than a name—indicated in the organization's minutes or in newspaper accounts—is known about most of them.[59] Ironically, through popular writing, academic publications, and mass printings of the *Blue Book*, more is known about the women of Storyville than the women who led these various reform groups and those they aided. The *Blue Book* details the opulent interiors of the sporting houses and the exceptional charms of madams, such as Lulu White, who possessed "the largest collection of diamonds, pearls, and other rare gems in this part of the country," or Antonia P. Gonzales, who was the "only Singer of Opera and Female Cornetist (*sic*) in the Tenderloin."[60]

And thus we return to Storyville, now glamorized in the name of a boutique hotel, a T-shirt company, and a production facility, among others, and known as the place where New Orleans jazz and musicians, black and white, once flourished. Forgotten are the thousands of women who were marginalized because they had few social or economic alternatives to prostitution and whose home addresses were determined by their occupation. Overlooked are the scores of elite women who were committed to saving others from prostitution by creating the in-between spaces where single women could live respectably and improve their lives through education and training. As Storyville's geographical dividing line became spatially and morally erased, so too did the borderlines of the public and private spheres, as more and more women entered the workforce. Yet neither the prostitutes, the reformers, nor the residents challenged the fundamental notion that women's rightful place was within the home as wife and mother, or that men should dominate political, economic, and religious institutions. Well into the 1970s, the Catherine, CWE, and YWCA offered the service of safe, affordable, and "homelike" surroundings to single working women in the interstitial space between the public and private spheres.

NOTES

1. E. J. Bellocq, *Bellocq: Photographs from Storyville, the Red-Light District of New Orleans* (New York: Random House, 1996). Quotes from the introduction by Susan Sontag, 7–8.

2. L'Hote v. City of New Orleans, 177 U.S. 587 (1900), http://laws.findlaw.com/us/177/587.html; Al Rose, *Storyville, New Orleans* (Tuscaloosa: University of Alabama Press, 1974), 1, 185–90; Alecia P. Long, *The Great Southern Babylon: Sex, Race, and Respectability in New Orleans, 1865–1920* (Baton Rouge: Louisiana State University Press, 2004), 105; Emily Epstein Landau, *Spectacular Wickedness: Sex, Race, and Memory in Storyville, New Orleans* (Baton Rouge: Louisiana State University Press, 2013), 1; Shannon Lee Dawdy, *Building the Devil's Empire: French Colonial New Orleans* (Chicago: University of Chicago Press, 2008). The number of blocks comprising Storyville varies: Landau mentions nineteen blocks, Long and Rose sixteen.

3. Long, *Great Southern Babylon*, 158, 195; Rose, *Storyville*, 38–39, 177. According to Rose, the Uptown District was never referred to as Storyville. See Campanella, chapter 7 of this volume, for a more detailed discussion of the city ordinances and geographical boundaries relating to prostitution.

4. Landau, *Spectacular Wickedness*, 157; Long, *Great Southern Babylon*, 210, 171.

5. Rose states that approximately two thousand prostitutes were working regularly, 31. Cribs were bare one-room structures that opened onto the street and contained little more than a bed, table, and chair. It would have been nearly impossible for a woman to live in one. Strung together along a street, they often had a common roof and low-hanging eaves—in stark contrast to the luxurious bordellos along Basin Street. *The WPA Guide to New Orleans: The Federal Writers' Project Guide to 1930s New Orleans* (New York: Pantheon Books, 1983), 218; Rose, *Storyville*, 173, 174.

6. Charles L. "Pie" Dufour, *Women Who Cared: The 100 Years of the Christian Woman's Exchange* (New Orleans: Christian Woman's Exchange, 1980), 7.

7. Andrea Pactor, *A Sense of Place: A Short History of Women's Philanthropy in America* (Indianapolis: Indiana University Lilly Family School of Philanthropy, 2010), http://www.cfgnh.org/Portals/0/Uploads/Documents/Public/A-Sense-of-Place-FINAL.pdf

8. Karen V. Hansen, "Feminist Conceptions of Public and Private: A Critical Analysis," *Berkeley Journal of Sociology* 32 (1987), 105–28; Ulla Wischermann and Ilze Klavina Mueller, "Feminist Theories on the Separation of the Private and the Public: Looking Back, Looking Forward," *Women in German Yearbook* 20 (2004) 184–97; Marise Bachand, "Gendered Mobility and the Geography of Respectability in Charleston and New Orleans, 1790–1861," *Journal of Southern History* 81, no. 1 (2015); Pactor, *Sense of Place*.

9. Barbara Welter, "Cult of True Womanhood: 1820–1860," *American Quarterly* 18 (1966), 151–74.

10. Landau, *Spectacular Wickedness*, 2, 101–4.

11. Long, *Great Southern Babylon*, 90–94; Christine Wiltz, *The Last Madam: A Life in the New Orleans Underworld* (New York: Faber and Faber, 2000), 16.

12. Quoted in Long, *Great Southern Babylon*, 216.

13. Rose, *Storyville*, 96, 90.

14. Long, *Great Southern Babylon*, 171–78.

15. Katy Coyle and Nadiene Van Dyke, "Sex, Smashing, and Storyville in Turn-of-the-Century New Orleans: Reexamining the Continuum of Lesbian Sexuality," in *Carryin' On in the Lesbian and Gay South*, ed. John Howard (New York: New York University Press, 1997), 66–67.

16. Social Explorer (SE) dataset of US census data from 1880, 1890, 1900, 1910, 1920, 1930, 1940, digitally transcribed by the Inter-university Consortium for Political and Social Research and edited and verified by Michael Haik, 2003–2014.

17. Data on families prior to World War II is sparse. See James R. Wetzel, "American Families: 75 Years of Change," *Monthly Labor Review* (US Bureau of Labor Statistics), March 1990, 5–6. It was not until the 1950s that residential construction, favorable tax laws, and easier financing raised the homeownership rate in Louisiana to 50 percent.

18. Dufour, *Women Who Cared*, 6. The Christian Woman's Exchange (renamed the Woman's Exchange in 1999) was the first association to be established and chartered in the city of New Orleans by women, for women. It is now one of the oldest continuously operating women-owned nonprofit organizations in the region.

19. Kathleen Waters Sander, *The Business of Charity: The Woman's Exchange Movement, 1832–1900* (Urbana: University of Illinois Press, 1998), 21, 45, 61, 121–23. The New Orleans Christian Woman's Exchange was the twelfth woman's exchange to be organized in the country and the first in the deep South; Christian Woman's Exchange records, Manuscripts Collection 257, Louisiana Research Collection, Howard-Tilton Memorial Library, Tulane University, New Orleans, hereinafter CWE.

20. Dufour, *Women Who Cared*, 7.

21. Quoted in Sander, *Business of Charity*, 72. Sander states that the gifts were two of the largest given to charitable organizations by women in their own names during the late nineteenth century (67). In 2010, $674,000 had the same purchasing power as $28,500 in 1887. Lawrence H. Officer and Samuel H. Williamson, "The Annual Consumer Price Index for the United States, 1774–2015," MeasuringWorth, 2017, http://www.measuringworth.com/uscpi/. The CWE had a limited number of rented rooms at their earlier location in the French Quarter for women staff and travelers to the 1884 Cotton Exposition.

22. Boarding houses were commonly defined as places where the rent covered a single furnished room along with meals served "family style." Rooming houses offered tenants a furnished room but no meals. The rooming house gained popularity over the boarding house because of its greater privacy and choice of where to take meals. In both cases, housekeeping services were provided, bathrooms were down the hall, and only rarely did a room contain a washbasin. Also in both cases, the space was highly gendered, with men predominating as tenants, and women, often widows, as landladies.

23. "Travelers' Aid Society History (Draft)," Travelers' Aid Society of Greater New Orleans records, Box 1, Manuscripts Collection 365, Louisiana Research Collection, Howard-Tilton Memorial Library, Tulane University, New Orleans, hereinafter TAS.

24. "Working Provisions of the Charter and By-Laws of the Travelers' Aid Society: Incorporated before Albert Guilbault, Notary Public, May 30, 1913," Box 1, TAS.

25. "Over-Night Home Plan for Girls: Travelers' Aid Discusses 'Clearing House' Not to Be Reformatory," *New Orleans States*, September 19, 1918; "'The Lodge' Home for Girls, Is Now Open," *New Orleans States*, November 5, 1918; "Traveler's (*sic*) Aid Plans New Home," *New Orleans States*, May 22, 1919.

26. "Travelers' Aid Saves Woman from Con Man: Gallantry of Flashy Gent to Old Lady with Bank Roll Fails; Unfortunate Girls and Needy Helped," *New Orleans States*, November 21, 1920.

27. "Negroes Plan to Aid Wayward: Colored Volunteers Seek Fund to Assist Delinquent Girls of their Race," *New Orleans Item*, September 21, 1919, 62.

28. "Grima Mansion Bought as Home," *Times-Picayune*, November 25, 1923; Minutes of the Board, August 3, 1923, p. 13, Box 6-A, CWE.

29. Wiltz, *Last Madam*, 10, 17–18.

30. Letter to members, 1924, CWE.

31. See table 1 for the occupation of residents in 1920. In 1930, among the fourteen CWE residents were three business owners and managers, several sales clerks and secretaries, a teacher, and a solicitor. One woman had no recorded occupation. All residents were white, native born, and predominantly single; five of the fourteen were widows. US census data, 1930, Ancestry.com.

32. Mary S. Ferguson, "Boarding Homes and Clubs for Working Women," *Bulletin of the Department of Labor* III, no. 15 (Washington, DC: Government Printing Office, March 1898): 141–96.

33. Quote from Jeanne Catherine Lawrence, "Chicago's Eleanor Clubs: Housing Working Women in the Early Twentieth Century," *Vernacular Architecture Forum* 8 (2000), 219–47; Minutes of the Board, December 2, 1927, CWE.

34. "Where Young Women Get All the Comforts of Home," *Times-Picayune*, November 23, 1919. Other homes for working women existed at other times, including the Boarding Home for Working Women founded by the Women's Parsonage and Home Mission Society in 1898 (closed 1925), and the Louise Boarding Residence for Working Girls. The Louise house had begun as a Catholic orphanage for white girls, New Orleans Female Orphan Asylum, built by Margaret Haughery between 1840 and 1861, but some time after 1920 and before 1930, its mission shifted to being a residence for employed young women.

35. "Where Young Women"; New Orleans YWCA, Manuscripts Collection 847, Louisiana Research Collection, Howard-Tilton Memorial Library, Tulane University, New Orleans, hereinafter YWCA.

36. Lawrence, "Chicago's Eleanor Clubs."

37. "Policies Pertaining to Permanent Residents," January 15, 1952, YWCA. The date when the policy actually was instituted is unknown.

38. Mrs. J. R. Morton, "New Orleans Woman's Club—Oldest Club in the City," *New Orleans Life*, November 1925, 17. The article states the Woman's Club was organized in 1884 as the first woman's club in the South. However, the CWE preceded the founding by three years.

39. "Stories from the Catherine, Big Sister to Worthy Girls," *Times-Picayune*, May 1, 1919; "Mrs. Ellsworth Woodward Heads Catherine Club," *Times Picayune*, May 5, 2017, 9.

40. "Where Young Women"; "Stories from the Catherine."

41. Lawrence, "Chicago's Eleanor Clubs."

42. Claudia Goldin, "The Work and Wages of Single Women, 1870–1920," *Journal of Economic History* 40, no. 1, 81–88, http://www.jstor.org/stable/2120426.

43. "Classes Are Announced," *Times-Picayune*, April 28, 1919, 7; "Catholic Woman's Club Schedules Many Classes," *Times-Picayune*, October 17, 1920, 67; "Where Young Women."

44. "Where Young Women"; the purchasing power of ten cents in 1919 had the value of $1.26 in 2010 (MeasuringWorth).

45. Joseph A. Hill, *Women in Gainful Occupations, 1870–1920*, Washington, DC: Government Printing Office, 1929), tables 92, 137, 161, 168, and 170; Goldin, "Work and Wages."

46. US census data, 1920, Ancestry.com. The *New Orleans City Directory* shows a listing for the home for the years 1920 to 1923 only. *Efforts for Social Betterment Among Negro Americans*, ed. W. E. B. Du Bois (Atlanta: Atlanta University Press, 1909), shows there to be no listings in New Orleans for homes for working girls or rescue homes for women.

47. The *New Orleans City Directory* was not published in 1943 or 1944. There is no listing for the "YWCA (colored br)" in the 1945 directory, and 2436 Canal Street is listed as "vacant."

48. Box 41, YWCA.

49. Long, *Great Southern Babylon*, 232.

50. "Facts About the Travelers' Aid Society of New Orleans," TAS.

51. Goldin, "Work and Wages."

52. US census data, 1920 and 1930, Ancestry.com.

53. "Stories from the Catherine." See also Elizabeth Kirkland, "A Home Away from Home: Defining, Regulating, and Challenging Femininity at the Julia Drummond Residence in Montreal, 1920–1971," *Urban History Review* 34 (2006).

54. "Y.W.C.A. Girls to Hold 'at Home' Reception Today," *Times-Picayune*, February 22, 1920; "'Come and See Day' for Y.W.C.A. Wednesday," *Times-Picayune*, March 14, 1920.

55. Kirkland, "Home Away from Home"; Truth Thomas, "The Catherine Club," *New Orleans Life*, July–August, 1926, 14; "Maid's Duties," Box 67, CWE.

56. "Stories from the Catherine."

57. Goldin, "Work and Wages."

58. Anne Firor Scott, *The Southern Lady: From Pedestal to Politics, 1830–1930* (Chicago: University of Chicago Press, 1970), 154; "Christian Woman's Exchange," *Daily Picayune*, April 9, 1881; "Exchange Notes," *Daily Picayune*, September 24, 1881.

59. For a narrative of several of the board members and residents of the Christian Woman's Exchange, see Beth Willinger, "The Women of the New Orleans Christian Woman's Exchange (1881–Present): From 'Helping Women Who Help Themselves' to a

Mission of Historic Preservation," in *Louisiana Women: Their Lives and Times*, vol. 2, ed. Shannon Frystak and Mary Farmer Kaiser (Athens: University of Georgia Press, 2016), 308–34.

60. *Blue Book*, 5th ed. (New Orleans, ca. 1907–1915). Louisiana Research Collection, Howard-Tilton Memorial Library, Tulane University, New Orleans. The *Blue Book* was a free publication distributed to would-be clients containing advertisements from the various brothels and listing the name, race, and dwelling of each woman residing in the District.

CHAPTER NINE

Congo Square as a *Lieu de Souvenir* in New Orleans

Race, Place, and the Complexity of Blackness

—*Angel Adams Parham*

In the rear of the town . . . Africans collected together to perform their *worship* after the manner of their country. They have their own national music. . . . These amusements continue until sunset, when one or two of the city patrols show themselves with their cutlasses, and the crowds immediately disperse. (1808)[1]

An ordinance changing the name of Congo Square to Beauregard Square. Adopted. (1893)[2]

Beauregard Park commissioners stopped blacks from walking through the park on Saturday nights on the way to a dance hall that had existed for some time in the vicinity. (1906)[3]

[We celebrate] the music and culture of the African diaspora at the seventh annual Congo Square New World Rhythms Festival. . . . This free event celebrates the cultural diversity of New Orleans and the melting pot of traditions. . . . We feature the music and dance of Africa, the Caribbean, the American Gulf South and beyond in this two-day, family-friendly festival. (2014)[4]

The epigraphs above are drawn from distinctive periods in the history of Congo Square. They demonstrate how this small public space, pressed between the old city of New Orleans on one side and its expanding suburbs on the other, casts new light on enormous shifts in the social, cultural, and political lives of African Americans. The first quotation highlights ethnic diversity among the Africans inhabiting the Square; the second and third bear witness to a somber middle period where diversity in the Square was suppressed as the era of segregation limited Blacks' access to the area; and the last shows a return to the flourishing of the Square as a space to celebrate diverse African diaspora traditions.

By examining the fate of the Square during different historical periods, this essay uncovers the ways that Congo Square can be read as a *lieu
de souvenir*: a space for remembering the rich, diverse strands of African
diaspora identity and practice that are sometimes hidden beneath the
overarching category of "Blackness" in the United States. The word *souvenir* comes from combining the Latin words *sub*, "under," and *venire*,
"to come." To *souvenir* is, therefore, to invite issues, experiences, or practices, to *come up from under* the place where they have been buried.

This kind of disaggregating remembrance is one that helps us to
uncover and appreciate the complexity and hybridity that underlie many
taken-for-granted identities and practices. This remembrance is particularly important when it comes to the politics of race and place. In
his excellent work on the history of Tremé—the larger neighborhood
of which Congo Square is a part—Michael Crutcher emphasizes the
importance of what he describes as "critical geographies." He writes:

> Critical geographies go beyond . . . [literally describing] the world. . . .
> [They] seek to understand how places, spaces and landscapes are the prod-
> ucts of uneven power relationships . . . [and] attempt to comprehend how
> the lives of those not in power are governed in those spaces and how those
> people resist their oppression.[5]

By examining the patterns of oppression and resistance that have occurred
in Congo Square over the course of its history, we can better appreciate
those relationships of power and their consequences. The importance
of engaging in such critical memory practices is amply demonstrated by
recent events on college campuses and in cities throughout the United
States: the debate at Yale University concerning the slave-owning legacy of John C. Calhoun, after whom a residential college is named; the
conflicts at Princeton University over the racist and segregationist views
of Woodrow Wilson, for whom the school of public and international
affairs is named; the tumult in New Orleans after a vote by the New
Orleans City Council to remove the statue of Confederate general Robert E. Lee from a prominent section of the city.[6]

Critical memory practices that unlayer the contested or forgotten
pasts of specific places are also crucial today, given the discussions and
debates about the so-called "new" Black diversity.[7] In a recent review on
the impact of Black immigrants on African American communities in
the United States, sociologists Mary Waters and her coauthors describe
"the growing diversity within the Black population, driven largely by
the presence of Black immigrants from the Caribbean and Continental
Africa."[8] They also explain that this growth in Black diversity has been

supported by the end of Jim Crow segregation and the concomitant rise of a more substantial Black middle class.[9]

While it is certainly true that changes in immigration policy and the decline of legalized segregation have increased the social and cultural diversity of Black communities in the mid-twentieth and early twenty-first centuries, this era of increased diversity is rarely placed within the larger historical context of African American heterogeneity that has existed for centuries. Without this larger historical context, Black diversity is seen as new and unusual and those immigrants who are contributing to this diversity are seen as cultural outsiders whose histories and societies are completely separate from and foreign to our own.[10]

Without this larger context we are treated to the implicit assumption that the Black community was more or less homogeneous until changes in immigration and segregation policy ushered in greater diversity in the 1960s. The alternative narrative presented in this chapter, however, helps us to see the ways that diversity has always been the default of African American communities in the United States and further demonstrates how this heterogeneity was suppressed for a relatively brief period from the late nineteenth through the mid-twentieth centuries through exclusionary immigration policies and injurious programs of legalized racial segregation. The former kept voluntary immigrants of color out of the country, while the latter literally reduced differences among African Americans to a single salient characteristic—Blackness in phenotype or descent.

With the rescinding of these policies, the underlying diversity that has always characterized Black communities has resurfaced and is now being reinforced by new waves of Black immigrants. While the difference in these ways of framing social change in Black communities may seem subtle, what is at stake here is a politics of belonging where alternative historical narratives can either invite identification with others whose histories and cultures are seen as intertwined with our own or, conversely, solidify differences by framing these others as new and foreign.

The concept of the lieu de souvenir, with its approach to uncovering the social and cultural layers embedded in the histories of specific places, helps to expose the often forgotten and diverse roots that have shaped what we think of today as native Black American cultures. Recent scholarship on Congo Square, for instance, clearly illustrates the diverse African and Caribbean contributions that have helped to shape Black community and culture in New Orleans. There are, moreover, many other lieux de souvenir that illustrate the long-standing diversity among Blacks within the United States. These include the Tremé in New Orleans, where descendants of the Haitian Revolution organized the *Plessy v. Ferguson*

Figure 9.1. Historical plaque in Congo Square, Louis Armstrong Park, just outside the French Quarter. Photograph by Jan R. Oyebode, *Mindreadings: Femi Oyebode's Musings*, 2013, femioyebode .wordpress.com/.

case; Overtown in Miami where Bahamians and other West Indians helped to build the city; Franklin Square in Savannah, Georgia, where a monument recalls the role Haitian soldiers played in 1779 in supporting the American quest to win independence from Britain—and many others.

The value of highlighting and examining these lieux de souvenir is that they set current debates about Black diversity into historical context while simultaneously encouraging us to see those who are typically portrayed as outsiders as historically significant players whose social and cultural presence in the past has helped to shape many aspects of contemporary American experience. When we look at the short list of lieux de souvenir above, for instance, the idea that Caribbean influences are new is revised by the ways that they have long shaped regional Black histories and cultures—well before the 1960s. Such an approach also invites those from different locations and origins in Black communities to appreciate the diverse roots of "native" African American communities and identities. Appreciation of the presence and negotiation of past diversity may then become a springboard to work toward overcoming ethnic and social differences in today's Black communities.[11]

The lieu de souvenir is a conceptual cousin of Pierre Nora's *lieux de mémoire*. Nora describes lieux de mémoire as objects, spaces, or images that help to fix memory, capture it, and hold onto it in the service of bolstering identity. On the social desire for lieux de mémoire, he explains:

> *Lieux de mémoire* originate with the sense that there is no spontaneous memory, that we must deliberately create archives, maintain anniversaries, organize celebrations, pronounce eulogies, and notarize bills because such activities no longer occur naturally. The defense, by certain minorities, of a privileged memory that has retreated to jealously protected enclaves in this sense intensely illuminates the truth of *lieux de mémoire*—that without commemorative vigilance, history would soon sweep them away. We buttress our identities upon such bastions, but if what they defended were not threatened, there would be no need to build them.[12]

What Nora describes here is the near desperation that drives people to construct lieux de mémoire. This sense of desperation is communicated in the idea that "certain minorities" act defensively to protect a memory that "has retreated to jealously protected enclaves." But even once the precious memory has been enclaved, one must still exercise "vigilance" lest the forces of history "soon sweep them away." Such defensive and vigilant work is necessary, Nora explains, because the memories are "threatened."

Lieux de mémoire provide, therefore, the materials and experience needed to continually renew one's sense of identification with a particular community or identity that no longer engages in unconscious communal practices that help it to simply *be* a community imbued with a particular identity but must instead consciously *cultivate* community and identity. Thus, Nora explains, "The less memory is experienced collectively, the more it will require individuals to undertake to become themselves memory-individuals, as if an inner voice were to tell each Corsican 'You must be Corsican' and each Breton 'You must be Breton.'"[13]

In many ways, lieux de souvenir are, in fact, quite the opposite of lieux de mémoire. Rather than fixing memory—and thereby bolstering conventional identities—they invite us to uncover the hybridity and complexity of memories, identities, or events that have long been fixed or taken for granted as simple, pure, or unidimensional. The different perspectives encouraged by lieux de souvenir and lieux de mémoire lead to quite different social and political tendencies. Lieux de mémoire tend by their nature to purify through exclusion. The disadvantaged or threatened memory community closes ranks and continually unearths or produces documents, memorials, or events that reinforce what the community is and who belongs. We can see lieux de mémoire active in today's Black American community among the kinds of people Touré takes issue with in his book *Who's Afraid of Post-Blackness*. He quotes, for example, the photographer Lorna Simpson, who explains the sense of constraint she has experienced with other Black people: "I find within the Black community we can be so striated in expectations of how you're supposed to live, who you're supposed to date, how you're supposed to operate, how you wear your hair, and I never felt that I wanted to play by those rules because that's not what I wanted out of life."[14] We see among the folks Simpson speaks of here a quite circumscribed view of what it means to be Black. This narrow view is then accompanied by efforts to police the borders of Blackness.

In contrast, the disaggregating nature of lieux de souvenir tends to encourage inclusion and communication across differences. Rather than simply celebrating or protecting a specific identity, they instead call to mind the many historical contexts, cultural strands and social origins woven into seemingly simple places, identities, and communities. This characteristic of the lieu de souvenir will appear prominently as we peel away the social and cultural layers of today's Congo Square in New Orleans.

New Orleans: African, Caribbean, and American

New Orleans is, for many reasons, an ideal place from which to consider the history of Black diversity; and within that city, Congo Square provides a rich site of inquiry. In the eighteenth century, Louisiana was a struggling, bedraggled colonial territory where everyone fought for survival, including white slave owners. One of the tools whites used to survive was to grant slaves relative degrees of freedom that were unusual compared to wealthier areas of North America. Moreover, because slave owners were often too strapped financially to provide many resources for their slaves, Africans became instrumental in supporting and feeding themselves and the colonists.

On Sundays, many of the enslaved congregated in the large area just on the outskirts of the French Quarter that is today known as Congo Square. There they conducted a large market that included foodstuffs and engaged in music and dance that retained distinctly African characteristics. In some cases, they were able to keep the profits of their sales to cover their own necessities. In this sense, the white colonists' difficulties provided an economic opportunity for slaves as well as a space to cultivate the endurance of African cultural practices.

While the economic difficulties of the Louisiana colony provided one of the conditions for the persistence of African culture in New Orleans, this endurance was also abetted by the fact that the colony was ruled by the French and the Spanish until 1803. The French and Spanish approached African populations and their cultural practices quite differently than the Anglo-Americans who followed them after the Louisiana

THE BAMBOULA.

Figure 9.2. "The Bamboula," one of the few nineteenth-century illustrations of Congo Square, published in George Washington Cable, "Creole Slave Dances: The Dance in Place Congo," *Century* 31, no. 4 (February 1886), 517–32. This image is courtesy of the Making of America Digital Collection, Cornell University Library.

Purchase of 1803. They exercised a less heavy hand, for instance, over the regulation of music and dance traditions that were visibly non-Western and non-Christian. While African cultural practices were thus still denigrated and seen as un-Christian, there were few efforts to crush them. In fact, when the government in Spain decreed in 1789 that Sunday activities at Congo Square should be abolished, Spanish colonial authorities refused to enforce the edict.[15] They saw the marketing activity in the Square as crucial to the area's survival and were unmoved by critiques of the cultural practices it supported. Sundays at Congo Square were an entrenched part of the city's life, and colonial authorities were unwilling to squash them.

Diversity among the participants in the Square is well documented. In the earliest years, Africans from many different ethnic groups frequented Congo Square, including Bambara, Mandinga, Wolof, Fon, Yoruba and, certainly, Kongo. The Kongo were, in fact, the largest single African ethnic group in New Orleans from 1770 to 1803.[16] In addition to participants coming directly from Africa, there was also a strong Haitian and Cuban influence on the participants and activities in Congo Square—especially after 1800 when nearly ten thousand refugees from Haiti and Cuba flowed into New Orleans, nearly doubling the population. Most of these newcomers stayed in or near New Orleans, and one-third of them were enslaved persons, many of whom would have been drawn to the activities in Congo Square. [17]

Ned Sublette notes that the French and Spanish approach to cultural regulation helped the enslaved in New Orleans to retain African practices that were subdued or eradicated in other parts of the United States. He explains:

> The one place where drumming and other direct manifestations of Africanness continued to be openly displayed in public, albeit on a limited basis—and it was the legacy of the Spanish period—was New Orleans. . . . All across Spanish America, including New Orleans, Sunday was the day for the slaves to dance. . . . In New Orleans, Africans gathered to drum and dance as soon as there were Africans in the colony and—unique in the United States—these gatherings continued at least until the 1840s.[18]

The situation would gradually change, however, with the coming of Anglo-American rule in 1803. The Anglo-Americans were much less sanguine about the African cultural practices occurring in Congo Square. In part, a more ascetic Protestant Christianity made the Anglo-Americans less congenial than French and Spanish Catholics to non-Christian cultural practices.[19]

From the beginning, Anglo-Americans set out to anglicize the Louisiana territory culturally, politically, and racially. They were particularly aggrieved by the social conduct and cultural practices they observed in Congo Square. In his brief history of the Square, Jerah Johnson highlights an illustrative Anglo-American reaction: "Benjamin Latrobe's reaction was typical. . . . He betrayed his amazement and apprehension at the sight of five or six hundred unsupervised slaves assembled for dancing when he added, in a tone of relief, 'there was not the least disorder among the crowd, nor do I learn on enquiry, that these weekly meetings of negroes have ever produced any mischief.'"[20] Not only was there fear of such large numbers of slaves, there was antipathy to the African dances themselves. On observing the dancing and singing, Latrobe wrote in his journal: "A man sung an uncouth song to the dancing which I suppose was in some African language, for it was not French, and women screamed a detestable burthen on one single note. The allowed amusements of Sunday, have, it seems, perpetuated here, those of Africa among its inhabitants."[21]

Despite such disapproval, marketing and dancing continued in the Square well after the 1803 Louisiana Purchase. Participants continued to include native Africans, Creole slaves who had been born in Louisiana, an increasing number of Anglo-American slaves brought into the territory following the Purchase, and, after 1809, slaves from Haiti and Cuba whose owners had fled the revolution in Saint-Domingue.[22] Given these many different points of origin, the early nineteenth century represented perhaps the height of diversity among the Africans and people of African descent who gathered in that space.

Color and class diversity are also part of the story of Congo Square. Freddi Williams Evans illustrates this diversity by citing the experiences of nineteenth-century observers: "James Creecy, who travelled to the city in 1834, reported that 'the lower order of colored people and Negroes [*sic*], bond and free, assemble in great numbers in Congo Square, on every Sunday afternoon in good weather, to enjoy themselves in their own peculiar manner.'"[23] George Washington Cable also affirmed that house servants were less likely to be found in Congo Square than those working in the fields.[24] But while higher-status slaves may have preferred to gather indoors with others like themselves, some of their number did frequent the Square, as did free people of color. In his discussion of the interaction between Congo Square and the adjacent neighborhood, Faubourg Tremé, Johnson paints a portrait of the area's social and cultural life as experienced by both free and enslaved participants:

> In the Faubourg Tremé [as the area stretching back from Congo Square came to be called] most of the free-colored population not only lived but also established the city's major free-black schools, benevolent associations, social clubs, and literary and musical societies. Consequently, Congo Square's Sunday crowds came virtually entirely from the city's Creole community. . . . It also served as the Faubourg Tremé's public meeting ground. During the circus and carnival off-season, neighborhood youths used the square as a playing field, particularly for *raquettes*, a lacrosse-like Choctaw Indian game that remained popular in New Orleans throughout the nineteenth century. The slave and free-black vendors continued to set up there on Sunday morning, and to mingle with the crowds of other slaves and free blacks who gathered on Sunday afternoons for the square's famous, and historically significant, African dances.[25]

Here we catch a glimpse of how the area was used before Anglo-American racial and cultural transitions were completed; black and white, free and enslaved lived and intermingled freely. While the enslaved could not claim to own their own bodies, many did have freedom of movement unusual in other parts of the continent. This free access and loose monitoring would change, however; by 1820 city officials had enclosed the area with wooden railings, providing two turnstile gates for entrance.

Gating the Square obviously made it easier to regulate and commodify the space, which had come to be used by a circus. It also, however, facilitated the more precise imposition of the color line by keeping Blacks out, since the circus was for whites only. In the excerpt above, for example, the youths of the Faubourg Tremé played *raquettes* and engaged in other amusements only "during the circus and carnival off-season"—the times when they had access to a space already becoming restricted in its use and population.

By the 1830s and 1840s, two changes—one demographic, the other political—decisively turned the tide toward narrowing the diversity once observed in the Square. First, as a result of the decline in the introduction of persons born in Africa, the enslaved population became increasingly American-born. Driving home the significance of this demographic shift, Jerah Johnson cites observers' contrasting experiences in the early and mid-nineteenth century. When Pierre de Laussat visited the Square in 1808, he observed "two circles of Black dancers side by side, one group performing an African *bamboula* and the other a French *contre-danse*."[26] By 1843, however, a local writer noted in his piece in the *Daily Picayune* that he had never seen "pure African dances" in the Square. Then, in 1845, writer Benjamin Norman noted that the "unsophisticated" old dances of the "Congo" from the Square's "primitive days" were no longer being practiced.[27]

An 1879 *Daily Picayune* article made similar comparisons between past and present activities in the Square:

> [In the past] about eight negroes, four male and four female, would make a set and generally they were but scantily clad. It took some little time before that tapping of the drums would arouse the dull and sluggish dancers, but when the point of excitement came, nothing can faithfully portray the wild and frenzied motions they would go through. . . . As the dance progressed, the drums were thrummed faster, the contortions became more grotesque until sometimes in frenzy the women and men would fall fainting to the ground. . . . Subsequently . . . the descendants of the original Africans got up an imitation, but it could not compare to the weird orgie of their progenitors. . . . The tomtoms have long since been laid away.[28]

There is much to remark on in this description. First, it is clear that the writer stands very much outside of the social and cultural context he writes about. There is evidence here of a kind of troubled fascination with what the writer clearly sees as exotic practices—not uncommon in such nineteenth century descriptions where whites are observing Blacks. Given this social context, we must be careful about the kinds of conclusions we draw. The writer here assumes that because later dances were not as "frenzied" or "orgy"-like, they were less authentic. However, Congo Square was host to different kinds of dances, and some may indeed have seemed frenzied while others were observed to be slower and more measured. In any event, the concluding sentence makes clear that the beating of the drums had faded away by 1879, a dramatic change corroborated by many other sources.

The second change that led to transformation in Congo Square was the decline in the French and Creole ethos of the city as a whole. By the 1830s, Americans and other non-Creole immigrants were gaining in numbers and—just as importantly—in economic strength. The most vibrant economic area was the Faubourg St. Mary, which included large numbers of Americans and American businesses. The Americans took advantage of their growing numbers and wealth to turn the tide decidedly against the Creole population. In 1836 citizens were able to use anti-French sentiment in other parts of the state to win legislative approval to divide the city of New Orleans into three separate municipalities. This change allowed them to autonomously administer their own section of the city. They had sought this freedom in order to escape what they saw to be discriminatory treatment by Creole administrators whom they accused of denying their section of the city timely services such as street paving and gas lighting. But the Americans' freedom also spelled the Creoles' political and economic decline. The American sector had the best-managed, most lucrative businesses and, consequently, higher and better-used city income. Within two decades, the Americans had definitively consolidated their gains over the Creoles.[29]

By 1852 the three municipalities were dissolved and the city returned to a single municipal whole. The historically Creole sections of the city then came firmly under Anglo-American control. In 1856, just a few years after this transformation, the Americans began to exert cultural control over the city as a whole and over Congo Square in particular. First, they disciplined the loose, unfettered Mardi Gras celebration by reorganizing it into the krewes that are familiar today. Next, they adopted an ordinance that sounded the death knell to activities in the Square: it became illegal to beat a drum or to blow a horn or trumpet in public, and public balls and dances were outlawed without the mayor's permission. Added to these restrictions was a beautification plan for the Square, which meant the planting of more trees—and the Sunday gatherings were effectively squelched. Sublette observes that it is no coincidence that Sundays at the Square declined during the same period that the Creoles were overpowered and the Anglo-Americans asserted their influence over the city. With the city's Creole leadership came their cultural affinities and tolerances; as the Americans rose to ascendancy, so did their more stringent ways of living and governing.

If the 1850s ended with the Anglo-Americans politically and culturally triumphant, the years during and after the Civil War saw the Anglo-American racial structure, with its one-drop rule, become firmly entrenched. Any person with any perceived African heritage was categorized as Black. Indeed, even if a person appeared to be white, but documentation showed that she had a Black ancestor, she would still be categorized as Black according to the one-drop rule.[32] As the practical application of this rule took place, earlier distinctions of color and class, as well as distinctions between Creole and non-Creole, became less sharp, and the pressure to assimilate to Anglo-American style Blackness increased manyfold.

Exile from Congo Square and the
Cauldron of Black Assimilation

By 1860 the drums were silent and the dances had ceased in Congo Square. By the time the Civil War was over, the Square was largely abandoned and derelict. Other than a brief cleaning of the space for the 1884–85 Cotton Exposition, the area lay in waste. Even when an effort was finally made in 1893 to clean it up and restore it to public use, the thumb of Anglo-American racial structuring was clearly evident. The old Congo Square was renamed Beauregard Square in honor of Confederate general P. G. T. Beauregard, who had recently died. New trees were planted and sidewalks were laid. Then, in 1905, a public school was built for white children and the entire space was reserved for whites. What an irony that a place that had once beat vibrantly with African drums was now restricted to whites, while Blacks were refused entrance. This period of Anglo-American racial ascendance was the nadir of Black diversity in the Square.

For in this period, from the late nineteenth century until the mid- to late 1960s, a general assimilation to Anglo-American Blackness occurred in New Orleans. The fall of Reconstruction in 1877 led to a vicious backlash against people known or suspected to fit the one-drop criterion—regardless of their color, class, education, or cultural background. Where once there had been social distinctions between Anglo-Blacks—many of whose ancestors had been slaves—and Creole Blacks, who were shaped by French language and culture and more likely to have had free ancestors, now having any African ancestry, no matter how minute, made one "black." As a result, it became more difficult, if not impossible, to find or express forms of Blackness that did not fit the Anglo-American social, cultural, or political mold. For New Orleans's Creoles of color, many of

Figure 9.3. Congo Square, Louis Armstrong Park, the circular pattern of the paving stones recalling the circle dances once performed by early African residents. Photograph by K. C. Smith, 2013, stevesmittens.wordpress.com.

whom wanted to preserve their distinctive identity and community, this was a particularly challenging time.

Wendy Gaudin records the struggles of this community in the many interviews she conducts with those who lived during the eras before and after the civil rights movement. While the generation of Creoles coming of age in the early twentieth century generally worked to distinguish themselves from African Americans, the forces of assimilation grew much stronger for those who came of age in the 1950s and 1960s during the civil rights movement. Although the older generation recognized the violence and oppression of Jim Crow segregation, they cognitively separated themselves from African Americans.

We can see this distancing in the language that Gaudin's older black Creole interviewees use. One woman, Mrs. Mercedes Prograi Barthé, affirmed how poor most people were during the Depression but also explained that although she and her Creole family were poor, they were "not like the ... [pauses and lowers her voice] ... blacks ... they didn't have nothing." [33] By pausing and lowering her voice, Mrs. Barthé signals the stigmatized status of non-Creole blacks. Another interviewee, Mrs. Bernadine Bart Moore, also affirmed the community's general state of poverty during the Depression, but she too employs distinguishing language to underline the difference between her Creole family and non-Creole blacks. This effect is conveyed when she discusses the ways her mother took pity on poor neighbors. Mrs. Moore describes these neighbors as "one black family that lived way in the back, about two blocks down the street. . . . they were black people that we didn't associate with at all."[34] The "at all" that concludes this quote places an emphasis on the social distance Mrs. Moore put between herself and Anglo-Blacks.

As a survival mechanism, Creoles of color living in Jim Crow Louisiana carefully preserved Creole social institutions that provided a protected space which helped them to weather the racial storms raging around them. These institutions included Creole-of-color schools, churches, and social clubs. A third Gaudin interviewee, Mr. Ferdinand Delery, experienced this protected circle as so all-encompassing that he maintains that he and others in the Creole community barely felt the denigrations and deprivations of Jim Crow. Instead, he observes, "We had our own way of living, our own group and all." When referring to segregation, he notes, "We didn't feel that we missed anything, really. . . . We didn't feel that we were segregated."[35]

While it worked for the generation coming of age in the early twentieth century to make distinctions between Creoles of color and Anglo-Blacks, this way of drawing social boundaries became much harder to sustain as the civil rights and Black Power movements began to affect the larger culture. These movements for justice made a powerful appeal to a younger generation of Black Creoles who began to embrace a unified conception of Blackness. As they entered college and began to construct their own politics, many became committed to working for justice under the banner of Blackness.

In Gaudin's study of the *Xavierite*, a student-run publication at Xavier University, young black Creoles published a manifesto of sorts for their 1970 edition. With this manifesto, the young people urge their fellow students to reimagine themselves as part of a larger Black community. They made their appeal in these words: "Within these pages, fellow Xavierites, is a reflection of you. . . . Now as we approach the reality of Blackness in its fullest and most effective sense, the word relate [*sic*] assumes a new connotation—relate to MY world, relate to MY people, relate to ME. . . . To whom do we owe the privilege of voicing at last this long-smothered identity?"[36] It is instructive to note that the students describe Blackness as a "long-smothered identity." One senses that they had long struggled with how to relate to Anglo-Black identity and politics, and that now that they were testing their independence, they were free to declare their unabashed Blackness.[37]

These selections from the *Xavierite* articulate the result of nearly one hundred years of assimilative pressures that helped to craft a more or less unified Blackness out of formerly diversified roots in New Orleans. In the 1870s, many—perhaps most—of the Xavier students' ancestors would have spoken French or Creole and would have identified as Creole. In 1907, Creole community leader Rodolphe Lucien Desdunes penned a letter in response to a speech given by W. E. B. Du Bois.[38] The latter had given his speech in New York where he described Negroes of the South as lacking in book knowledge. [39] Desdunes, the descendant of generations of literate and French-speaking Creoles of color, protested, quick to explain Creoles' literary accomplishments and to draw social and cultural distinctions between French-identified Creoles and Anglo-American Blacks.

But as the twentieth century proceeded, with few new French-speaking immigrants of color, the changing demographics made French-speakers a minority in New Orleans. In addition, the realities of segregation made being identifiably Black the primary determinant of one's well-being and future—and they placed severe political pressure on anyone in this category to identify as Black. One had either to jettison or to suppress alternative identities like "Creole" and "French." While many did assimilate, dropping French language and Creole identity, the seeds of difference lay dormant beneath the soil of conformity, waiting for the right conditions to push forward and sprout again.

Renaissance of Congo Square and Black Diversity

The roughly one hundred years from the 1870s to the 1970s was manifestly a period of great assimilation, one that departed from the earlier reality of Black diversity in Congo Square, in New Orleans, and beyond. But, in the longer-term view of nearly four hundred years of US history, this one-hundred-year flattening of black diversity was short-lived.[40] As more people of African descent immigrated to the United States, and as the gains of the civil rights movement eased the oppressive and repressive atmosphere under which Blacks had been living, the shoots of Black diversity began to flower again. This flowering is evident in the renaissance of Congo Square.

In 1968 the parade for the International Jazz Festival began in Congo Square, in celebration of the 250th anniversary of the founding of New Orleans. This event marked the beginning of the increased pace of transformation in a space that had been rarely used for several decades. In 1970, in an effort to place New Orleans more firmly on the tourist map,

Figure 9.4. Contemporary drumming in Congo Square, New Orleans. Photograph by Bart Everson, 2011, https://www.flickr.com/photos/11018968@N00/6215960749.

business leaders reached out to George Wein, a top festival producer who had experience producing the Newport Jazz Festival in Rhode Island. Wein partnered with local musicians like Ellis Marsalis to locate the talent for the first New Orleans Jazz and Heritage Festival. Congo Square was chosen as the location: though it had slipped into disuse, it was still known locally as a sacred space for New Orleans music, going back to the time that enslaved Africans had danced and drummed there. Although the initial 1970 jazz festival was small—only three hundred and fifty tickets were sold—it was deemed a musical success and promoters were able to raise more money for a second festival the following year. Thus began a tradition that has grown substantially over the course of forty years.

The 1980 New Orleans Jazz and Heritage Festival was special in that it occurred in the newly renovated park, which had been renamed for Louis Armstrong. The Congo Square portion of the park had also been renovated, and paving stones had been set in a circular pattern in remembrance of the dance circles formed by Africans in early New Orleans. In 1990, the Congo Square Foundation was formed to promote the preservation and positive use of the space. Although Hurricane

Katrina dealt a heavy blow to the city and to the Square, in 2007 the first annual Congo Square Rhythms Festival was held in the park. But the symbolic high point of Congo Square's renaissance occurred in 2011 when the city council voted to officially change the name from Beauregard Square back to Congo Square. After more than a century, Congo Square was restored to itself.

As of this writing, the Square is used routinely as a lieu de souvenir, providing regular opportunities to remember and celebrate the diverse roots of Black communities. It has been my pleasure to participate in this remembrance with my daughters and other young people who are learning the stories of Congo Square for the first time. In April 2014, we attended the Congo Square Rhythms Festival, where several groups—including my daughters' African dance company—shared music and dance from across the African diaspora. That same month, many children from across the city came to Congo Square to take part in the Umoja Village Celebration of the African American Child. In addition to seeing performances, children were invited to make their own goat-skin drums, create jewelry, and express themselves through music or dance during the open mic times.

A more somber event occurred on Mother's Day 2014 when community leaders organized a Bring Back Our Girls rally to express solidarity with the Nigerian families who lost their daughters to Boko Haram. The timing of this event was significant in several ways. First, Mother's Day offered a symbolic occasion for making a statement of solidarity with other mothers. But the rally was also scheduled for three o'clock on Sunday—precisely when the Congo Square Preservation Society sponsors a regular time of drumming and dancing. This time was itself chosen, no doubt, to remember and mark solidarity with the African peoples who had built New Orleans. The day and time of the rally thus extended that solidarity across the water.

During the period that Congo Square has experienced this renaissance, there has also been a re-identification with Creole identity among many Creoles of color. In 2004 the Louisiana Creole Research Association was formed to provide support and community to Creoles of color researching their family histories. In addition to assisting with private genealogies, however, the association also sponsors events to educate the community about who Creoles are and their unique history and culture. Such events encourage pride in a Creole identity that had been on the defense since the 1960s, both because of an earlier generation's intentional separation from non-Creole African Americans and because of pressures to "be Black" in the Anglo-American mold. Now, with a buffer of a few decades, it has become possible to step back from some of the separatism and rancor that marked those earlier decades in order to acknowledge and celebrate the distinctive social life and cultural contributions of this group, which is so central to New Orleans history.[41]

Within the context of the long history of New Orleans, today's flourishing celebrations of African, African American, and Creole cultures at Congo Square mark a profound reclamation of a place that had once allowed for complex expressions of diversity and hybridity—the in-betweenness that was once a pervasive element of Black identity, until it was submerged beneath the social and economic pressures of the late nineteenth and early twentieth centuries. Placing Congo Square into this larger historical context allows us to see today's era of Black diversity, not as a sharp departure from the past, but rather as a continuation of this rich earlier history, resonant with possibility.

NOTES

1. Freddi Williams Evans, *Congo Square: African Roots in New Orleans* (Lafayette: University of Louisiana at Lafayette Press, 2011), 138.

2. The City Meeting, *Daily Picayune*, Wednesday, March 29, 1893, p. 3, column 3.

3. Evans, *Congo Square*, 161.

4. See the announcement "Congo Square New World Rhythms Festival," 2014, New Orleans Jazz and Heritage Festival and Foundation, accessed July 22, 2016, http://www .jazzandheritage.org/congo-square/2014-congo-square-new-world-rhythms-festival.

5. Michael E. Crutcher Jr., *Tremé: Race and Place in a New Orleans Neighborhood* (Athens: University of Georgia Press, 2010), ix.

6. See news accounts for summaries of these controversies: Isaac Stanley Becker, "Yale Keeps the Calhoun Name despite Racial Controversy but Ditches the 'Master' Title," *Washington Post*, April 27, 2016, accessed July 22, 2016, https://www.washington post.com/news/grade-point/wp/2016/04/27/yale-keeps-the-calhoun-name-despite -racial-concerns-but-ditches-the-master-title/; Gabriel Fisher, "Princeton and the Fight over Woodrow Wilson's Legacy," *New Yorker*, November 25, 2015, accessed July 22, 2016, http://www.newyorker.com/news/news-desk/princeton-and-the-fight-over-woodrow -wilsons-legacy; Jessica Williams, "Confederate Monument Removal Bid Process Stalled amid Threats," *New Orleans Advocate*, May 23, 2016, accessed July 22, 2016, http://www .theadvocate.com/new_orleans/news/politics/article_bddd1a7f-b8b1-50c7-bcfa-7f1456d c6bc3.html.

7. There are a number of books on increased Black diversity and even on the idea of "post-Blackness." See, for example, Eugene Robinson, *Disintegration: The Splintering of Black America* (New York: Doubleday, 2010); Touré, *Who's Afraid of Post-Blackness? What It Means to Be Black Now* (New York: Free Press, 2011); and Ytasha Womack, *Post Black: How a New Generation Is Redefining African American Identity* (Chicago: Chicago Review Press, 2010).

8. Mary Waters, Philip Kasinitz, and Asad L. Asad, "Immigrants and African Americans," *Annual Review of Sociology* 40 (2014), 370.

9. Ibid.

10. For an alternative approach to thinking about the influence of Caribbean peoples on the United States, see Michel Laguerre, *Diasporic Citizenship: Haitian Americans in Transnational America* (New York: St. Martin's Press, 1998). His section on the history of Haitians in the United States provides a particularly Haitian view of what we often think of as purely US history; he writes, for example, of the role of direct descendants of Haiti in the organization of the *Plessy v. Ferguson* case.

11. Many of these differences lead to criticism of different Black groups' culture and values. In *Black Identities: West Indian Immigrant Dreams and American Realities* (Cambridge, MA: Harvard University Press, 1999), Mary Waters provides many examples of West Indians' negative perceptions of African Americans. One Grenadian interviewee, for instance, says: "In conversations with other black Americans—not all, mind you, some. I see that some of their basic concepts are so strange, that it keeps them back. You know, their values," Waters, "Immigrants," 152. But another interviewee, a Black American worker, reflects the tensions between West Indian immigrants and American Blacks and clearly articulates the lack of understanding and empathy between them. She explains, "They [West Indians] think that we're lazy. . . . But you try to teach them how some of the black people feel, you know. . . . Lots of times when you sit down and they learn from history, they can say, yeah, I can see why some of them black Americans are like that, you know. . . . I think you have the confrontation between black Americans and the black islanders because the black Americans are not trying to understand the islanders and the islanders are not trying to understand the black Americans," ibid., 133.

12. Pierre Nora, "Between Memory and History: *Les Lieux de Mémoire,*" *Representations* 26, Spring 1986, 12.

13. Ibid., 16.

14. Touré, *Who's Afraid*, 24

15. See Jerah Johnson, "New Orleans's Congo Square: An Urban Setting for Early Afro-American Culture Formation," *Louisiana History: The Journal of the Louisiana Historical Association* 32, no. 2 (Spring 1991), 117–57.

16. See Evans, *Congo Square*, 47. On the Kongo influence on New Orleans, see "The Kongo Period," in Ned Sublette, *The World That Made New Orleans: From Spanish Silver to Congo Square* (Chicago: Lawrence Hill Books, 2008), 106–15.

17. On the 1809 migration, see Nathalie Dessens, *From Saint-Domingue to New Orleans: Migration and Influences* (Gainesville: University Press of Florida, 2007); and Carl Brasseaux and Glenn Conrad, eds., *The Road to Louisiana: The Saint-Domingue Refugees, 1792–1809* (Lafayette: University of Southwestern Louisiana, 1992).

18. Sublette, *World*, 114–15.

19. These different approaches were reflected even in the ways the Spanish and the French lived out their Christianity. The Catholic residents of Louisiana had an attitude to religious and cultural life that was forcefully repudiated by the Anglo-Americans who succeeded their rule. As Benjamin Latrobe noted about life in New Orleans in 1819, the white residents of the city used the Sabbath to engage in drinking, dancing, and feasting, behaviors that shocked the consciences of the Anglo-Protestants who came to the Louisiana Territory after the purchase; Benjamin Henry Latrobe, *Impressions Respecting New Orleans: Diary & Sketches, 1818–1820* (New York: Columbia University Press, 1951), 130.

20. Johnson, "New Orleans's Congo Square," 36

21. Evans, *Congo Square*, 145.

22. Ibid., 48.

23. Ibid., 49.

24. Ibid., 49.

25. Johnson, "New Orleans's Congo Square," 35–36.

26. Ibid., 41.

27. Ibid., 41–42.

28. *Daily Picayune*, October 12, 1879. Gary A. Donaldson helpfully mentions this article in "A Window on Slave Culture: Dances at Congo Square in New Orleans, 1800–1862," *Journal of Negro History* 69, no. 2 (Spring 1984): 63–72.

29. See Joseph Tregle Jr., "Creoles and Americans," in *Creole New Orleans: Race and Americanization*, ed. Arnold R. Hirsch and Joseph Logsdon (Baton Rouge: Louisiana State University Press, 1992), 131–85.

30. Johnson explains that "Sunday dancers, intimidated by the presence of the militia, harassed by the police, and hampered by what had become a veritable forest of saplings, came in fewer and fewer numbers after 1856, and before the end of the decade, ceased to come at all," "New Orleans's Congo Square," 47.

31. Sublette, *World*, 115.

32. On the history of the one-drop rule, see James F. Davis, *Who is Black? One Nation's Definition* (University Park: Pennsylvania State University Press, 1991).

33. Wendy Ann Gaudin, "Autocrats and All Saints: Migration, Memory, and Modern Creole Identities" (PhD diss., New York University, 2005), 57.

34. Ibid., 58.

35. Ibid., 96.

36. Ibid., 84.

37. This inner struggle about how to position oneself with respect to blackness is documented by interview data in chapter 6 of my *American Routes: Racial Palimpsests and the Transformation of Race* (New York: Oxford University Press, 2017).

38. Rodolphe Lucien Desdunes, "A Few Words to Dr. DuBois with Malice toward None," 1907, Folder 38, A. P. Tureaud Papers, Amistad Center, Tulane University.

39. For a summary of Du Bois's lecture, see "Mixed Blood Aided White Geniuses," *New York Times*, February 18, 1907, accessed July 22, 2016, http://partners.nytimes.com/books/00/11/05/specials/dubois-mixed.html.

40. I include in this history areas that were technically colonies or territories before being fully incorporated into the United States.

41. Some separatism and rancor still exist, but there is, on the whole, more social and mental space for embracing Creole identity and culture now than there was thirty to forty years ago.

INTERSPACE FIVE ❧ *In-Betweenness in Motion*

Angel Parham's concern with past and current performances in Congo Square transects the reflections that follow by jazz historian Bruce Boyd Raeburn and American cultural studies scholar Joel Dinerstein. Raeburn, obliquely criticizing the scholarly obsession with the "authenticity" of early jazz's sound, traces the adaptability of early New Orleans jazzmen—in search of the "sweet spot"—to varied city spaces, ranging from music halls filled with dancing bodies to moving wagons along city streets. Dinerstein, in his wide-ranging essay, invites us visually and rhythmically to experience a second-line parade, and traces the ways in which second-line paraders, in their continually shifting modes and sites of dancing, highlight and celebrate some dimensions of in-betweenness, while criticizing and literally overrunning others. For Dinerstein, second-line performance engages interstitial built elements—stoops, roofs, poles, porches, freeway overpasses, and indeed the neighborhood streets themselves. In doing so, second-lining explicitly highlights and celebrates "in-betweenness" itself as a concept possessing liberatory, border-crossing dimensions.

CHAPTER TEN

Into the Between

Interstitial Soundscapes in Early New Orleans Jazz

—*Bruce Boyd Raeburn*

For some, an interstice suggests uncertainty or foreboding, as in the lyrics to the Stealers Wheel's 1973 hit recording "Stuck in the Middle with You," and in that song's subsequent application to a torture scene in Quentin Tarantino's 1992 film *Reservoir Dogs*. But for jazz musicians, venturing into the between is more like entering a comfort zone: indeterminacy and risk are precisely what they seek to engage. As an improvisational musical style and genre, and as a musical intervention, jazz is thus inherently interstitial, both theoretically and practically inhabiting a state of perpetual becoming between what a given musical composition has been and what it can be.[1] In the case of early New Orleans jazz, the original jazz idiom, such in-between factors were especially pronounced as the style was coalescing, while musicians experimented with variable instrumentation, repertoire, and technique, prior to the development of a terminology and a canon. The new music no longer conformed to the categorical imperatives defining "ragtime" or "blues" but did not definitively come to be known as "jazz" until after the first recordings by the Original Dixieland Jazz Band, a band of white musicians from New Orleans, were produced in New York in February 1917. Their release created a sensation around the term based on record sales and the band's popularity among dancers, ultimately establishing a dominant paradigm. Vernacular terms such as "ratty" and "gutbucket" that had been used by New Orleans musicians to differentiate their music from ragtime quickly disappeared, although some stalwarts, such as the clarinetist Sidney Bechet, resisted the shift to "jazz." Bechet continued to refer to his music as "ragtime" throughout his long career, and despite almost a century of predominance, the term is still contested, particularly by some African American musicians who view it as an imposition representing white exploitation of black creativity.[2] In recent years, the New Orleans trumpeter Nicholas Payton has argued that "Black American Music" is a more palatable and appropriate label for the music he makes.[3]

Yet jazz can also be understood as interstitial in relation to its synthesis of distinctly different racial and cultural roots, inhabiting the syncretized middle ground between Afrocentric and Eurocentric approaches to making music. In the nineteenth century, professional musicians who performed Eurocentric art and popular music were expected to be musically literate, responding to the conservatory tradition. The Afrocentric vernacular—from which ragtime, blues, and jazz derived—was more akin to an amateur folk music in which intuitive, expressive practices predominated. Each system had its own rules and standards, with jazz musicians practicing an eclectic bricolage in selecting the best tools for their respective musical visions. Some jazz musicians therefore became known as "fakers" because they could not read music but compensated with superior expressive power and versatility. In New Orleans jazz, almost all bands required an admixture of varying skill levels in order to satisfy a wide range of clients with differing stylistic preferences: sight readers who could read the latest scores and thus introduce the newest popular songs into band repertoires, which then became fodder for improvisation; "fakers" or "get off" men (and sometimes women) who memorized parts as needed before reconstructing them to maximize their expressive potency; and "spellers," musicians who could not sight-read notes but could extract enough information from a score to negotiate the chord changes and contribute effectively.[4] By inhabiting the middle ground between conservatory and amateur methodologies, jazz musicians established their own sweet spots, developing personal voices on their instruments and in playing styles that served as markers of individuality, much like musical signatures. Bands adopted similar strategies, marketing themselves according to the chemistry achieved by the collective membership, while remaining ever mindful of a potential upgrade if a gifted player became available. Such imperatives balanced aesthetics with economic practicalities, ensuring not only artistic satisfaction but also continuous work in a competitive market.

In New Orleans, people love to hear drums: the beats of second-line parades, Mardi Gras Indian gangs, and ambient jazz bands performing in the streets animate their daily existence. The introduction of the trap drum set in the late nineteenth century was a technological innovation that guaranteed the acceptance of jazz as dance music in New Orleans because of the allure of a big, pronounced beat—what the jazz pianist and composer Jelly Roll Morton called "plenty rhythm." Over time, jazz drummers developed a rhythmic concept of swing by learning how to play slightly before or after the beat, shaping an interstitial nexus of space and time to evoke a visceral reaction, compelling compensatory movement in the listener's feet, hips, shoulders, and head.[5] Moreover, within the African American vernacular, brass, reed, and string musicians employed "blue notes," which were microtones falling between standard Eurocentric scales.[6] These practices led to a plethora of problems for transcribers attempting to document jazz solos with standard classical musical notation, but the expanded expressive power that resulted from such tampering and the visceral joy it evoked in listeners is what mattered most in the minds of consumers. For them, pedagogical reconstructions after the fact in the form of written solos played by sight or by rote could never match the magic of a uniquely ephemeral, spontaneous musical creation.[7] Some scholars have applied the same reasoning to jazz records, characterizing them as imperfect artifacts or "obstacles" to historical understanding: "Recordings have the status of an impressive testimony that is, regrettably for the historian, a secondary substitute for the 'living presence' of actual performance."[8] We will return to this issue in due course.

Since early New Orleans jazz was dance music, it was intrinsically participatory, constituting a shared "living presence." Jazz placed the reality of performance somewhere between musicians and audience members and fostered a dynamic of interaction that involved improvisation on multiple levels and on both sides of the divide. When Charles "Buddy" Bolden used his cornet to "call his children home" to band performances at Lincoln and Johnson parks in Carrollton, circa 1900–1906, erasing distance with sound, he was indulging in a time-honored clarion call that had biblical antecedents. Like Joshua, he was tearing down walls, delivering his people from the strictures of a polite and moribund Eurocentric musical canon and introducing them to the sensual pleasures of a dance known as the slow drag—described by some as "vertical copulation." Other band leaders refined the strategy in such a way as to actually bring the audience *into* the music. In Chicago during the mid-1920s, the members of the New Orleans cornetist King Oliver's band, the Dixie Syncopators, were instructed by their leader to put sand on the dance floor of the Plantation Cabaret to magnify the sound of dancing feet, adding additional percussion to which they could react as they played.[9] Even in concert settings, jazz audiences were often encouraged to yell, stomp their feet, and clap as the spirit moved them, so that the musicians could respond to their efforts. Oliver's ploy revealed the high value that jazz musicians place on fostering human connection but also

Figure 10.1. Kid Ory's
Woodland Band in
a sugarcane field in
LaPlace, Louisiana, ca.
1905. Courtesy of the
Hogan Jazz Archive,
Tulane University.

demonstrated an abiding interest in fully exploiting the sonic possibilities of the environments in which they perform.

New Orleans jazz is based on the practices of polyphony and heterophony, with various instruments improvising collectively and often simultaneously as part of an ongoing musical conversation, blending various timbres and sonorities into a unified, coherent sound. The acoustical properties of the spaces (or soundscapes) in which they played therefore factored significantly in such negotiations. Seeking to achieve what they heard as a "natural balance," the musicians who developed the jazz idiom in the early twentieth century thus found ways to adapt to the acoustical possibilities of a wide variety of soundscapes. Through a process of experimentation, they arranged players in different configurations depending on the nature of the engagement and the environmental circumstances they were confronting, including performances in dance halls, on riverboats (which were essentially floating dance halls), and on furniture wagons and in brass bands playing on the streets.

Using their own ingenuity to compensate for limited technologies, musicians tinkered with various approaches to determine the most effective ways to integrate the front line (consisting of trumpet, clarinet, and trombone) with a rhythm section (incorporating piano or guitar, bass, and drums) in various built and open-air spaces in order to achieve what they heard as an effective blending of instruments. For the bands that performed in dance halls and saloons and for picnics at camps on Lake Pontchartrain, the standard format became drums at far left (to the

Figure 10.2. The Eureka Brass Band performing for the Young and True Friends Benevolent Association in New Orleans, 1961. Photograph by William Russell, courtesy of the Hogan Jazz Archive, Tulane University.

viewer), then trombone, clarinet, trumpet or cornet, violin, guitar, and bass at far right, combined with a suitable elevation. The New Orleans drummer Warren "Baby" Dodds recalled that this bandstand configuration resulted from continuous trial and error until a workable solution was found:

> The band lined up . . . in a straight line, with the bass at one end and the drums at the other; a band with the drums in the middle will not be balanced. . . . Music is more even when it comes down on people's heads, because it hits the ceiling and comes down on them. The balcony bandstands in some New Orleans halls are good because they are up high. The music will sound too far away if the bandstand is too high or too low, but music from a too low stand will sound better than from a too high one. . . . A band will sound better if the best place in the room is picked out to set up the band.[10]

A myriad of photographs, including those of Edward "Kid" Ory's Woodland Band (1905), the Superior Orchestra (1910), the Peerless Orchestra (1911), and the Eagle Band (1916), depict this configuration. However, a dance band playing an advertisement while on a moving furniture wagon would always place slide trombone over the tailgate at the back of the wagon to protect the other musicians, thus acoustical issues could be offset by other functional imperatives. The open space behind the tailgate became a no-man's-land because of the danger of being hit by the trombone slide.[11]

Figure 10.3. Recreation of the first jazz recording session with the Original Dixieland Jazz Band and engineer Charles Sooy (top right) for *The March of Time*, 1937. Courtesy of the Hogan Jazz Archive, Tulane University.

Brass bands marching in the streets positioned trombones in front for the same reason, followed by clarinets and trumpets, with brass bass to the side and snare and bass drummers in the rear. Unlike an enclosed environment, an open-air setting disperses sound waves, which go straight up, requiring a format that will consolidate the sound accordingly.[12] A newsreel film of the Eureka Brass Band from Mardi Gras in 1929 demonstrates the difficulty involved. The camera and sound recording equipment were positioned at the corner of Basin and Canal Streets and captured only parts of the band as the musicians marched by in succession, thus failing to achieve an integrated documentation of the band as a whole. To make matters worse, the trombonists rested while the band made its turn from Canal to Basin, which subtracted crucial elements from the mix. By the time the bass and snare drummers at the rear arrived, the front line was inaudible.

As the Eureka case demonstrates, finding effective ways to record a band "in the wild" or even in a studio became a challenge fraught with a range of acoustical problems, the solutions to which depended on toying in potentially complicated ways with the space between the musicians and existing recording devices, until the electrification of sound recording made things easier. How such issues would be addressed therefore depended primarily on the technology available at the time, although human ingenuity and resourcefulness always mattered. The first jazz recording, made in New York City by the Original Dixieland Jazz Band from New Orleans in February 1917, predated the electrification of recorded sound. In this case, the ingenuity of the recording engineer, Charles Sooy, became the crucial factor in achieving a successful record-

Figure 10.4. Rebirth Brass Band and second line celebrating the band's tenth anniversary, 1993. Photograph by John McCusker, courtesy of the Hogan Jazz Archive, Tulane University.

ing within the limits of what is usually referred to as "acoustical" recording technology. Sooy experimented with moving the musicians around in relation to the recording horns, attempting to establish sweet spots, locations that were the most conducive to producing the desired aural result according to the tone and volume of the instruments involved. If the trumpet player was too loud, Sooy pulled him back from the recording horns; if the clarinetist was too soft, he pushed him forward. The result was a balanced recording that effectively blended the trumpet, clarinet, trombone, piano, and muted drums. Sooy's attention to the sweet spots between the musicians and the recording equipment produced a 78-rpm record that sold in excess of 1.5 million copies and introduced many Americans to what thereafter became known as the Jazz Age.[13]

In the mid-1920s, the introduction of electrical recording technology using microphones expanded the strategic options available to jazz musicians and the engineers who sought to record them, enabling accurate documentation of all the requisite instruments, including guitar, string bass, and drums. Still, ingenious spatial experimentation to achieve the best musical effects and ensure bonding with the audience remains a part of the culture to this day. This tendency is particularly pronounced in the traditional outdoor second-line parades where brass bands play for hours in the streets—in such cases, microphones are not an option and the sound goes where it wants to go, as do the people involved. Second-line parades can radically transform the normative interstitial zones variously separating or connecting musicians from audiences found in indoor settings. In some cases, boundaries of demarcation cease to exist. The second line surrounds the musicians and envelops them. Every dancer does his or her own thing, yet everyone is united by the beat the brass band drummers are providing and the melody projected by the brass and reeds. This is, in short, pandemonium tempered by a common groove. Especially when the band stops marching, the exchange among dancers and musicians can intensify dramatically. The more furious the dancing becomes, the more the musicians seek to match the energy, and then they, in turn, raise the sonic stakes. The collective reverie that results is the ultimate objective, and under such conditions the interstitial zone between players and dancers can evaporate entirely. All become one. When everyone is exhausted, the band and the crowd will disperse, usually making their way to the closest bar for a drink.

New Orleans brass bands are well aware of the value of finding and manipulating open-air sweet spots to enhance their sound and heighten audience gratification. In his book *Roll with It*, Matt Sakakeeny explores the strategies used by members of the Rebirth Brass Band to maximize their aural impact when parading on the streets of New Orleans, choosing certain songs and styles for when the streets are narrow, others when they are wide. During funerals and second-line parades, the Claiborne Avenue–Interstate 10 on-ramp and overpass (known locally as "the bridge") acts as a reverberation chamber (a sweet spot par excellence) that enables brass bands to raise the volume threshold dramatically— something they are wont to do to work an audience into a frenzy. The tuba player and sousaphonist Philip Frazier, a cofounder of the Rebirth Brass Band, explains:

> When you get to a certain intersection or a certain street where there's an opening, if the street is really wide, you know that's more dancing room for everybody, you wanna keep everybody upbeat. When you get to a street where it's more closed, and the parade might slow down at a pace, you slow it down 'cause you know everybody's trying to get through that small street. . . . When you get under an overpass, 'cause of the acoustics, you know the band gonna be loud anyway, and the crowd knows that gonna be like some wild, rowdy stuff and you want to get everybody hyped.[14]

This kind of experimentation to achieve the best sound for a given moment and particular environment has been occurring since the dawn of jazz and continues because New Orleans musicians enjoy the challenges and processes entailed in spatial adaptation—an aspect of jazz improvisation that has often gone unnoticed.

If the streets offer one series of challenges, dance halls have long provided another. Under the tutelage of cornetist Buddy Bolden in the period 1900–1906, jazz emerged as a preferred form of dance music catering to the imaginations of people who were seeking thrills and freedom of self-expression. According to various observers, his clients tended to be gamblers, pimps, off-duty prostitutes, hustlers, and other denizens of the sporting-life demimonde out to let off some steam. Band jobs typically lasted from eight o'clock in the evening until four in the morning, with the younger "night people," who wanted to dance to the blues until dawn, predominating after midnight. The buildings that served as dance halls, such as Economy Hall in Tremé (the headquarters of a benevolent association, Société d'Économie et d'Assistance Mutuelle, also known as Cheapskate's Hall), Funky Butt Hall (originally called Union Sons Hall, after a labor union, or Kenna's Hall, which alternated as a church on Sundays) in the Third Ward, and Come Clean Hall in Gretna on the West Bank, were essentially large wooden boxes, the equivalent of a very live reverb chamber with an elevated stage for the musicians.

In the 1940s, the jazz record producer and historian Bill Russell made a host of recordings in Tremé's San Jacinto Hall, documenting trumpeters Bunk Johnson and Avery "Kid" Howard and the clarinetist George Lewis. Russell used a mobile Presto disc recorder with a single microphone. He believed that the key to making an authentic recording of a jazz band was to find the "sweet spot" for placement of the microphone that would yield a balanced capture. As in the case of the first jazz recording that used acoustical technology in 1917, musicians would be resituated in various positions on the bandstand in a series of experiments with test recordings to achieve a desirable mix. Russell found that the distortion produced by the hall's natural reverb continued to be an ongoing problem, one that he never satisfactorily solved, but for the acolytes who followed in his footsteps, that signature sound, though imperfect, could inspire emulation. In a blog entry titled "New Orleans '61 (The Journey Begins)," record producer Chris Albertson writes about Société des Jeunes Amis Hall, the Seventh Ward site of Riverside Records' January 1961 New Orleans: The Living Legends record series: "The hall's acoustical sound was exactly what I wanted to recapture; the same kind of ambience that lent such character to Bill Russell's 1940's American Music recordings from San Jacinto Hall." With Russell's productions at San Jacinto in mind, in the 1960s Richard B. Allen and Paul Crawford of Tulane University's Archive of New Orleans Jazz organized recording sessions there featuring the traditional jazz of George Lewis, the husband and wife team of pianist Billie Pierce (née Wilhelmina Good-son) and trumpeter Dede Pierce, and trumpeters Peter Bocage, Avery "Kid" Howard, and Kid Thomas Valentine. Allen and Crawford shared an expectation that recording in San Jacinto Hall would lend an air of authenticity to their efforts—it was, after all, hallowed ground from the heyday of traditional New Orleans jazz in the 1920s when Sam Morgan's Jazz Band played there—but they, too, were hampered by the booming echo that went with the space. Why, they pondered, did a dancehall that served as a focal point for jazz in its prime sound so bad? Yet in his liner notes for *Kid Howard at the San Jacinto Hall* LP (1963), Tom Bethell brushed that issue aside and praised the Bunk Johnson sides made there by Bill Russell in 1944 as "the finest recording session in jazz history . . . the most authentic band of them all."[16]

The heavy reverb on these recordings thus became lauded as a positive aesthetic standard unto itself for some observers (somewhat akin to the emperor's-new-clothes syndrome), connoting an idea of authenticity that had little to do with how New Orleans jazz bands actually sounded when they were performing in dance halls. Russell's intent had simply been to make as balanced a recording as possible based on the strategic placement of a single microphone. He was, in essence, translating Bunk Johnson's view of authenticity regarding instrumentation, style, and repertoire into a comparably basic (some might say "primitive") approach to its documentation using the most minimal electrical technology available. In 1944 when he was recording Bunk Johnson's band in San Jacinto Hall, he had some concerns that the hall "may have been a little too 'live' as far as the acoustics went, but probably we couldn't have done any better elsewhere. At least we had our run of the place and could take our time." At an alternate location, Artisan Hall, where he recorded Wooden Joe Nicholas's Band in 1945, Russell experienced similar problems:

> As soon as we got inside Artisan's Hall and somebody whistled, I knew the acoustics were bad, so we opened all the windows, restroom and cloakroom door. . . . The acoustics were so bad I even thought of moving the band up to the balcony. . . . We could hardly hear the band properly for the echo. I moved the microphone back and we took off any extra clothes we had, like sweaters and jackets and things we had wrapped around the records, and hung everything over chairs to absorb the sound. . . . We invited people from the neighborhood to come in, as people absorb sound too.[17]

As the years passed, even less effort was expended in solving the echo problem, because the negative aspects had been transformed into positives by the jazz cognoscenti. Significantly, film of Allen and Crawford's

Figure 10.5. Dancers on the opening night of the Pythian Temple Roof Garden in New Orleans, with Manuel Perez's band elevated on the gallery, 1923. Courtesy of the Hogan Jazz Archive, Tulane University.

Kid Howard recording session on August 2, 1963, shows an entirely empty hall, save for the musicians and producers. In their quest for an authentic locale, Russell, Allen, and Crawford had forgotten about a major ingredient of what made jazz bands that performed in New Orleans dance halls sound so good.

What was lacking was the intervening presence of human bodies—the dancers—a dynamic, weighty mass of flesh to dampen the reverb effect by absorbing the sound. Without them as an interstitial element, the formulas developed by early New Orleans jazz musicians for maximizing the sound in dance halls were rendered meaningless. In a typical dance hall situation, the elevated stage ensured that the band's music would project directly over the heads of the dancers to the back of the hall, while the interaction of audience and band—mutually creating the sweet spot that connected them—absorbed just enough echo to produce a pleasant listening and dancing experience. The result was audible without being too loud, somewhat soft around the edges, yet still clear and robust. The modern ideal of recording jazz bands "authentically" in empty halls was thus very far removed from the dance hall realities that most New Orleans jazz musicians had experienced historically. Some-times, it seems, the desire for an idealized version of the past can only lead to distortion in the present. In fact, in the final analysis, when it comes to New Orleans jazz, no recording can ever substitute for actually being there, literally, in the flesh, jammed together with a sea of dancers moving in unison to the rhythmic, sonic effusion for which New Orleans jazz bands are so famous.

Yet, times must change. The musicians who perform at New Orleans Jazz and Heritage Festival today routinely rely on the talents of sound technicians at mixing boards with an almost infinite array of electronic gadgets for adjusting volume, pitch, reverb, and balance among instru-ments. For many contemporary New Orleans jazz musicians, however, these technological advances are not viewed as progress. One often finds among them a nostalgic longing for a time when jazz musicians used ingenuity and patience to tackle the challenges that a variety of ambient soundscapes presented. Their mission was to venture into the between—to locate the interstitial space that both separated and con-nected them to their audiences—in order to achieve the most memo-rable musical performance possible with the tools at hand. In so doing, they not only came to know their own capabilities in combining art and science but also revealed their need to establish a powerful human con-nection with the people who danced or listened to their music. It is a truism among jazz musicians that the value of a jazz performance can-not be judged by the notes that are played but always by the feeling, the emotional content, that animates them, compelling an audience to dance, clap, snap their fingers, or tap their feet. It took years for New Orleans musicians to learn how to tweak the sweet spots between mind, heart, and ear to maximize performance, but once learned, these lessons can never be forgotten. This is why the New Orleans style is so often referred to as "traditional" jazz, invoking a continuum of experience and innovation that is available to veteran and newcomer alike and that remains susceptible to infinite variation and expansion.

NOTES

1. For a detailed explication of the improvisational nature of jazz, see Paul F. Ber-liner, *Thinking in Jazz: The Infinite Art of Improvisation* (Chicago: University of Chicago Press, 1994). Jazz musicians engaging in improvisational interaction seek to connect with each other across interstitial zones, voids that they fill with sound and spirit, just as they do with audiences—all of which qualify as reciprocal relationships, at least in the ideal. See Ingrid T. Monson, *Saying Something: Jazz Improvisation and Interaction* (Chicago: University of Chicago Press, 1996).

2. Sidney Bechet with Joan Reid, Desmond Flower, and John Ciardi, *Treat It Gentle* (New York: Hill and Wang, 1960), in which he states, "But let me tell you one thing: Jazz, that's a name the white people have given to the music. . . . When I tell you ragtime, you can feel it, there's a spirit right in the word" (8).

3. For Payton's views on "Black American Music," see his blog: http://nicholaspayton.wordpress.com/2008/06/30/hello-world/.

4. For a fuller discussion of the integration of amateur and conservatory practices in jazz, see Bruce Boyd Raeburn, "Stars of David and Sons of Sicily: Constellations beyond the Canon in Early New Orleans Jazz," *Jazz Perspectives* 3, no. 2 (August 2009), 123–52.

5. See Theodore Dennis Brown, "A History and Analysis of Jazz Drumming to 1942" (PhD diss., University of Michigan, 1976).

6. For an analysis of the integration of blue notes into New Orleans jazz, see Vic Hobson, *Creating Jazz Counterpoint: New Orleans, Barbershop Harmony, and the Blues* (Jackson: University Press of Mississippi, 2014).

7. See John Joyce's discussion of issues related to jazz transcription in John J. Joyce Jr., Bruce Boyd Raeburn, and Anthony M. Cummings, eds., *Sam Morgan's Jazz Band: Complete Recorded Works in Transcription* (Middleton, WI: A-R Editions, 2012), xxxv–xlv.

8. See Jed Rasula, "The Media of Memory: The Seductive Menace of Records in Jazz History," in Krin Gabbard, ed., *Jazz among the Discourses*, (Durham: Duke University Press, 1995), 135.

9. Bruce Boyd Raeburn, "Dancing Hot and Sweet: New Orleans Jazz in the 1920s," *Jazz Archivist* 7, no. 1–2 (December 1992), 10–13; Albert Nicholas, interview with Richard B. Allen and Lars Edegran, June 22, 1972, Reel 1 transcript, p. 3, Hogan Jazz Archive, Tulane University, in which he recounts how Oliver instructed his Dixie Syncopators to play softly in certain passages so that the sound of dancing feet could be utilized for percussive effect.

10. Warren "Baby" Dodds, interview by William Russell, May 31, 1958, transcript, p. 3–4, Hogan Jazz Archive, Tulane University.

11. For detail on the stylistic ramifications of "tailgate" trombone, see John McCusker, *Creole Trombone: Kid Ory and the Early Years of Jazz* (Jackson: University Press of Mississippi, 2012), 70, 119, 150, 166.

12. Warren "Baby" Dodds, *The Baby Dodds Story*, as told to Larry Gara, rev. ed. (Baton Rouge: Louisiana State University Press, 1992), 16–17.

13. For details see H. O. Brunn, *The Story of the Original Dixieland Jazz Band* (Baton Rouge: Louisiana State University Press, 1960), 66–70.

14. See Matt Sakakeeny, *Roll with It: Brass Bands in the Streets of New Orleans* (Durham: Duke University Press, 2013), 23–25.

15. Chris Albertson, "New Orleans '61 (The Journey Begins)," accessed June 3, 2016. http://stompoff.blogspot.com/2009/11/new-orleans-1961.html.

16. Tom Bethell, liner notes for *Kid Howard at the San Jacinto Hall* LP (San Jacinto Records, SJ 1, 1963).

17. See *Bill Russell's American Music*, compiled and edited by Mike Hazeldine (New Orleans: Jazzology Press, 1993), 45–46, 54.

CHAPTER ELEVEN
The Cultural Democracy of the Second Line
A View from beyond the Ropes

—Joel Dinerstein
With photographs by Pableaux Johnson

For more than 150 years, working-class African Americans of New Orleans have created and sustained a second-line culture of pleasure, parading, and aesthetic performance, with all three *P*s intertwined in service to raising the community spirit. It has been common enough in US history for community organizations to provide social aid for their members, often along ethnic lines or for recent immigrants. Making pleasure a community objective marks the mobile signature of the New Orleans vernacular.[1] There are a few analogous dance walkabouts powered by music in the African diaspora—in Cuba, the Caribbean, and West Africa—but there's only one in the United States. The second-line parade is a rare example of in-group ethnic expression that creates the conditions for a broader cultural democracy.[2] Here I will call it a *citizenship of the streets* as it manifests in the specific neighborhood spaces of New Orleans.

You will never hear the phrase *first line*, but of course there is one, and all second-lining is dependent on it. The unspoken first line of a second-line parade consists of (1) the sponsoring social aid and pleasure club (SAPC), with its members dressed in that year's spectacular suit, and (2) the club's chosen local brass band, such as Rebirth, the Hot 8, or the Stooges. At noon or one o'clock on every Sunday between Labor Day and July 4, the tuba's first downbeat lays down a sonic brass carpet for the SAPC members to "come out the door" of their headquarters (usually, their home bar). Each member rocks his or her suit on the threshold of the club and then descends single file, *Soul Train*–style, solo dancing down the concrete alley in between forty foot-long ropes that define their elite space for the day. In dancing down the rope line, the SAPC members dead-sanctify the street as hundreds of folks fall in around and behind them to "ease on down / ease on down / the road" for over four hours over four or so miles. These are the second-liners.

A second line is a ritual that recognizes life as a combination of work and play and survival and then reproduces it on Sunday for the *pleasure* of music and dance, of food and talk, of mood elevation and dance meditation. The devout practitioners of this street-level dancing mass raise the spirit of their neighborhoods, the city, and themselves every Sunday afternoon. Not for nothing does photographer Pableaux Johnson call his self-assigned weekly engagement "going to church."

I have been a member of the Prince of Wales Club, the second-oldest SAPC (founded in 1928), on and off for eight years. On my very first second line after moving to New Orleans in 2003, I found myself dancing along until I was miles from my neighborhood; I simply had to know how this weekly ritual came to exist and how it was sustained. Here I was, an American studies scholar with expertise in African American music, dance, and culture—how was I unaware of the long history of Sunday second lines? I later wrote a journal article for *American Quarterly* about the Prince of Wales Club's first major second line after Hurricane Katrina—I interviewed all the members who paraded that year—and I was invited to join the following year.[3] In contrast to that article, this impressionistic essay is drawn from what I have learned about African American participatory democracy both inside and outside the ropes.

Consider the second line an ongoing march that moves through the streets as a weekly dream of past time and an imagined future, history and the American dream. The second-liners march with symbolic associations that go back in time to civil rights demonstrations and forward to a nonracist future when an entire city might use an African American–led community ritual to regenerate its social bonds. The Sunday second-line splits the difference between the sacred, static space of church and the unholy public spaces often pejoratively called "the streets."

The second line is a cultural version of the body politic expressing the freedom of kinetic assembly. Second lines originated some 150 years ago, and I submit it is a musical ritual that creates a version of Mircea Eliade's concept of sacred time: in other words, it harks back to the origins of a national African American expressive culture as a built-in resistance to oppressive Southscapes, affirming community vitality, embodied possibility, and the temporal power of the present. The streets, the music, and the bodies in motion flow together to become mutually constitutive. The music shapes the moving space, but it needs the streets as the foundational, concrete element (literally) for the alchemical transformation of Sunday afternoon spirits, bodies, and minds.[4]

Claiming the Streets as
Culturally Expressive Space, ca. 1910

A second line is an event that presumes a participatory ethos on the part of all who gather on Sunday afternoons. For certain communities, music is itself a form of "social life," as ethnomusicologist Thomas Turino theorizes in his indispensable work, *Music as Social Life: The Politics of Participation* (2008). Where such a cultural formation has been established as a baseline, there are "no artist-audience distinctions," since such expressive performances simply function as extensions of walking and conversation. Rather than the "presentational performance" of artistic spectacle with its (spatially) elevated artists and seated crowd of passive listeners, in events that partake of participatory framing, "the primary goal is to involve the maximum number of people in some performance role." The success of a musical event is gauged by how "participants *feel* during the activity" rather than the formal qualities of the music or dance. On any given second line, for example, random people will walk right behind the band, adding extra layers of percussion by playing cowbells, tambourines, or even empty pint whiskey bottles. The brass band musicians neither encourage nor discourage them. On any given second line, when the band plays a recognizable cover song, the entire musical army on the march will start singing "Backstabbers," "Beat It," or "I'll Fly Away," without any sign from the band. On any given second line, there are high-level dance-offs along the sidewalks equal in quality and expressiveness to the dancing provided by club members. Most people never see them.[5]

In fact, the second line is a rare ritual named not for its star performers but for its celebrants—the audience, the community, the everyday people (to invoke Sly Stone). "The Second Line is a bunch of *Guys* who follows the parade," Louis "Satchmo" Armstrong recalled of his childhood. "They're not the members of the . . . Club. Anybody can be a Second Liner, whether they are *Raggedy* or dressed up. They seemed to have more fun than anybody."[6] Just as rare, second-lining is a ritual that has remained true to its roots—and substantively the same—for more than a century and a quarter, as documented by Armstrong and Sidney Bechet, the first two musical geniuses of New Orleans jazz. Armstrong also mimicked the first line in his recollection: "To watch those clubs parade was an irresistible . . . experience. All the members wore full dress uniforms and . . . beautiful silk ribbons. . . . They were a magnificent sight. The brass band followed, shouting a hot swing march as everyone jumped for joy." *Second line* was already invoked as both verb and noun. "Every time one of those clubs paraded," Armstrong recalled, "I would second-line along with them all day long."[7]

In Sidney Bechet's *Treat It Gentle*, an indispensable memoir of New Orleans, jazz, and Afro-modernism, the Creole clarinetist gives over an entire chapter to the ritual. Bechet invoked the participatory event as a symbol of the vitality of New Orleans's black culture: "Even when I was just a little kid I was always . . . chasing after the parades," Bechet wrote of the first decade of the twentieth century. "One of those parades would start down the street, and all kinds of people . . . would forget all about what they was doing and just take after it, just joining in the fun." He describes in detail all the elements familiar to anyone second-lining today: SAPC club names such as "the Swells or the Magnolias . . . [with] their full dress suits on with sashes"; the strutting leader carrying the club's standard; the designated stops, "maybe six places they was scheduled to go"; and crucially, people joining all along, "coming from every direction."[8]

While sponsors would put in a dollar or so, the poorer community members just joined in, and "they enjoyed it just as much" as the first line—"more, some of them." Bechet recalled of New Orleans circa 1910: "They were called 'second liners.' . . . [They made] their own parade with broomsticks, kerchiefs, tin pans, any old damn' thing. And they'd take off shouting, singing, following along the sidewalk." When chased off the main route by the first line, they would go "off on side streets." If the police tried to break them up, "they'd go off one way and join the parade away up [later]."[9]

In short, the demand of second-liners for a space of cultural democracy would not be denied in the Jim Crow era. Second-liners were neither imitating the better-off, better-dressed first-liners nor simply having fun. Along sidewalks and streets, they created their own moves and styles, radiating and reflecting *back* the energy, pleasure, and kinesthetic of the first-liners and so *signifyin'* on their parade. "They'd be having their own damn' parade," Bechet admired in retrospect, "taking what was going on in the street and doing something different with it, tearing it up."[10] The first line struts through the streets between ropes that mark the boundaries of their mobile street stage. The second-liners follow, walking and dancing in undulating parallel lines in a mass outside the ropes and behind the band. Even more than the first line, they embellish, dramatize, and galvanize the energy of the entire event.

In the concentric layers of interstitial spaces outside the ropes—on sidewalks and porches, on church steps and rooftops—second-liners perform African American vernacular culture as a counterforce of community participation. In these negative spaces, the positive rejuvenation of this secular Sunday ritual comes to light. Off stage and outside the scope of photographers', videographers', and tourists' lenses, their reverberating energy constantly primes the second-line pump.

Here are four examples that characterize almost all second lines: when someone climbs a roof and dances above the crowd, creating a satellite point for the parade's energy; when the loose, serpentine crowd turns a corner and flows into a new street like water, as if to colonize all paths; when second-liners jump with joy under the Interstate 10 overpass on Claiborne Avenue, ramping up the energy of the parade through this makeshift concrete amplifier; and when the crowd hits a main thoroughfare such as St. Charles Avenue and streetcar tourists gawk and snap photos.

In their everyday lives, these second-liners are consigned to the sidelines through economics. Yet from the sidewalks and side streets, through makeshift props from kerchiefs to tin pans and improvised dramatic physical gestures, their reaction and refraction become central to the main action. This citizenship of the streets is formed (and performed) mostly by those on the economic margins of African American life.

The Afro-Caribbean Challenge Jumps the Ropes

There are many angles through and by which to participate in second lines: as club member, culture bearer, walker, dancer, and street watcher. Some people just walk along as if it's a mobile beer garden or an outdoor pub crawl—but this is the wrong way to second-line. When I say "wrong," I only mean it marks you as a spectator and a consumer in an event of participatory cultural democracy meant to rejuvenate the community spirit (and your own). To treat it like an outdoor DVD is to miss the point. The music is a call to dance and stroll, to socialize and harmonize with the urban environment. And if you're someone who says, "I don't dance," then give of your spirit in other ways. It may be a cliché, but not for nothing goes the African proverb, "If you can walk, you can dance." And this is an African American ritual more in line with an Afro-Caribbean cultural sphere than a North American one. At such parades, Afro-diasporic peoples challenge one another to dance contests of deep play, as when an elder evaluates the ability of dancers, sometimes nonverbally and sometimes with such expressions as "show me what you're working with."

The ropes are, in fact, a permeable boundary not just because you can duck under them. Often enough, a downtrodden second-liner dressed in a dirty tank top will jump inside the ropes and just start pelvis-popping next to a suited-up club member, singling the first-liner out for cultural battle. As a challenge dance, this action makes African

American aesthetics and kinesthetics the coin of the second-line realm. It is a way of saying, "Let me see what you got, all dressed up like that," and a club member must answer the call. It may be friendly or not; it may be between acquaintances (or not); it may be an implicit accusation of coasting or laziness of spirit in the role of a culture bearer. This is the deepest form of call-and-response: there is no refusing the call of the community, even when it comes from a member of lower social status. The second line is a ritual in which the crowd often swallows up the day's host figures.

I will testify here from my experience as a member of Prince of Wales. We were closing down the bar at one of our dances around two o'clock in the morning. Trell, whom I knew only in passing, beckoned me over. A woman in her mid-thirties, she was intense and funny, with deep brown eyes that were often bloodshot. She was suspicious of my reasons for being in the club. "You dance?" she asked. "Yeah," I said simply. "You got rhythm?" she asked with a hard edge. "Yeah," I said. "You second-line?" "Yeah." "We'll see," she said. "I'm gonna test you." Then she put out her cigarette and walked away without taking her eyes off me.

I saw her next a month later on the broad boulevard of Louisiana Avenue, bending low to instruct her jubilant, princessed-out five-year-old daughter. She was passing on the vernacular dance tradition: showing her how to clap on the two and four, stopping her when she went off time to reinforce rhythmic discipline, encouraging certain individual moves, and discouraging others. When the girl's energy for the lesson waned, Trell lifted her athwart her hips and they strolled on together. It was a second-line Madonna-and-child image, Trell's daughter dancing in her mother's arms.

"Oh, hey," she waved when she saw me. "OK, I told you I would test you." She stopped and nodded towards the street, where I was to show my second-lining skills. I felt self-conscious for a second but I'd just been dancing anyway, so I turned and went back to grooving to the tuba's bassline. I bent lower into a near-limbo crouch, came out into a slow spin, and then rocked my arms and pelvis. Trell kept her eyes steadily on my hips and legs, evaluating my fluidity, intentions, and footwork (I'm guessing here). At one point, I jumped perpendicularly—facing Trell. "Uh-uh, that's Joe's move," she said, referring to fellow Prince of Waler Joe Stern, "you can't do that." I laughed (she was right) and sunk into one of my signature moves, a low-center-of-gravity squat where I shift my hips and then roll ball-to-toe, and then I rose up halfway into a long-striding low strut in which I imagine myself to move something like Robert Crumb's Mr. Natural. By the time I turned back around, she had moved on. I figured I'd passed the test since she never challenged me again and dropped her suspicion about my presence at Prince of Wales meetings.

Such challenges go back to the beginnings of African American culture to colonial-era slavery when the threat to spiritual evisceration was palpable. Beginning in the eighteenth century, certain culture bearers ensured the survival of African-derived dance moves and physical gestures at ritual events such as cornhusking, Christmas, or Jonkonnu (John Canoe) festivals. "Give me that knee-bone bent," an elder would call, a recognition of African dance gestures: Africans dance with every part of their bodies, often with each part crooked at the joints, or pumping or shimmying a specific part of the body. This was in stark contrast to the rigid upright postures of then-prevalent European courtly dances (such as the pavane or waltz) and folk dances (like the Irish jig or Scottish fling). At such events, though circumscribed by slavery and oppression, African retentions and culture survived on the body long after drums were legally banned and tribal languages collated into African American Vernacular English (AAVE). The polyrhythms of African music were retained through clapping out rhythms, patting juba on the torso, or reinforcing the sacred circle in the ring shout.[11]

Of central importance is the democratization of the body moving in public space—every part equally valued, every part in motion, moving in relation to the groove. Often enough, two or three parts of the body move in opposition, creating aesthetic and dramatic tensions—shoulders versus feet, head versus hips—by moving with and against the groove. Such cultural transmission made possible the survival of central aspects of African heritage. I refer here to fluid arm, neck, hip, and head movements, explosive jumps and spins (as in break dancing), and fast, repetitive motion of a single body part (whether hips, shoulders, or butts).[12]

You can still see nearly every African American move ever appropriated into American and global social dance on any given Sunday second line, from the turkey trot to the twist to the hustle to twerking. Moreover, the pervasive influence of Afro-diasporic moves and grooves remain visible and influential in global culture: this is how global youth hits the dance floor and the streets. West and central African movement practices transformed nearly all social dances in the twentieth century.

Jazz drummer Jo Jones of the Count Basie Orchestra described Kansas City in the 1930s as a place where "people used to walk in time down the street"—meaning to the beat, in the groove, as if dancing. Jones said they walked "in swingtime" in Kansas City, in that buoyant 4/4 groove invented by musicians of that time and place. He meant that the music shaped individual movement on the streets.[13] Clearly, the entire city had been musicalized by the presence of the innovative big-band swing in its all-night clubs and jam sessions. African American musicians often discuss "the tempo of the time." In this case, the interplay of bands and dancers created a new urban tempo for a specific geographic location (Kansas City) and a specific ethnic group (African Americans) as it reflected a specific urban experience in one of the few cities that were prosperous during the Great Depression.

Similarly, a generation earlier, jazz had begun in a land where people marched to a specific street-level tempo created by brass bands on and off the street. Brass bands have since been musically revised by funk and then hip-hop, but New Orleanians still walk their streets in time on Sunday second lines. Before Katrina, I heard this chant more than once: "if you're not gonna roll / I say if you're *not* gonna roll / then get the fuck on outta the way." In other words, don't come to a second line for flava or to feel cool walking along at some funky ritual. This is serious business, the deep play of cultural rituals. Learn the rules and participate ("roll") or create your own ritual if you think it's important enough ("get the fuck outta the way"). Don't dilute or commodify this one.

My use of "deep play" here is indebted to Diane Ackerman's revision of Clifford Geertz's concept as she inflects it toward "ecstatic play" or secular transcendence. Ackerman's theory braids together a few classic sociological and anthropological concepts: Johann Huizinga's sense of "play" as a festive activity and mood outside of the quotidian accompanied by "a feeling of exaltation"; Emile Durkheim's concept of "collective effervescence," when a group participates in a single activity and raises community morale; Victor Turner's concept of "communitas," when a given activity creates a temporary ritual space for the suspension of everyday social roles and stratification. On second lines, perhaps the most important aspect of deep play is Mihaly Csikszentmihalyi's sense of "flow" in the midst of creative physical activity—whether sports, dance, or music. It is this immersion into improvisatory action through multiple sensory exchange that produces "the special pleasure that comes from using one's body and senses to the fullest."[14]

African American dance is not simply about freestyling or doing whatever you want. There is always a space for improvisation, but it is within an aesthetic framework with emblematic, culture-bearing moves, steps, rules, and rhythmic attunement. As for me, how else would I dance except within an American social dance tradition invented mostly by African Americans, from the Charleston to the robot to krumping? There are no white American dance styles in Brooklyn where I grew up, except perhaps the square dancing I learned in summer camp or doing the hora at Jewish weddings. African American social dance is an oral tradition grounded in a set of aesthetics and kinesthetics that people outside the tradition often misinterpret in order to conform it to their own (often racist) aesthetic hierarchy of what constitutes beautiful or compelling physical movement.

Mobility and Modernity

A second line is a kaleidoscopic pattern of clothing, music, and dance—of color, movement, and Sunday struttin'. African American dancers work every limb, creating a shifting series of angles upon which the light plays. Though the main show between the ropes will always generate striking photographic images, the experience cannot be adequately captured by the camera. While the second-liners are an equivalent part of the show, they are rarely photographed: they are the embodiment of cultural democracy on the periphery, the sonic echo chamber of the first line's party-time second gear. They strut in rough, very loose parallel lines alongside the ropes and on the sidewalks, each person doing his or her thing, walking in time and walking *on time*, as musical time is created (and kept) by the brass band.

We all walk, step, wiggle, and slide down the streets and sidewalks. We're all struttin' with some barbecue, I often think, especially when the aroma of smoked meats from the truck grills hits at a designated stop. And yet the song by which we remember the phrase "struttin' with some barbecue" does not mean that at all. As written in 1927 by Lil Hardin Armstrong—pianist, composer, and Satchmo's second wife—"Struttin'" is one of the definitive recordings by Louis Armstrong's Hot Seven. At the time, *barbecue* meant a beautiful girlfriend in AAVE: the song projects the feeling of rolling down the street with your woman on your arm.[15]

Yet it remains an equally redolent phrase for all the stylin' on the second-line—and *stylin'* is an even older, nineteenth-century AAVE term. A polyvalent term, it referred to how African Americans "communicate meaning through gesture, dance, and other forms of bodily display," according to historians Shane White and Graham White in their superb study. Even today, to be *stylin'* means to encode the spirit of cultural and social evolution in one's public self presentation and kinesthetic movement. *Stylin'* does not refer simply to a sharp sartorial sense but to one's singular, hip, signature style of dress. One may dress for the spectacle but all the rest of the stylin' is done on the fly, in the streets, by and sometimes on the seat of your pants. Dancing in time to the brass band's polyrhythmic attack, second-liners "make the rhythms visible" (in Jacqui Malone's vivid phrase) in personalized movement displayed in and across a range of mundane, inconsequential, and often blighted spaces.[16]

Second-liners can make the ubiquitous rhythms visible on corners and vacant lots and porches. The music is in the space between the sprung legs of a dancer in mid-jump, for example. It is the sonic bellows of air pumped by a woman's right arm, hand on her hip—then out and back, out and back—in a kinesthetic quote of the funky chicken. To invoke two AAVE terms gathered by folklorists almost a century ago, in these spaces music remains akin to an invisible "rainbow wrapped around one's shoulders" for every dancer who is "eagle-rocking" on the fly.[17]

The music is a challenge to raise your spirit to its full volume, power, and flexibility. To engage and respond to all others on the line, reflecting the horns and drums in conversation. To challenge yourself to improvise physically in the groove while maintaining a calm center—what jazz musicians call "in the pocket"—as a model for flexibility of mind and emotional improvisation. If your mind could improvise as quickly as a tenor saxophonist, or as a second-line dancer, where is the advantage? It might translate to and facilitate better mental flexibility, expanded capacity, creative movement. You might become *groovy*, in the way that term once signified as a positive metaphor—to be in the groove, on track, relaxed and ready, buoyant in spirit, and fluid in thought. This was back before *groovy* became a joke, a pejorative term, a dead metaphor of a once hip cultural flux centered in postwar African American music and culture.[18]

A second line demands copresence; it demands your presence. A second line is a walking dance meditation, a dancing walk. Five hundred people—sometimes two hundred, sometimes a thousand—all doing that locomotion, baby. You have to go to a second line and second-line; you have to physically improvise and participate rather than spectate. The second line demands your personal, singular energy for its mix. Without participation, there is no understanding of the event. That is the cultural cover charge for this weekly free street spectacle.

We now turn Pableaux Johnson's camera to "the sideshow," as it is sometimes called, of the second line.[19] For comparison, consider the artistic project of going to a boxing match but keeping the camera on the audience for the entire bout. In analyzing each photo or pair of photos below, there is a single implicit question: What can we learn by focusing on the people in the spaces between the boundary ropes and the houses passing by, the ones supposedly on the periphery of the main event?

Figure 11.1. *Stayin' Alive: Woman over the Fence*. Photograph by Pableaux Johnson.

Stayin' Alive: Woman over the Fence

New Orleans is culturally thick but topographically flat. The music diffuses ahead onto the next block, around the corner, in between the shotgun houses, out towards the lake, and back towards the Riverbend. The music carries through the low-slung city since there are no tall buildings to trap the sound and lots of buckled pavements to bounce second-liners up into the groove. In short: the music carries, now as then.

She has been able to hear the second line coming from a mile away. The neighborhood has been roiling with movement for the past hour.

She watches it pass from inside her own gate, content to echo back the second line's energy with a relaxed, open smile. In the city's African American neighborhoods—Central City, Tremé, and Carrollton—the second line is both an event and an opportunity to catch up with friends, neighbors, former classmates, and relatives. Second-liners step out of line to hug observers and people shout greetings as they pass by. Looking at the parade over the fence, one sees a community performing its vitality as a multigenerational, multiethnic, multicultural citizenship of the streets, a tuba-powered mobile universe.

The legendary jazz saxophonist Lester Young grew up in Algiers on the West Bank in the 1910s and chased every flatbed truck carrying a band. "I just loved this music so well. . . . In New Orleans they got these trucks that advertise these shows. . . . I'd be running [after the bands] until my tongue was hanging out. Anything I was doing, they'd start playing some music and I'd run to catch it." He chased the trucks so industriously that a few bands made him a so-called handbill boy, since he already knew all the routes and "how they'd stop on certain corners."[20] As a youthful apprentice drummer in his father's carnival band, Young was already becoming a conduit for the acoustic musical revolution of jazz then electrifying the city—and soon to change the nation's, and then the world's, popular music—in the midst of the First World War.

The Man from Sudan

Roderick "Scubble" Davis of the Sudan SAPC sinks low to avoid an unmarked ditch, arms swinging low for balance, eyes down scanning the scarred ground, one knee tricked out, kicking it to the off-camera beat of the Hot 8 Brass Band, one of New Orleans's most acclaimed brass bands. Apart from the main action, no one watches him: this is self-expression for its own sake and pleasure, unmonitored grooving, dancing while no one is watching. He doesn't need to look at or follow the musicians; none of the dancers do. The music is on the air. The music is in the air. The music *is* the air. The air has become music.

Figure 11.2. *Sudan Man I.* Photograph by Pableaux Johnson.

Figure 11.3. *Sudan Man II*. Photograph by Pableaux Johnson.

Once on level ground, Scubble takes a wide crossover step. Looking up, he finds Pableaux Johnson's familiar camera trained on him: he smiles spontaneously and spreads his arms wide, crane-style, creating a colorful wingspan worthy of a tropical bird of paradise. The yellow and royal blue blocks of color ground the plaid sleeves that drape loosely on his deep brown skin. Striking a pose, his upper body remains relaxed while his lower body progresses in dynamic forward motion. Caught mid-step, he smiles broadly and lightly, unforced, a microcosm of the ritual: an existential affirmation of self, second line, sunshine, and Sunday afternoon, the secular Sabbath of New Orleans's working-class blacks.

Many of the line dancers at a given second line are members of one of the sixty-odd social aid and pleasure clubs. It's your club's week only once a year, and the second-line calendar marks the secular year—from Labor Day to mid-June—much like an academic calendar. Second-liners all know that the Sudan SAPC parades on the second Sunday of November, the Young Olympians the last Sunday in September, the Revolution the fourth Sunday in March, the Big Nine the second Sunday in December. So here, Roderick Davis of the Sudan SAPC simply gets down with his bad self, as James Brown once suggested, a directive to keep the organism psychologically healthy. The phrase is an unacknowledged bit of American biophilosophy in practice on the second line.

Cultural Transmission on the Streets

The kid in figure 11.4 can't be two years old, yet he already reaches out as if to attune himself to the kinesthetic of the rolling block party passing by. It's all in the stance and the photographer's timing. The camera catches the toddler's head cocked slightly, attentive to the passing brass band, denim shirt open as if for style. His feet planted, legs leaning slightly in, his left arm extended to hold the door, right hand poised behind for balance. He seems both planted and leaning over too far at the same time.

The second line's kaleidoscopic revelry is available to any toddler on the route, two layers removed from the first line. Below him, the choogling dancers rock the sidewalk as they tap on the fence; inside of this line of dancers, the marchers glide along the ropes and turn to dance with the club members; inside the ropes and behind the band, men tap out rhythms on cowbells and empty whiskey bottles. The first line is only twenty feet away, and next year, this boy may just walk down the steps and join the party. Children kick off many second lines, having learned the tradition by the age of seven or eight. Maybe in a few years this child will march with his father's, mother's, or uncle's club.

In figure 11.5, the seven-year-old yearns to slip under the ropes to show that he already knows how to second-line. In a blood-red T-shirt and camouflage pants, he already adds color, style, and participatory energy to the parade, there to second-line in mind, body, and spirit, if not yet dancing. He is neither an observer nor just some cute kid. He's in full apprenticeship to this vernacular tradition of music, dance, style, and kinesthetics.

His arms and shoulders hang straight yet slightly inflected to the music, head and left leg leaning in, fingers of his right hand captured in mid-snap. The camera catches him on the upbeat, mind-grooving between two passing members of the Single Men SAPC dressed in the year's sky blue and canary yellow suits, matching hats, and ribboned streamers. Adults around him shoot pictures on their smartphones; his sister seems bored. Second-lining is not for everyone. But this boy is a

Figure 11.4. *Cultural Transmission on the Streets I.* Photograph by Pableaux Johnson.

Figure 11.5. *Cultural Transmission on the Streets II.* Photograph by Pableaux Johnson.

slice of cultural transmission in process, attentive to the adult men sinking low to the ground as they pass him at arm's length, his ears cocked to the brass band driving everyone forward down the streets, down *his* streets.

In 2009, the eminent musicologist and American studies scholar Charlie Keil came to New Orleans and was awed when taken on a second line. Keil invented a certain subgenre of cultural analysis called "groove-ology" in the late 1960s, jumpstarting a theoretical revolution in the study of African American, ethnic, African, and popular musics. Musicology had been enslaved to a Western classical model of hierarchy that valued harmony, melody, and rhythm—in that order—as well as composed music over improvisation, solo lines over rhythmic complexity, classical music over world-music traditions, and mind over body. And then came Keil's groundbreaking work, *Urban Blues* (1966). As music critic Robert Christgau reflected, "It would be difficult to overstate how significant *Urban Blues* was for rock criticism and popular music studies, neither more than a gleam in a nerd's eye when he wrote it." In addition, Keil founded Musicians United for Superior Education, an organization that produced and implemented an elementary school curriculum geared towards teaching children to dance.[21]

A drummer and tuba player himself, Keil thrilled to the percussive ritual. He was incredulous marching alongside the tuba player over five miles as he pumped out a groove for four hours. "I didn't realize what an endurance contest it was! *I* was exhausted," he said. This is quite a compliment: Keil has an impressive record of fieldwork and ethnography with the Tiv in West Africa, with polka bands and blues musicians in Chicago, and with bouzouki musicians in Greece. What impressed him most was the intergenerational social range on the streets and the cultural transmission: "How do you have this here [in New Orleans]? In other places kids Twitter and techno-cocoon. . . . [H]ere you have mothers and grandmothers teaching their five year olds how to dance on the street to live music. I got weepy yesterday [watching them]. I'm gonna get weepy now."[22] The value of the second line ritual and its rarity in US culture impressed itself on Keil immediately.

How we in New Orleans have this unique experience is because, since the end of Jim Crow and until Katrina, New Orleans had been a dysfunctional, depressed, deindustrialized southern city, socially and economically segregated down to the ground. Until quite recently, neither middle-class whites nor many middle-class blacks cared about the crazy organic street-dancing parties of working-class black people, nor would they have considered second-lines culture, art, or community in any sense. New Orleans tourism has always capitalized on a fantasy version of jazz history and cosmopolitan partying, not majority-black street parties through the roughest neighborhoods of the city.

Even as Keil and second-line celebrants see cultural continuity, many others simply see the practice through the lens of social class or cultural elitism: an escapist ritual for impoverished people, a walk through dilapidated neighborhoods, wild, crazy dancing of an exotic nature, an idiosyncratic style easier to mock than understand or appreciate. Community music and dance traditions—as well as Keil's old-school humanistic beliefs in them—are now more often considered by academics to be utopian or nostalgic holdovers than African American strategies and technologies of survival and cultural transmission. Keil has always believed that these survival techniques constitute an important cultural heritage for the entire human race, as he discusses at length in the essays of *Music Grooves*.

Two months after Keil's visit, he sent around an email to a few New Orleans music scholars to consider starting a "second-line revolution." He wanted to create "some sort of missionary headquarters that would convert the entire world" through SAPCs, such that "all the world's neighborhoods currently in need of 2nd line capacity would get some! And quick." Here's what Keil thought could be changed by a second-line revolution: (1) a revival of the "knowledge of strut, bounce, prance, twist & shout, jivin & jukin, breaks," that is to say, a conscious knowledge of the kinesthetics of social dance in the global music revolutions of jazz, swing, rock-and-roll, funk, and hip-hop; (2) a way to convince "really curious kids" to learn dance and movement; and (3) an awareness of the social fact that "body knowledge [is] just not there any more" and might become desirable. As Keil once wrote with sad clarity, "Blacks create the new moves and grooves of every generation." He regretted the loss of awareness of this social and cultural fact.[23]

Still, African Americans in New Orleans keep passing down the moves and grooves of their vernacular pan-African American culture, confident of its cultural importance, significance, and existential affirmation, as well as of their aesthetic power and beauty. Parents pass this cultural tradition onto children through directed learning. I have seen second-lining seven-year-olds who have already integrated the fundamental moves of the African American vernacular while adding some significant moves of their own.

I imagine the musical repercussions of the second line as themselves interstitial, filling in cultural knowledge between disciplines and heritage, and sacralizing the streets as historical sites of public memory and resistance, art and aesthetics.

Elevate Your Consciousness

A second-line is a grounded and grounding ritual, yet the music produces an entrancing soundtrack for the mind as well. In a city with potholed streets and buckling sidewalks upended by century-old tree-root systems, second-liners are either looking ahead at the folks in front of them or looking down. Yet despite being happily buzzed in the flow of people and sound, everyone remains alert to the topography of asphalt and concrete.

Figure 11.6. *Elevate Your Consciousness I.* Photograph by Pableaux Johnson.

Figure 11.7. *Elevate Your Consciousness II.* Photograph by Pableaux Johnson.

It takes a bit of the spectacular to interrupt this collective choogling. This action comes from individual dance mavericks who constantly scan the landscape for adventurous platforms. You hear a slow whoop from the crowd and turn to see a topless young man shaking a low-lying billboard with a heavy-footed soft shoe over a dilapidated garage on St. Claude Avenue. Or in the midst of a stop-time trumpet solo, a joyous murmur snakes through the crowd until all eyes are turned to the top of a two-foot flight of concrete church steps on Tulane Avenue. On this small concrete stage, a half-dozen teenagers dance both for us and for themselves, signifyin' at the church door in favor of this unholy secular street parade dedicated to the pleasures of the feet and the streets. Or a sudden shout cuts through the music ("Ho!"), fingers point, and we all look directly into the sun where an iconic white man in a suit and a ZZ Top–level beard stands high in the sky on the fourth floor of a construction site. Known only—and oddly—as Bin Laden, this iconic dancer seems pierced by the April sun as he tightropes along the *I*-beams with the same dancing force and derring-do with which he pounds the streets, truck roofs, or trash cans.

On the second line, young urban explorers seek to transform any flat surface into a stage: billboards, flatbeds, church steps, cars, porches, and roofs. Once enacted, this commandeering of private or public space has two effects: (a) it affirms the relationship of the dynamic individual to the community as a figure of change; (b) there is a temporary raising of consciousness through a literal raising of the heads to a higher elevation.

In a play of horizontal dancing lines, the man in figure 11.6 moves laterally along the low roof-like overhang of the Circle Food Store as if guided by the ridged notch on the stucco of the larger building above his head. Arms out for balance, left foot lifted to jump for the next move, his hips centered and knees bent, he works his way laterally back against the second line, bringing crosscurrents to the crowd's forward movement. Visually and aesthetically, the lines of his body create an almost Egyptian play of gestures.

In the second image, against the sky, a shirtless man in camouflage shorts and high-tops boogies slowly up an incline to plant his spirit flag at the apex of a vintage brick house. He scales the roofline in time, dancing his way to the top. It is important to underscore again the flatness of the city's topography. A man we see him climbing up a roof, lifting our eyes and spirit, extending the breadth and hold of the second line to the high lines of the city. At the top, he will claim the peak with his own signature dance routine that will always include the traditional syncopated New Orleans dance steps. Focused on the area between the knees and heels, in patterns of two and three heel drops, with a hesitation skip on the offbeat, the street moves of black New Orleans bear a distant relation to the quick flurry of rhythmic leg movements of the Afro-Brazilian samba.

When even a single person claims a part of the built environment with his or her feet, it sends a rippling message down the line: now this commercial structure, too, is inside *our* thing today. Now this sacred structure belongs to the second line. Now even the sky is inside the second line. The ritual absorbs all it touches.

Gena Dagel Caponi's theory of black aesthetics is instructive here. In her important essay "The Case for an African American Aesthetic," the American studies scholar marked out six elements or principles by which we can read a distinctively African American event or performance through its exemplars, whether athletes, musicians, or dancers. She found these elements, listed below, present in live events from sports (basketball) to music (jazz, blues, hip-hop) to dance (tap, swing, hip-hop) to ritual. All six are present in and on the second line.

(1) rhythmic and metric complexity;
(2) individual improvisation and stylization;
(3) active engagement of the whole person and the whole
      community;
(4) dialogic interaction or call-and-response;
(5) social commentary or competition through indirection and
      satire; and
(6) development of a group consciousness or sensibility.[24]

The Cool Cat on the Street

Among African American tap dancers in the 1930s, to be known as a "cool cat" meant you were poised, balanced, and light on your feet; you were ready to improvise and never surprised by a new drum lick or a rival dancer's moves. The African American concept of "cool" derives from western and central African cultures, where there are thirty-five languages with variations on the concept. In western Africa, cool represented an ideal mode of inner (spiritual) composure expressed through a self-presentation that signals transcendent balance (literally, physically, and figuratively).[25]

Among black tap dancers of the 1930s, Fred Astaire was known as a cool cat. It is little known that Astaire created a revolution in how Hollywood filmed dancers. In the films of the 1930s, dancers' bodies were cut up by the camera to show different parts of the body—to show just

Figure 11.8. *The Cool Cat on the Street.* Photograph by Pableaux Johnson.

footwork or just the torso or just women's long legs or just an individual's facial expression. This was especially true in Busby Berkeley films, where dancers were simply arranged in interesting geometric patterns as at a halftime show. Astaire demanded that, in his films, all dance numbers were to be shot of the whole body flowing across the floor from the front. He won this battle due to his box-office clout, and for this reason, the films of Astaire and Rogers retain their ability to enchant us through the flowing aesthetic beauty of the human body.[26] The man in figure 11.8 sports a bit of Astaire's charm here as his entire dancing body fills the frame, harking back to Astaire's cinematic victory.

The cool cat dances with his whole being. It is not a matter (simply) of footwork or flashy it is about individually integration controlled from a drum control by an inner governor. It is about using motor memory for intricate movements, creating new combinations in the moment, and stylin' on the fly. From small, precise gestures, a resonant persona emerges up from the ground. To catch this holistic set of techniques, the camera must capture a person's whole body in relationship to the ground itself (as Pableaux Johnson has here)—not just undulating torso or artful arms, not just head and shoulders or hips and legs.

Set against the forward stroll of second-liners, he turns to honor the music with a sweet crossover step. There is the sly confidence in his quasi-feminine curtsy pull below the hips of his shorts, his left hand behind for balance. And dig the stylin' of his innovative street tux: a black beret, a short-sleeve shirt, and midi shorts; a grey bowtie and white vest; black and white argyle socks extended into black and white sneakers. A signature style, rendered. He gives his elegance and nuance to the street in style, movement, and creative individuality, a subtle dance of uplift from a cool cat.

A dancer's cool is the outward sign of an inner grace—and, as Africanist art historian Robert Farris Thompson has long theorized, cool is the master trope of African America. Thompson drew on his own ethnographic fieldwork in dance and language across central and western Africa to theorize "the aesthetic of the cool" in 1966. Cool manifested in dancers who always kept a calm center and facial expression in the midst of fast, precise, athletic motion—"facial serenity," Thompson called it—and this gesture received the greatest shouts of praise and encouragement. Such successful dancing has always sent—and still sends—an aspirational message written in dance to the far-flung communities of the African diaspora: This is how we do it, baby. Now it's your turn.

In the Seams of the Groove: A Coda

What is the second line about? It's about rhythmic connectivity within and without, connections made at the speed of sound. It's about the social function of music for stayin' alive—mentally, physically, spiritually, psychologically, organically. You carry your enlightened self away from the streets with enough spirit to last until the secular church is called into mobile order by the tuba again next Sunday.

Why is the second line important? I submit the following to cultural studies, American studies, and dance scholars: the second line is the most significant ongoing weekly ritual in American culture. Rugged individualism was an American myth: creative individuality on the street remains a living tradition in New Orleans.

The call: listen to find your own sweet spot in the polyrhythmic mix.

The response: add your moves to the rolling second-line beat, doing your patriotic part in expressive cultural form, voting with your feet in this weekly citizenship of the streets. The crowd supports and liberates individuals for rhythmic attunement to the beats of the street but it also demands your energy for others. If there is a bill of rights, there is also a bill of obligations. In short: get down with your bad self because your good self will be healthier for it—as will the entire community.

This is your mind on a second line: two metaphors.

(1) In the human brain, with all its seeming rivers, streams, and grey matter, consider the effect of escalating brassy riffs against underlying snare- and bass-drum rhythms pushing neurons around to dance with other neurons such that we stay physiologically vital and spiritually present. In each individual brain, neurological connections recommit to each other, rejuvenating an inner drive to live another week. That's my long-winded translation of the phrase "raising the spirit."

(2) Conjure up that iconic image of the earth hanging in space, our blue planet against black interstellar infinity. Now reimagine it as a disco ball refracting music instead of light. That's what a second line is like on a Sunday afternoon on the streets of New Orleans, where everyone trips the light fantastic in his or her own way, catching a ray of light in the color spectrum from this disco maypole and swinging into the future one city block at a time.

NOTES

1. Nick Spitzer, interview by author, September 10, 2007.

2. This concept deserves further theorization. See Don Adams and Arlene Goldbard, "Cultural Democracy: Introduction to an Idea" (1995), last modified 1998, http://www.wwcd.org/cd2.html.

3. Joel Dinerstein, "Second-Lining Post-Katrina: Learning Community from the Prince of Wales Social Aid & Pleasure Club," *American Quarterly* 61, no. 3 (2009), 615–37. Reprinted in Clyde Woods and Kalamu ya Salaam, *In the Wake of Hurricane Katrina: New Paradigms and Social Visions* (Baltimore: Johns Hopkins University Press, 2010), 189–211.

4. See Thadious M. Davis, *Southscapes: Geographies of Race, Region, and Literature* (Chapel Hill: University of North Carolina Press, 2011).

5. Thomas Turino, *Music as Social Life: The Politics of Participation* (Chicago: University of Chicago Press, 2008), 26–38.

6. Louis Armstrong, *Louis Armstrong in His Own Words: Selected Writings*, ed. Thomas Brothers (Oxford: Oxford University Press, 1999), 17.

7. Louis Armstrong, *Satchmo: My Life in New Orleans* (New York: Prentice Hall, 1954; repr. with intro. by Dan Morgenstern, Cambridge, MA: Da Capo Press, 1986), 225.

8. Sidney Bechet, *Treat It Gentle: An Autobiography* (New York: Twayne, 1978; repr. with intro. by Hugh Hlawka, Cambridge, MA: Da Capo Press), 61.

9. Ibid., 62.

10. Ibid.

11. For more on these topics, see Jacqui Malone, *Steppin' on the Blues: The Visible Rhythms of African American Dance* (Urbana: University of Illinois Press, 1996); Katrina Hazzard-Gordon, *Jookin': The Rise of Social Dance Formations in African American*

Culture (Philadelphia: Temple University Press, 1992); and Thomas F. Defrantz, *Dancing Many Drums: Excavations in African American Dance* (Madison: University of Wisconsin Press, 2001).

12. See Brenda Dixon Gottschild, *The Black Dancing Body: A Geography from Coon to Cool* (New York: Palgrave Macmillan, 2005).

13. Jo Jones, quoted in Nat Shapiro and Nat Hentoff, *The Story of Jazz as Told by the Men Who Made It: Hear Me Talkin' To Ya* (New York: Rinehart, 1955; repr. New York: Dover, 1966), 294.

14. I use "deep play" more in the vein of Diane Ackerman and Albert Murray by way of Johann Huizinga than of Clifford Geertz. See Diane Ackerman, *Deep Play* (New York: Vintage, 2011), esp. 1–27. But see Johann Huizinga, *Homo Ludens: A Study of the Play-Element in Culture* (London: Routledge, 1949); Emile Durkheim, *Elementary Forms of the Religious Life* (1912; trans. Karen E. Fields, New York: Free Press, 1995); Victor Turner, *The Ritual Process: Structure and Anti-Structure* (1969; New York: Aldine Transaction, 1995); and Mihaly Csikszentmihalyi, *Flow: The Psychology of Optimal Experience* (New York: Harper Perennial Modern Classics, 2008).

15. Louis Armstrong, "Struttin' With Some Barbecue," *Portrait of the Artist as a Young Man: 1923–1934* (Columbia, C4K-85670, CD, 1995). In the quasi-official guide to interwar African American Vernacular English, *Cab Calloway's Hepster Dictionary*, *barbecue* is defined as "the girlfriend, a beauty." See Open Culture, http://www.openculture.com/2015/01/cab-calloways-hepster-dictionary.html, accessed December 23, 2016.

16. See Shane White and Graham White, *Stylin': African American Expressive Culture from Its Beginnings to the Zoot Suit* (Ithaca: Cornell University Press, 1998); and Malone, *Steppin' on the Blues*.

17. See Arna Bontemps and Langston Hughes, eds., *The Book of Negro Folklore* (New York: Dodd, Mead, 1958).

18. Like *groovy*, many emblematic words and concepts of African American culture are adapted, appropriated, and then discarded by bohemian and youth cultures. African American terms such as *cool*, *hip*, *beat*, *deep*, and *heavy* become exhausted through appropriation and replaced.

19. Matt Sakakeeny, *Roll with It: Brass Bands on the Streets of New Orleans* (Durham: Duke University Press, 2013), xi.

20. "Lester Young: Interview with Francois Postif," February 6, 1959, in *The Lester Young Reader*, ed. Lewis Porter (Washington, DC: Smithsonian, 1992).

21. Robert Christgau, "Charles Keil: Up from Darien," *Village Voice*, 1998, http://www.robertchristgau.com/xg/bkrev/keil-96.php, accessed December 23, 2016. See Charles Keil, *Urban Blues* (Chicago: University of Chicago Press, 1966).

22. Charles Keil, email exchanges with the author, 2009.

23. Keil, emails to the author, 2009; Charles Keil and Steven Feld, *Music Grooves: Essays and Dialogues* (Chicago: University of Chicago Press, 1994).

24. Gena Dagel Caponi, "The Case for an African American Aesthetic," *Signifyin(g), Sanctifyin', and Slam-Dunking: A Reader in African American Expressive Culture* (Amherst: University of Massachusetts Press, 1999), 10.

25. Robert Farris Thompson, *Aesthetic of the Cool: Afro-Atlantic Art and Music* (Pittsburgh: Periscope, 2011).

26. "Cool Cat," Marshall Winslow and Jean Stearns, *Jazz Dance: The Story of American Vernacular Dance* (New York: Da Capo Press, 1968), 220. See Joel Dinerstein, *Swinging the Machine: Modernity, Technology, and African American Culture between the World Wars* (Amherst: University of Massachusetts Press, 2003), 237–46.

INTERSPACE SIX ❧ *"Authenticity," Simulacra, and Apocalypse*

Our contributors' shared concern with what entangled forms of historical and cultural awareness may be revealed or contested in depictions of in-between spaces in New Orleans carries over in a different register to the two final essays. Concerned with exploring general dimensions of what he calls "airportness" at Louis Armstrong New Orleans International Airport, currently slated for demolition, literary critic Christopher Schaberg runs smack dab into the old airport's fascinating simulacrum of the city it serves. At once generic and local, authentic and ersatz, the airport slips between categories in ways that plans for a new "seamless" airport experience seek to erase. For philosopher John P. Clark, our concluding essayist, New Orleans has always been, and until its final moments defiantly will be, the enemy of fixed categories. A twelfth-generation New Orleanian, Clark imagines the entire city as irrepressibly "interstitial"—situated between physical, political, and cultural structures against which its in-betweenness continually pushes. In Clark's understanding of apocalypse, interstitial pressures may well result in the "antistitial," giving rise to a terrible, transformative, but potentially liberating breakdown of all confining structures.

CHAPTER TWELVE
Airportness in New Orleans

—Christopher Schaberg

At Loyola University New Orleans, when the weather is nice, I often teach my classes outside. Invariably, they are interrupted by a roar in the sky: usually a Boeing 737 or Airbus 320 on descent into our local airport. We pause, glancing up, knowing that the plane is bringing economy-fueling tourists to town or local travelers homebound. There is something about the city that lends itself to a travel mentality. And coincidentally, the Danna Student Center, the student union on Loyola's campus, vaguely resembles an airport. This architectural quirk occurred because in the 1960s the building was originally planned for a new site in the expanding suburbs west of town, near the airport. When that arrangement fell through, the university administration apparently stuck with the same building design, but just placed it on the original campus. And so, out of sync with the surrounding neo-Gothic brick buildings, but at home with the airliners on final approach above, the student union emanates a strange aura of *airportness*, the ambient vibe of air travel. Airportness is evident in floor-to-ceiling windows, lounge chairs that call to mind layovers rather than study sessions, and bustling cacophonous concourses that seem better suited to roller bags than sorority bake sales. There's even a pedestrian bridge on the top floor, traversing the space as if in an efficient maneuver—though without last minute boarding calls, the transit space seems eerily quiet and unnecessary.

All this airportness exists on a century-old university campus in the uptown neighborhood of New Orleans. Meanwhile, the city's actual airport lies just upriver, eleven miles west of downtown. The call sign for the Louis Armstrong airport, KMSY or just MSY, refers to an earlier name for the airport: the Moisant Stock Yards. The airport was originally

Figure 12.1. Statue of Louis Armstrong in the
Louis Armstrong New Orleans International
Airport. "A New Orleans Mardi Gras: Statue of
Louis Armstrong," Lauren Loves Good Food,
February 24, 2012, accessed December 26, 2016.

named after John Moisant, a legendary daredevil aviator who crashed
and died in 1910 on the agricultural site upon which the New Orleans
airport would later be built. Given that flying as a human pursuit seems
prone to superstition and overabundances of caution, I am always struck
by how a fatal crash lurks behind the airport's simple, pragmatic call
sign, evoked countless times each day as aircraft depart and arrive.

In 2001 the site was renamed Louis Armstrong New Orleans International Airport, on the one-hundred-year anniversary of the musician's
birth. Travelers today are greeted in the main terminal by an oversized,
cartoonish statue of Armstrong—a garish idol betraying the fraught
relationship between the airport and its heritages, be they a crashed aviator or a local musician whose legacy seems stitched to the transit hub
in order to capitalize on a certain caricature of jazz, entertainment, and
hedonistic pleasure. And interestingly, the statue is in fact advertising
a tertiary tourist site, Blaine Kern's Mardi Gras World. It is Louis Armstrong's airport—as long as the name lends currency.

Toward the very beginning of Spike Lee's four-hour documentary
about Hurricane Katrina, *When the Levees Broke: A Requiem in Four Acts*

(2006), the film introduces viewers to Phyllis Montana Leblanc, whose story of survival becomes a through-line for Lee's cinematic dirge. It is at first unclear where this interview is taking place; it vaguely resembles a church or a cathedral of some sort. But New Orleans residents will recognize the grand, illuminated room behind Leblanc as none other than the arching main terminal of Louis Armstrong International. For New Orleanians during and after the storm, the airport became both a point of escape and a point of refuge. But it is also haunted by its history as a refugee camp: the supposed-to-be transit zone that became entangled with the bare lives of thousands of evacuees after the flood.

This isn't the only time that the airportness of Louis Armstrong International has been used for cinematic effect—even when it is not about New Orleans. The 2012 film *Killing Them Softly*, starring Brad Pitt and directed by Andrew Dominik, was shot in New Orleans and used MSY's baggage claim area to introduce us to the late James Gandolfini's downward-spiraling hit man character, Mickey. *Killing Them Softly* is a movie about how the economic downturn of 2008 seeps into organized crime and the business of killing, with grisly results. In this brief scene at the New Orleans airport, the fate of Mickey is crystalized: once a sought-after killer, now he has been flown to town in coach class, on the cheap; he drags an absurdly off-scale roller bag through the baggage claim; no one is there to greet him. His sad shuffle says it all: he's pathetic, a mere tool of his own doomed destiny. For nearly a decade, audiences grew used to James Gandolfini in the guise of Tony Soprano, acting as the centerless center of a vortex of violence and power beyond the law. In *Killing Them Softly*, it is not so: Mickey is barely coherent, and because he can't do his job adequately, he is phased out of the narrative without even an on-screen departure. In the introductory scene when we meet him at the airport, the shabby luggage carousels, worn-out blue columns, existential fluorescent lighting, and low ceilings prefigure Gandolfini's own nondramatic demise in the film. MSY's dingy baggage claim area reeks of airportness, with all its worst connotations.

Shortly after *Killing Them Softly* was filmed, Louis Armstrong International actually received a facelift in anticipation of the 2013 Superbowl championship football game. By early 2013, it appeared as though the airport had entered a new era: soft burgundies, leathery yellows, and dull oranges festooned the terminal across grids of curvaceous lounge chairs and wrapped columns, a tradition drawn in dim of a Christo and Jeanne-Claude installation. The airport looked good again, if slightly old-fashioned. Indeed, strangely, the style of the airport renovation resembled an older period, closer to the era of the popular television show *Mad Men* than to our own digital age (which, paradoxically, *is* the

era of *Mad Men*, too). The redesign included tasteful commercial art
such as colorful, wavy panels suspended from the main terminal ceiling; when my toddler Julien looked up and saw these for the first time,
he exclaimed, "Pillows!" Airiness at the airport is always a sure sign of
airportness at work.

The renovation deployed highly detailed touches, such as strategi-
cally placed cypress bark strips in the handrails of the pedestrian bridge
that stretches from the parking structure to the main terminal—as if to
say, Don't forget: you're in the bayou. My son loves to walk across these
pedestrian bridges: those tenuous elevated connectors that take travelers from the dim and dank parking structure to the brightly lit space
of the terminal. Occasionally we go to the airport just to pass the time.
Airports, as the environmental psychologist Robert Sommer notes in
his book *Tight Spaces: Hard Architecture and How to Humanize It*, are
places that lend themselves in surprising ways to spontaneous child play:
in spite of the airport's rigid layout, "the exploratory urges of the child
propel him to the only flexible, movable, manipulable objects available."[1]
For some time, MSY seemed to consciously accommodate this impulse
by passing out complimentary balsa-wood gliders and palm-twist heli-
copters for child play. The airport became a miniature of itself, a vast
aerodrome for myriad hand-propelled journeys, as children discovered
the miracle of flight.

One particular time Julien and I were at the airport to pick up my
parents, who were flying into town for a visit. We'd arrived at the airport
a good hour early to explore, before their plane was to land. We walked
around the baggage carousels and went up and down a few escalators
and elevators. We spotted a shiny "Welcome Home!" helium balloon
that had escaped someone's grip and had floated to the top of the main
terminal. Julien would talk about that balloon for weeks, wondering how
it would ever get down, eyes brimming with tears.

Julien had ice cream on his mind, and so we went on a mission in
the main terminal area, searching for a cold treat. But we were informed
that the only ice cream in the airport was past security and far down into
the nether regions of B Concourse, where the Southwest Airlines flights
come in. Not only were we removed by physical distance, then—we were
also prohibited by the airport's own post–September 11 protocols, a sad
closing of the commons. We ended up at a beignet shop nearby, and
Julien was successfully distracted by the allure of fritters smothered with
powdered sugar.

While we were waiting for the beignet dough to puff and float in
the fry oil, a Delta captain strutted up and ordered a dozen. I started
chatting with him and learned that he piloted an MD-80. I inquired if

he was perhaps taking the beignets to his crew. Sure enough, they were in the middle of their day, and he said the beignets would help the flight attendants "power through" the final legs of their trip. I have nothing against the decadent tradition of beignets in New Orleans, but I couldn't help but to "think critically"—as we are trained to say in American universities—about this scenario. A pile of deep-fried pouches of dough doused in sugar in the middle of the day: this does not exactly conjure a corollary image of tight aisle maneuvers, lithe cabin movements, and hefting carry-on luggage. Rather, these treats suggest a long afternoon of lethargy, nausea, and maybe even a nap.

Nevertheless, the Delta pilot strolled off with his darkening bag of beignets, and I can only imagine that they were consumed with delight and gratitude, if also felt in aftershocks of roiled bellies upon takeoff. But I couldn't blame the flight attendants or the Delta captain. For how many of us have succumbed to McDonald's or the like while negotiating the constraints and distortions of airport space-time?

The beignets at the New Orleans airport function as a naturalizing part of air travel. The presence of these foodstuffs serves to some degree to transport people somewhere else outside the end-to-end flow of a plane trip, to ground travelers (and workers) in the place they are traveling through or to. Part of airportness is the steady—if tenuous—connection to the outside world, where things are recognizable, be they destination items or blandly generic fare. At most large airports in the United States, travelers can expect to be able to sit down at a chain restaurant during a standard hour-long layover and enjoy a gigantic beer or soda and some form of familiar fried food—and thereby feel something like what they would spending an evening at the local sports bar or mall food court. The beignets at the New Orleans airport are similar and different: they entice passengers and airline employees with a taste of the city without ever having to head to the French Quarter—in many cases, these treats likely serve those poor souls nursing a hangover on their way back home. Never mind that everyone knows the only "real" New Orleans beignets are supposed to come from Café Du Monde. The beignets confirm presence and location, conferring on the airport the authenticity of their city and, as they are eaten, the stable being of the traveler. You have arrived somewhere, somewhere *really* real. At the same time, the Coke machine and other mainstream items in the cooler do the work of reassuring passengers that they are back in the airport, back in the generically familiar—gratingly or calmingly so.

The beignets also dabble with what Jean Baudrillard once termed the "hyper-real": this is a feature of postmodernity that unsettles easy relations between real and unreal, simulacrum and original.[2] These airport

Figure 12.2. The Mississippi River and the New Orleans airport. Photograph courtesy of the Louis Armstrong New Orleans International Airport.

beignets do not just lead to a simple or pure gustatory experience; they also function as exaggerated forms of an already mass-produced thing, echoing and reinforcing an *idea* of beignets. Beignets in New Orleans cannot help but be somewhat fake—a kind of tourist trifle or come-on—and yet the beignets in the airport play a strange trick, confirming the as-if reality of those outside, beyond. In Louis Armstrong International everyone knows that they are eating "beignets" in postmodern scare quotes, wink, wink. But moreover, in a perverse turn, the beignets, like Disneyland for Baudrillard, turn out—exactly by being obvious simulacra—to prop up all the normal, unquestionable operations of everyday air travel. The costume of the Delta pilot, the security line rituals, the beeping metal detectors, and the sanctioned "layers of shouting" (as the ecotheorist Timothy Morton once described the security checkpoint to me)—all of these matters pass under the radar of the real, while beignets bubble and spurt in their fry-oil baths. It should come as no surprise, of course, that the postmodern airport serves as an apt site in which to see postmodernity on full display. Airportness in the New Orleans airport is like the city it serves: precisely and deliciously ambiguously a pastiche of real and fake, dressed up and totally stripped down. The architect Le Corbusier would have loved MSY for its "naked," bare-minimum aspects.[3]

But the New Orleans airport isn't just a multiply layered, hyper-real place. It has important ties to its region and to its surrounding and encompassing ecosystem. Looking out the window on descent into New Orleans, you cannot miss how the city exists as a sort of "minor outlying island" (as my colleague John Clark likes to call it), floating on the frayed and eroding edge of a continent. The runways of Louis Armstrong airport are only four feet above sea level, making it the second lowest lying airfield in the world, just a little higher than Amsterdam Airport Schiphol.

In the spring of 2013, travel writer Harriet Baskas asked me to take some pictures of souvenirs at the Louis Armstrong airport—she writes a weekly blog post called Souvenir Sunday and wanted to feature the New Orleans airport that particular week. Of course I was glad for an excuse to head out to the airport and wander around for a few hours. Up to that point I had mostly ignored the souvenirs at the airport, but I was curious to go with this explicit mission in mind.

At the airport I meandered around, looking for interesting things to frame, capture, and caption. What can possibly count at an airport that itself presents as a sort of humongous souvenir, a totem of its nearby place? At first I was stumped. Despite my self-assurance that there was good New Orleans–themed stuff at the airport, nothing jumped out at me—or at least, not beyond the beignets and the oyster restaurant, which didn't seem to count as souvenirs—not exactly. I drifted into a generic-looking airport newsstand–cum–convenience store, called Westwin News. There, amid the standard travel items available at any airport, I discovered shelves upon shelves of New Orleans foodstuffs and baubles: Shrimp, Crawfish, and Crab Boil in a box, Creole Étouffée Mix, Zapp's Spicy Cajun Crawtators potato chips, Pat O'Brien's Hurricane Cocktail Mix: just add rum and have fun!

It was a veritable cornucopia of instant New Orleans cuisine and other treats. I held a Jelly Belly Pet Gator gummi candy that stretched across my palm and over my forearm. Looking around, a theme started to emerge. There were actual taxidermy alligator claw backscratchers and taxidermy baby alligator heads full of razor sharp teeth. Like the cypress bark strips, these things made reference to the surrounding ecosystem: wetlands encompass our city and alligators abound. Sometimes when I'm fly-fishing in the Mississippi River just a few blocks from our home, alligators appear in the shallows. One recently popped its head up just about ten yards away from me. But this was out in "nature"—not in the technoculture of the airport. Or, do these alligators at the airport suggest a deconstruction of the very inside/outside dichotomy operating here, to expose deep culture as just plain nature, no more and no less?

Airportness often exploits the blurry borders *between* human and other, inside and outside, air and ground.

Back to the alligators: what are these creatures doing at the airport? Are they conferring a real place on this nonspace or merely adding another dimension of ironic distance, via a rather vulgar aesthetics? We know these are just gimmicks, gewgaws to take home, so we can then say, "Look, kids, I was in Louisiana, where wild alligators frolic! Careful, or it'll bite!" But there must be a threshold here—I can't imagine that the alligator claw backscratchers are really going to make it through the security checkpoint. For that matter, what about the Mardi Gras masks for sale in the gift shop? In an airport, where so much depends upon a real photo ID, are masks actually allowed? Louis Armstrong airport is thus in tension with itself; even as it proceeds smoothly, transporting tourists in and out, it also contains strange objects that obscure its status as a strictly functional site of transit. To rephrase Nietzsche, airportness loves a mask.

At this point I was drawing attention from the employees at the Westwin News. Though I tried to act nonchalant as I snapped pictures, eventually I was approached by a large man in a black track suit with a stern look on his face; he appeared to be a plainclothes police officer, or worse. It turned out that he was just the manager of the Westwin chain, and he was eager to learn what I was doing—quite thrilled that a travel blog would be featuring their items for Souvenir Sunday. He showed me object after object that I might be interested in photographing, proudly explaining the real Cajun meanings and sources of his products. Thus the experience was turned on its head yet again: the space of consumer items and New Orleans kitsch turned out to be rooted in a Cajun family business's authentic ties to and appreciation for the Tabasco sauce, the voodoo dolls, the jambalaya hobby kit in a box, and more.

One of the things I often hear from people about the New Orleans airport is how great it is: how the lines are rarely ever long and how even the Transportation Security Administration agents are friendly and laid back, ready to greet you with the vernacular "yeah, you right." The airport has *character*—even as it tarries with the necessarily generic functions and semiotics that accompany contemporary air travel anywhere. It has airportness, with a twist. There seems truly something authentic about the New Orleans airport, even as it comes somewhat masked in the form of nine-dollar pints of Abita Amber hawked in the center bar of D Concourse in flimsy plastic cups, or overpriced but nonetheless delicious oyster po'boys from the new old Dooky Chase in the main terminal.

But then, like James Gandolfini before it, this airport's days are numbered. In the spring of 2013, the New Orleans Aviation Board unveiled

Figure 12.3. Interior view of the lobby of the airport, formerly Moisant Field, which began commercial operation in May 1946. Photograph courtesy of the Louis Armstrong New Orleans International Airport.

plans for a complete redevelopment of Louis Armstrong International, which would see most of the old concourses demolished. In its stead, the aviation board has proposed to construct a brand new airport across the runways, closer to the main highway, Interstate 10, which leads into New Orleans. In the words of one report, the project would "thrust" the New Orleans airport "into the modern era—a reimagining of the sleepy, mid-century airstrip" for the city's three hundredth anniversary in 2018. The goal, of course, is to make it a "world class" airport—or something like what John Kasarda and Greg Lindsay have famously termed an "aerotropolis": an airport-qua-multiplex city center, designed from the ground up to facilitate vast and digitally enabled networks of logistics, transport, commuters, and mobility flows—networks that are pitched as becoming constant for an immediate present, a notion of progress at its peak that is simultaneously projected forward into a bizarrely static-while-booming future.[4] This vision of New Orleans imagines concentric circles of productivity and corresponding economic chains leading into and out of the airport. Taken to the extreme, this kind of airport would displace downtown New Orleans as the city's center and move everything, for all intents and purposes, eleven miles away. The city would become just one of many minor destinations radiating from the airport's newly central place in the region. More realistically, the new Louis Armstrong airport will ostensibly use its space more efficiently, effectively shrinking the airport's footprint while increasing passenger volume; and it will integrate the airport into the city's cultural life more fluidly, both in terms of actual traffic flows and in terms of the art that will be brought in to adorn it.

What will the new airport be like? What will it feel like? Judging by the architectural concept renderings made public in late 2013, the new building will have predictably vaulted ceilings and an ambience of murmuring hushes—that muted din of progress that new airports manage to facilitate at all times, no matter if it is during peak travel hours or in the dead of night, with only a stranded slumbering traveler contorted on a seat here and there. The new airport will feature "a consolidated security checkpoint, concession stands placed closer to gates and an automated baggage screening system"—all to make more seamless the increasingly "natural" stages of commercial flight. There will be more natural light throughout, as opposed to the low-ceiling caverns that currently vex certain corridors in the existing structure. And green space: there will be trees, geometric wedges of grassy bogues. Plus, there will be jazz: musicians will be allowed (invited, or spontaneously?) to play in the terminal, entertaining and perhaps making money, thereby conceivably extending the vibe of the French Quarter into the alien realm of airspace. Instead of Eames Tandems or Eames Tandem knock-offs, we see cream-colored sofa chairs in the plans—seats with no armrests to foil sleepy travelers. From the pictures, it is a utopia of air travel, an upbeat and uplifted zone where travel seems to happen effortlessly, on-time, and in a way that makes the travelers seem to *want* to be there.

This is the wish image, anyway. And the developers, architects, planners, and builders might just pull it off. Still, I hope that the airport doesn't become *too* seamless. Even if it does become the perfect airport—what will this airport feel like to actually travel through, and how long will the feeling last? Amid the futuristic drawings and plans for swift transit, I find myself wanting to pursue and celebrate the *freeplay* that airports

Figure 12.4. Architectural rendering of the new airport, to be completed in 2018. Photograph courtesy of the Louis Armstrong New Orleans International Airport.

necessarily allow for, and without which they would not even be recognizable as structures of transport. We can think about this in terms of the geographic play of distances, locations, and destinations, or the broader wiggle room of weather patterns, air currents, and temperature—but I want to remain in the airport, on the human level, if just for now.

What would the Louis Armstrong airport be without occasionally empty abandoned gate areas for my son to run through? Or what if the security lines worked in such a way that they didn't suggest labyrinthine puzzles, maddening yet open to toddler transgressions? Or if there were no more weird rooms with old parts, doors left open for passengers to glimpse the airport's outmoding in action? Or what if communication technologies were so perfectly synced with the present that we would never have overlapping remainders of embarrassing prior modes of connecting, coping pay telephone stalls and outmoded early Internet communication ports? I'm heartened in MSY when I see something like a solitary seat uncoupled from its base and nestled in some obscure corner of the concourse.

In his seminal study *Non-places*, the anthropologist Marc Augé writes, "We have to relearn to think about space."[5] My continuing fasci-

Figure 12.5. The iconic façade of the Louis Armstrong New Orleans International Airport, partly obscured by renovations from the early twenty-first century. Photograph courtesy of the Louis Armstrong New Orleans International Airport.

nation with airports involves constantly relearning to think about these spaces—always paying attention anew to both how they work and when they get weird. I have found this to be especially worthwhile when thinking about Louis Armstrong International.

This all may sound very naïve, and I suppose in a way it is. But as much as I appreciate the efficiencies, marvels, and commonplaces of modern air travel, I am equally drawn to the moments and sites where things are a little off, misused or rubbed against the grain. J. G. Ballard picked up on this potential in his grotesque menagerie of a novel *Crash* (1973), with the London airport hovering over every conjunction of twisted metal and torn flesh. At Louis Armstrong International, the effect is more muted; you have to be ready to slow down and see the out-of-place as not only a symptom of New Orleans, but also maybe as a kind of subtle commentary on human flight in general. And New Orleans is good for slowing down and re-viewing things. What you will see at MSY are airport glitches on a more mundane level than in *Crash*, and in less spectacular form. These are the things that make an airport unique; Louis Armstrong International emerges from its oddities.

I like airports because they require awkward lingering, even as they also seem poised to squelch it at every turn. I like airports because they offer unique vantage points on our contemporary movements and transitions. Airports intrigue me because they *are* interstitial spaces, before or beyond any metaphor. They are perhaps best thought of as literal human ecotones or transition zones—and there's something striking about them for what they reveal about expected behaviors and normative patterns of perception and inhabitance as we travel from here to there. We think of rivers as obviously natural zones—flux, erosion, irrigation, drainage—but airports function similarly. They are sites of flow and impact. They facilitate any number of migration routes, and they, too, register and remark the passing of time.

I know that old airports must die and be replaced by newer and better super-modern sites—sites that will inevitably shorten our waiting times, speed up the time to the baggage claim, and hurry us to our flights with unprecedented ease. But let's not be too quick to kill off our old airports in the rush. An airport may be an aging non-place, but it is still also a place of its own, rooted in the ground and rife with possibilities for inquiry, wonder, slippage, and play. Louis Armstrong International embodies such qualities perfectly; you just have to look at it a little sideways to see them.

The morning that I finish this chapter, I am standing in the Mississippi River, several miles downstream from the airport, not far from where I teach my classes. I'm casting a streamer fly to finicky needlefish feeding where the current slows after this particular bend. Pink-bottomed, heavy clouds are exploding in slow motion on the horizon. Driftwood slats pile up, a mixture of pieces milled by devices human and nonhuman. Translucent grass shrimp tickle my toes but slide away as I pull my foot up to catch a glimpse of them. Concrete slabs jut up out of the mud. I hear the bell striking the hour in the church steeple on Loyola's campus, echoing across Audubon Park. A covered barge, contents unknown, is pushed upstream toward the airport, where baggage handlers sort and stack suitcases. In the control tower, a flight is cleared to land; I see the Airbus 319 banking above me, flaps being adjusted and landing gear emerging. It is another day, another mundane cycle at the airport. Beignets sputter in their fry oil some place between real and hyper-real, and Transportation Security Administration agents adjust the magnetometer for maximized metal detection. Frozen in time, Louis Armstrong blows his comical trumpet in the main terminal. Meanwhile, in a large shallow drawer, somewhere between here and there, plans await that will wipe away this place and promise smoother experiences for the traveler, for the worker. The old MSY will lie like so much rubble on the riverbank, as the muddy Mississippi insistently washes by. I've tried here to capture in miniature this passing airport, and its own qualities of airportness, musing on its capacity to slip between the generic and the unique, the thickly real and the ersatz. Standing in this space, watching as the powerful currents slide everything along, we can imagine Louis Armstrong International as another feature of the river and of the earth that is special in space and yet at the same time one of many, a fragile mile marker on a journey longer than we can ever know.

NOTES

1. Robert Sommer, *Tight Spaces: Hard Architecture and How to Humanize It* (Englewood Cliffs: Prentice Hall, 1974), 74.

2. See Jean Baudrillard, *Simulacra and Simulation* (Ann Arbor: University of Michigan Press, 1994).

3. See Alastair Gordon, *Naked Airport: A Cultural History of the World's Most Revolutionary Structure* (New York: Metropolitan Books, 2004).

4. John D. Kasarda and Greg Lindsay, *Aerotropolis: The Way We'll Live Next* (New York: Farrar, Straus and Giroux: 2011).

5. Marc Augé, *Non-places: Introduction to an Anthropology of Supermodernity* (New York: Verso Books, 1995), 36.

CHAPTER THIRTEEN
Carnival at the Edge of the Abyss
New Orleans and the Apocalyptic Imagination

—John P. Clark

The Mysterious Crescent

New Orleans is known as the Crescent City. According to conventional wisdom, the name refers to its position within a curve of the Mississippi River. But as long as 160 years ago, the geographer Elisée Réclus could already note that on such a basis it should already have been known as the "double-crescent city."[1] And now, all the crescents have disappeared; yet, the idea is alive and well in the local imagination. So, forsaking all literalist explanations, one might ask, What is the secret meaning of the crescent? Of course, there are as many secrets of the crescent as there are devotees of the city. But what is the relevant meaning for our purposes— purposes that are at once interstitial, antistitial, and apocalyptic? Perhaps it is the crescent itself that can best pose, and best answer, this question.

The crescent is the figure that results when a circle has a segment of another circle removed from its edge. It thus consists of an area enclosed by two circular arcs that intersect at two points. So there is a question, or mystery, implicit in the crescent itself: "What lies within the missing circle?" The crescent defines a relationship between two realities: the explicit one within the crescent and the implicit one inscribed in the crescent through the striking presence of its own absence. In a sense, it is the implicit that is most explicitly designated or pointed to.

Isn't the crescent a kind of monstrance, holding out to us and revealing some numinous reality that ordinarily escapes our attention? That reality, we will see, is the other side, the dialectical other, of the city, of the civic, and of civilization. It is the suppressed complementary or contradictory reality. It is the reality of forgotten nature, forgotten life,

Figure 13.1. O'SAN brand: an embossed cigar box label, reflecting the crescent iconography of New Orleans. Here the Nile River, visually reduced to an oasis, is seen through the Muslim crescent, which frames an operatic scene, replete with pyramid. The Mississippi River, which flows between New Orleans and orientalist-named Algiers and Arabi, resembles the storied Nile: both rivers suffer from misguided management with resulting collapsing deltas and eroding wetlands. Caption by Stephen Duplantier. Chromolithograph by unknown designers and artists of the Walle Corporation of New Orleans, ca. 1915. Public domain.

forgotten history, forgotten colonies, forgotten peoples, and forgotten depths of being.

This sacred realm of oblivion is the matrix out of which emerges the utopian promise of apocalyptic transformation. We should remember that the word "crescendo" comes from the same root, *crescere*, as "crescent." "Crescendo" connotes both a continual increase in intensity and also the peak or fulfillment toward which that growth in intensity aims. Loci of intensity and a qualitative leap in intensity may be our guides into the quest to uncover the secret of the crescent, the secret of interstitiality and antistitiality.

Interstitial New Orleans

When filling out forms online, I have often been required to choose from a menu specifying what "state" my city is in. Fortunately, I have sometimes been able to choose the option "Minor Outlying U.S. Island

Possessions." This has seemed to say more about our local condition than any of the other choices. New Orleans is one of those edgy, border-linc, indeed interstitial places that are hard to pin down and confound conventional notions of place, position, and location. They defy standardized conceptions of core and periphery, Global North and Global South, first world and third world, empire and colony. While "edges" and "borders" are quite familiar concepts, "interstitial" is far less so. So it may be useful to reflect a bit on the meaning of this key concept. It may, indeed, offer the key to the city.

The term "interstitial" derives from the Latin *inter*, "between," and *stare*, "to stand."[2] Thus, interstices consist of what lies in the gaps between the "stitial," that which stands. What stands is conventional reality, and particularly those elements of the dominant reality that are raised up highest above all else. What stands includes hierarchies, structures of domination, social and ontological barriers, social statuses, sacred ideologies, and, not least of all, the state. Both "status" and "state," like "interstice," derive from the Latin *stare*, "to stand." The interstitial is thus not "in a state," but rather "between states."

The word "state" came to us via *l'estat*, an Anglo-French term that not entirely coincidentally evokes the famous fictional vampire from New Orleans. Nietzsche, in one of his most politically incisive moments, called the state "the coldest of all cold monsters." Long-time New Orleans writer Andrei Codrescu has argued that the first nation-state was Romania and that it was founded by Vlad the Impaler. This would make Dracula the father of the modern state, which is certainly true symbolically, if not entirely literally.

"Interstice" is also related to "static," which means "characterized by a lack of movement, animation, or progression" and "exerting force by reason of weight alone without motion."[3] The stitial is a realm in which Nietzsche's spirit of gravity prevails, weighing down not only the lightness of being but also all lightness of spirit. It is the domain of the object-like, the reified, and the ossified. The interstitial, in escaping this gravitational force, is a realm in which life, motion, and radical transformation find promising possibilities. The most crucial question about the interstitial and about New Orleans as an interstitial city is the degree to which interstices can and will become antistices. If the interstitial is that which lies between the stitial, that which stands, the antistitial challenges that which stands, and has the potential to overturn it.

Then there is the question (inevitable in view of the title of this collection) of what we might call "glycolocality"—the sweet spot. What are the relations between the interstice, the spot, and, more specifically, the sweet spot? Interstices might be described loosely as "spots," in the sense that they are locations. But we might ask whether they are necessarily sweet, or whether they might often be experienced as sour, bitter, salty, savory, pungent, or metallic? To help answer this question, we might consider the fact that the term "sweet spot" has at least three meanings. First, in acoustics, the sweet spot is the point at which something is heard "as intended." Interstices are in this sense quite the opposite of sweet spots. Interstices defy what is intended. They are the locus of the unintended, the mis-intended, and the anti-intended. Second, in sports, the sweet spot is the point at which there is maximum effect for effort. But this also has relatively little to do with interstices, much less antistices. The interstitial actually overturns accepted ideas of cause and effect, of instrumental rationality, of utilitarian calculation. It is the realm of shocks and surprises, where effect has an unexpected relationship to effort, and to effortlessness. Fortunately, there is a third realm, glycolocality, that offers a more promising degree of overlap with interstitiality.

In phonetics, the sweet spot is the point of maximum vibration, bringing us back to the crucial question of intensity. If the stitial is the realm of stability and stasis, or the quest for these, or the illusion of these, the interstitial is the sphere in which there is such intensity of motion and vibration that the possibility arises of destitializing the stitial, or shaking the stitial off its foundations. In other words, the possibility of the antistitial. Such antistitiality can be sweet music to the ears of some, but a bitter pill for others to swallow. Indeed, the interstice, when it rises to the level of antistitiality, takes on some of the qualities of the famous Hitchcockian anamorphic blot or stain explicated in Lacanian film analysis. The spot remains innocuously in the background until, at the decisive moment, it intrudes into the foreground, subtly and discretely at first, but ultimately with tremendous ontological force. For all its revelatory virtues, it is the bitterest spot of all from the standpoint of everyday, ordinary reality, since it disrupts and radically destabilizes that reality. Thus, to be as faithful as possible to the range of relevant phenomena, we might describe interstices as bittersweet spots.

The Social Ontology of Yat

New Orleans itself specializes in a kind of unruly disruptiveness, a quality that arises to a certain degree out of its interstitiality. The city tends to overturn many preconceptions, for example, those concerning North and South. I am not referring primarily to the preconceptions of outsiders who come to New Orleans expecting to hear a melodic, lilting accent exuding honeysuckle and molasses, and who are then shocked when they encounter Yat, the brash and rough-edged, working-class, quasi-Brookly-nese dialect. However, speaking of Yat: that dialect's classic self-referential query, "Where y'at?" can in fact initiate an investigation of the ambiguities of our psychogeographical and socio-ontological coordinates.

It is a cliché that New Orleans is "a southern city," even "the Queen City of the South." Nevertheless, it is also a northern city, and perhaps most significantly, it is a city on the boundary. It is located on the southern edge of North America, of the American nation-state, and of "America" as a cultural territory. Its most momentous earth-historical and geographical reality is its position at the southern end—the delta—of one of the world's great rivers, the Mississippi, the Gaealogical force that gave it birth. But New Orleans is also at the northern edge of its biore-gion, the littoral zone that runs from the Florida Keys to the northern coast of the Yucatan Peninsula. It is also at the northern edge of the great basin of the American Mediterranean Sea, which encompasses the Gulf of Mexico and the Caribbean. And finally, with its Mediterranean cultural heritage, including almost a century as a French and Spanish colony, it is at the shifting northern edge of Latin America. "Where y'at?" can be a very challenging question.

To take another approach, we might ask which world New Orleans inhabits. Is it located in the first world? The third world? The nonexistent second world? None of the above? At one time, I saw bumper stickers in New Orleans that proclaimed, "New Orleans: Third World and Proud of It!" It was popular because it evoked the city's Latin and African roots and its affinities with the Global South. It expressed a defiance of the Northern, Anglo-Saxon, Calvinistic work ethic and an appreciation of values like play, enjoyment, sensuality, desire, fantasy, celebration, wildness, and creativity. It represented the New Orleanian Dream as opposed to the American Dream. I never saw that bumper sticker again after the Hurricane Katrina disaster. We learned something that we had not fully understood about what it means to be a bit too "third-world"—on the fringes of empire in a time of extreme crisis and desperate need. Through our interstitial position between worlds, we (or at least those of us who didn't quickly retreat into the high, dry, elitist "bubble," as it was called) gained unique insight into what it means today to be "third-world" and a part of "the South," in a first-world, North-dominated global imperial order.

The more meaningful theoretical question is not whether we are third-world or first-world, but whether we are core or periphery. In world system theory, the core is the center of wealth, power, privilege, and prestige. Though the land area of the planet that this core occupies is proportionally a bit larger than the apple core that might come to mind, and although it is geographically dispersed over several continents, it can still be looked upon as the center of the global system of domination. The periphery, on the other hand, has relatively little wealth, power, privilege, and prestige, though it covers most of the earth's surface. We can also speak of a global semiperiphery. This is an interstitial geopolitical space that shares characteristics with both the core and the periphery yet is not predominantly one or the other.

A nation-state may be a core country yet contain within itself semiperipheral and even peripheral areas. In the United States, many Indian reservations and the most devastated urban zones qualify as periphery, however much the banner of the core may fly over them. New Orleans occupies a complex geopolitical space in that it is a part of the semiperiphery that lies at the edge of the core, not very far from the periphery, while also having islands of both core and periphery within it. It is strongly interstitial since it lies between parts of the core that stand high (the Houstons and Atlantas), and also lies between the core ("America") and the periphery (the other "Americas"). Its interstitial significance is further amplified by its expanding connections with Central America, especially Honduras and El Salvador, two peripheral countries that are among those most devastated by empire.

To live mindfully in New Orleans is to dwell dialectically on the edge, to border borders ambiguously, and to inhabit interstices precariously. This privileged position allows one to understand what lies either inside or over the edge, what exists on each side of the border, and what stands outside the interstices. It allows one to be both inside and outside at the same time. One can take the inside-outsider perspective: to be *in*, yet not *of*.[4] To be a New Orleanian who is fully awakened to the perspective of our place gives one a certain double vision, a certain privilege of parallax.[5] It makes possible the move from an interstitial topianism to the antistitial utopianism that is at the heart of New Orleans's apocalyptic nature.

Apocalyptic New Orleans

The term "apocalypse" originates, we are told, in certain Jewish and Christian writings from the period between 200 BCE and 150 CE that are "marked by pseudonymity, symbolic imagery, and the expectation of an imminent cosmic cataclysm in which God destroys the ruling powers of evil and raises the righteous to life in a messianic kingdom."[6] The word derives from the Greek *apokalyptein*, "to uncover." In the messianic Apocalypse, that which has been covered up, obscured, or occluded by layers of social domination and social ideology (that is, by the stitial) is "uncovered," in the sense of both "being revealed" and "being released into being."

Apocalypse implies cataclysmic change, but change that does not result in mere destruction and loss. Rather, the change opens up new utopian, antistitial possibilities that emerge out of what has existed all along within the interstitial gaps of civilization. The apocalyptic imagination envisions a return to a Paradise beyond the bounds and bonds of domination. A land of dreamy scenes. A Garden of Eden. A Heaven right here on Earth. This seemingly impossible return to the place where we have never been is indeed possible, but only because the roots of Paradise lie all around us, in the interstices.

As the invocation of these familiar phrases hints, the thesis here is that New Orleans is the apocalyptic city par excellence. If one looks into the history of New Orleans and the city's social imaginary, one finds that in both its fantasies and its reality, New Orleans is not only an apocalyptic city, in both the destructive and utopian senses, but also an edge city, poised at the brink of an abyss; an interstitial city, lying in the gaps between that which stands; and an antistitial city, always threatening, sometimes assisted by nature, always with the help of culture, to overturn that which stands.

An essential element of the apocalyptic nature of New Orleans is its position at the edge of the abyss. But what precisely does it mean to say that a city is situated "at the edge of the abyss"? Presumably, we are not interested in an exercise in vague dramatics or local-colorist exaggeration. Any decline into the mindless puffery that might be labeled Big Easyism is a betrayal of the city and its momentous destiny. In fact, the abyss above which the city is perched exists in two quite specific and clearly defined senses, both apocalyptic: the abyss of nonbeing and the abyss of becoming.

The abyss of nonbeing is the frightening apocalyptic nothingness of collapse, catastrophe, and fall. It is the loss of that fragile being that, when it is part of the structure of everydayness, assumes an illusory substantiality and concreteness. I have heard the phrase "the unbearable lightness of being" misremembered as "the incredible lightness of being." The concept is misremembered, if not entirely forgotten, for very good reason. The lightness of being is incredible precisely because it is so obviously credible. The expression designates a quality that in ancient Sanskrit was called *anitya*, "impermanence." It is, according to the ancient philosophy of awakening, one of the Three Marks of Existence that human beings always have so much trouble focusing on consciously.

New Orleans is an apocalyptic city because it exemplifies in such a striking manner the reality of impermanence. It announces impermanence to the world. Though some New Orleanians seem to require a state of permanent oblivion to avoid thinking about what they unconsciously know to be true, many are aware, either with full consciousness or with some degree of recognition, of the lightness of the city's being. The sometimes-unbearable truth is that the city could disappear at any time, and that it is indeed likely to disappear in the not-too-distant future. In any given hurricane season, it could be devastated by "the Big One." And beyond this looming disaster lies the Big One to end all Big Ones, the chain of social and ecological events that will almost certainly end the city's history entirely. It is highly unlikely that this three-hundred-year-old city will be around to celebrate its four hundredth anniversary. In fact, the odds are not so great for it to see 350 candles on its cake, if the present course of global climate change and sea level rise merely progresses as expected. As a result, the city is left with an apocalyptic fate and a correspondingly apocalyptic social imaginary. The probability of vast devastation increasingly shapes its conscious imaginary, while the inevitability of complete destruction slumbers uncomfortably in its unconscious imaginary.

Beyond this abyss of nonbeing lies another abyss, the abyss of becoming, the apocalyptic abyss of possibility. Nietzsche famously warned us to beware of looking into the abyss, because the abyss looks back into us. He might have warned us more explicitly against the problem of not looking deeply enough into the abyss and against preventing its return gaze. We should never settle for Abyss Lite. Those who look most profoundly into the abyss of nonbeing and allow it to gaze back into their own nothingness are able to do so because they recognize that there is a second moment of apocalypse, that of the abyss of becoming. This second face of apocalypse is the moment of possibility, of creativity, and of hope.

New Orleans, in expressing these two faces of apocalypse, takes its place as a prophetic city at the forefront of world history, increasingly revealing itself as apocalyptic, the story of the end of civilization. The city's prophetic message is this: "What we are, you shall be." We are the *mauvaise conscience*, the "bad conscience," or even the *mauvais inconscient*, the "bad unconscious," of civilization. Yet we are also the liberatory unconscious of what comes beyond civilization. Both these qualities are keys to the city's apocalyptic nature. We—all of humanity—are in the midst of an apocalyptic age, though awareness of its apocalyptic nature is just beginning to emerge. Precisely as the harbinger of this age is New Orleans a prophetically apocalyptic city. It is a city built on a foundation of impossibility, yet its impossible history and impossible destiny offer us indispensable messages of both possibility and inevitability.

The Other Face of Apocalypse

The apocalypse will not be televised, though attempts will certainly be made to capture it on the small screen. The apocalypse is untelevisable because it is inherently wild, and never can be domesticated or tamed. New Orleans is fertile ground for apocalyptic utopianism precisely because of its unconquerable wildness.[7] It is a wild place in several senses. Abandon your house for a few months or years and see what's there when you get back. Vines will have woven the back yard into a thick mat, interspersed with rainforest vegetation. Dozens of species of trees and bushes will have sprung up in what was formerly lawn, garden or even cracks in the sidewalk. Vines will have invaded every wall and colonized the roof, which will have turned into a bright green meadow interspersed with vivid yellow flowers. As art critic, photographer, and psycho-geographer Eric Bookhardt has said astutely of New Orleans, "The Jungle is Near."[8] This undeniable truth is meant in both a natural and a cultural sense. Abandon your narrow little prosaic mind for a while, let your wider mind walk on the wild side of the spirit, and the mythopoetic mental jungle will reappear. In New Orleans, the wild cultural rainforest vegetation seems always to be striving to take root and to spread across the landscape. In New Orleans, interstitiality is destiny.

Given such insistent interstitial and antistitial impulses, New Orleans has inevitably become the site of a never-ending war between the wild and the domesticated, the free and the dominated. It is the battleground in the "splace" wars. "Splace," a fundamental psychogeographical concept, is the battlefield on which space and place clash. Space is abstract, geometrical, analytical location. Space takes Pythagorean mathematical, Cartesian philosophical, Newtonian scientific, statist technobureaucratic, and capitalist economistic forms. In urbanist terms, space is the terrain for the designs and devices of developers. It is the privileged domain of development. In all its overlapping and mutually reinforcing forms, space reduces a location to its abstract parameters for instrumental ends and for purposes of political, economic, and technological domination. The dominant system has been obsessed with a space race, a compulsion to reduce everything to instrumental spatiality as rapidly as possible.

Place, on the other hand, is concretely dialectical location. It is the field on which physis, psyche, eros, pneuma, poesis, ethos, and mythos all unfold and manifest themselves. It is the plane on which the lives of persons and communities are lived. Ancient metaphysicians were right when they said that things have a natural place, but they were wrong in thinking that they could define that place or impose any general prin-

Figure 13.2. Float 8, "Enchantment of the Inner World," Krewe of Mid City. An interstitial moment as a carnival parade lines up just before rolling on its route. An invisible tractor driver pulls an empty float past disinterested porch-dwellers: even these giant, silverleaf-tipped, papier-mâché grapes cannot match the enchantment of the inner world. Caption and photograph (ca. 1975) by Stephen Duplantier.

ciple or arche on it. All beings have their own way of being, and they do in their own time and place. If you want to know the details, ask the persons and things themselves: Where y'at, *Ding-an-Sich*? Where things are at is where they are going, in their own way. Though everything must always be in its place, that place itself is always out of place. The thing in itself is always outside itself and beside itself.

Since the beginning of civilization, every location has been the site of the dialectic of space and place, the scene of splace wars. Today, antistitial New Orleans wages war against space on behalf of place. If Wordsworth warned astutely about the modern scientific spirit, "We murder to dissect," radical localists warn about postmodern gentrifiers: "We murder to develop." They fear that living New Orleans culture will be murdered, embalmed, and carried away in a Kabacoffin,[9] all to the accompaniment of a traditional brass band. They fear that carnival will be cannibalized.

New Orleans is known above all as the carnivalesque city, the city of Mardi Gras. Carnival is the dialectical festival par excellence, the temporary emergence of a world in which, quite manifestly, everything is what it is not, and everything is not what it is. In its New Orleanian incarnation, carnival is a particularly dialectical phenomenon. It radicalizes the fundamental cultural contradiction of New Orleans: an American city that is what America is not. Founded as a Latin, carnivalesque city, New Orleans has for two centuries been incorporated into a dominant Anglo-Saxon, decidedly anti-carnivalesque, capital-accumulation-obsessed culture.

The city's enduring saturnalian spirit therefore has a subversive, oppositional quality, which is central to its antistitiality and its utopian apocalypticism. It flaunts the subversive idea that *le pouvoir est toujours ridicule*. It confronts *le pouvoir* with its own powerfully ridiculous puissances. As a result of these antagonistic contradictions between power and powers, several carnivals have emerged, and at times a war of the carnivals even breaks out. On the one hand, there is domesticated carnival, the official carnival, a contrived spectacle, a festival of wealth and power, a mechanism for controlling the masses through repressive desublimation, a means of attracting tourists through the image of an ersatz bacchanalia and thereby contributing mightily to the grossly domesticated product. This is the Fat Tuesday of the fat cats. On the other hand (the left hand, of course), there is wild carnival, the popular carnival, dissident carnival, carnival with an edge, the festival of joy, creative self-expression, and defiance of convention.[10] This is the Fat Tuesday of the fat of the land, the overflowing abundance of natural richness and wild becoming.

Wild carnival functions as an ecstatically destabilizing force. It is the temporary collapse of normality and a temporary unleashing of unruly aesthetic and erotic forces. Carnival is antistitial in that it mocks all that stands. It tries to pull the rug out from under what stands. The roots of the city's unique expression of the carnivalesque lie in its original Latin heritage, and the African and Afro-Caribbean culture that was later superimposed, or, we might say, supersubversively subimposed. Its specific historical origins are in the medieval Feast of Fools, in which the dominant order is ridiculed and relativized, if only for a day. But what happens in a day has imaginary implications that can be very far-reaching. If the day is good enough, it might even lead to a *grand soir* The African heritage takes this insurgent antistitiality one step further with Mardi Gras's defiant affirmation of wildness, and their spirit of "won't bow down" to the dominant culture. Thus, one finds implicit in the carnivalesque the seeds of social transformation, the dream of a permanent carnivalesque community in which hierarchical power is permanently relativized and defanged. Power descends to the streets. Antistitial antistructures walk the streets.

Carnival produces the dream image of a community founded on wild beauty and mad love that can become a powerful imaginary counterforce to the dominant dream image of the commodity. Note that such a "permanent" carnivalesque community is anything but permanent. (In carnival, nothing ever is merely what it is.) It is a community that is constantly changing. It changes its costumes, of course, but it also changes its identities and imaginings. It is also constantly exchanging: gifts, experiences, and acts of creation. Carnival is the experience of finding enduring value in the free exchange of that which constantly changes hands, hearts, minds, and souls. Carnival is the ultimate evidence that samsara is nirvana, that the profane is profoundly sacred, that your own home is the promised land. In carnival, your feet won't fail to walk on sacred ground. In carnival, the very gumbo ground on which you walk, as Hakuin says, is Pure Lotus Land.

On Mystery Street

At the outset, it was said that the secret of the crescent lies in the revelation of mysteries. Nowhere have these mysteries been explored more intriguingly than in a little-known nineteenth-century novel, *The Mysteries of New Orleans*. This work, which might well be called *The Manifesto of Apocalyptic New Orleans*, was written in the 1850s by the Bavarian immigrant nobleman Baron Ludwig von Reizenstein.[11] The German title, *Die Geheimnisse von New-Orleans*, means literally "Secrets of New Orleans," but it was part of the mysteries genre that was the rage in the mid-nineteenth century. However, this extraordinary work explosively burst the limits of that genre and initiated the world into what might be called the literature of apocalyptic mysteries. In it, Reizenstein investigates strange, mysterious, subterranean, and surrealist elements of the city's culture and geography. This epic tale remains one of history's greatest examples not only of apocalyptic fiction, but of literary surregionalism and psychogeography.

Reizenstein explores an interstitial New Orleans that encompasses a multitude of regions and locations that defy the era's prevailing order of domination. Each embodies a mystery or secret that escapes the boundaries of conventional wisdom, challenges the dominant view of what can be recognized as real, and prefigures a new reality beyond the limits of all forms of domination. The mysteries exhibited by Reizenstein's characters and settings are radical breaks vis-à-vis the state, capitalism, patriarchy, heterosexism, racism, repressive morality, authoritarian religion, technological rationality, and the domination of nature. Thus, these subversive sites are both deeply interstitial and radically antistitial.

In the central plot, the mysterious two-hundred-year-old Hiram the Freemason contrives to bring together, magically, a mixed-race couple to produce an offspring who will liberate the enslaved people, thus making possible the regeneration of a corrupt and accursed social order. As translator and editor Steven Rowan summarizes, "Reizenstein's tale foretells the descent of a bloody retributive justice upon the American South. Slavery is a massive sin that would soon be made right by a bloodbath, heralded by the birth of a black messiah, a deliverer of his people." Rowan notes that the author "portrayed the coming revolution in frankly apocalyptic terms"[12]—and in terms that express precisely the conception of apocalypse developed here.

For Reizenstein, it was the deeply contradictory, indeed dialectical, nature of New Orleans that gave it a unique apocalyptic destiny. On the one hand, the city exhibited starkly the evils of brutality, exploitation, slavery, and domination. But on the other, it constituted an oasis of freedom that had certain redeeming qualities unique in American society.[13] It is the very intensity of the expression of evil that conditions the intensity of utopian possibility. Reizenstein describes the city as the scene of all forms of misery and degradation, but nevertheless as an exception to the repressiveness of the dominant American culture: "Much is forbidden, but much is also tolerated. This makes New Orleans the freest city in the United States."[14] He notes further that "New Orleans has always been the leader in the United States in everything that heightens enjoyment of life and makes the dullest people into Epicureans."[15] As a hotbed of corruption and oppression, New Orleans was particularly well-suited to be the scene of an apocalyptic fall. As a haven of freedom, the city was uniquely ordained to stage the ultimate redemption of society. So it is in New Orleans that Reizenstein imagines the emergence, out of the interstitial oases of freedom, a new world released from the chains of domination. In his apocalyptic imagination, New Orleans holds the promise of a passionate utopia whose subtropical wildness and earthiness would eclipse anything imagined by utopian socialists like Charles Fourier.

But Reizenstein was aware that many barriers would have to be broken before this utopia could emerge. His attack on slavery and racism is only the beginning of an assault on the manifold abuses of a vicious and brutal civilization. He condemns not only the South with its regressive, neofeudalistic slave system but the entire corrupt American soci-

Figure 13.3. A determined parade-goer, ghost-like, watches a post-apocalyptic, riderless, driverless parade. A second line of one, umbrella in hand, she may not be properly stylin'—but who blames her? The carnivalesque enthralls willy-nilly. Caption and photograph (ca. 1975) by Stephen Duplantier.

ety, which by the mid-nineteenth century had already shown itself to be deeply perverted by the forces of economic exploitation, racism, social repression and imperial conquest. Reizenstein presents a remarkable litany in which the evils of that society are enumerated and the cataclysmic revolt against them envisioned. Despite its length, this entire passage is worth quoting for the sake of its articulation of the forms of domination (forces of stitiality) to be abolished and the forms of liberation (forces of antistitiality) to be nurtured and protected:

> Wherever the law claps love in permanent manacles, where the Church proclaims sensual denial, where false modesty and inherited morality keeps us from giving nature its rights, then we lie down at the warm breasts of Mother Nature, listening to her secrets and surveying with burning eyes the great mechanism in which every gear moans the word Love. There is rejoicing in all the spheres, the fanfares of the universe resound, wherever love celebrates its triumph. But lightning bolts flash from dark clouds whenever tyrannical law and usurped morality seek to compel the children of earth to smother their vitality and entomb their feelings. How small and pitiful the nattering of parties seems, how petty the drama even of our own revolution,

against the titanic struggle of sensuality against law and morality. "Revolution!" the nun cries out in her sleep, throwing her rosary in the face of the Madonna. "Revolution!" the priest of the sole-salvific Church mutters as he rips his scapular into shreds. "Revolution!" thunders the proletarian when he beholds the fair daughter of Pharaoh. "Revolution!" the slave rattles, when he sees the white child of the planter walking through the dark passageway of cypresses. "Revolution!" the horse whinnies, mutilated by greed. "Revolution!" the steer roars, cursing its tormentors under the yoke on its shoulders. "Revolution!" the women of Lesbos would storm, if we were to rebuke their love.[16]

Thus, Reizenstein defends love, life, nature, sensuality, feeling, equality, and justice against capitalism, slavery, the state, authoritarian religion, repressive morality, sexism, heterosexism, racism, and even speciesism and the devastation of the natural world. In 1853, a specter was haunting the Mississippi delta—the specter of total liberation! While many specters have died since then, this one, as we shall see, still finds interstices in which to dwell, and still has some serious antistitial haunting to carry out.

Apocalyptic Urban Nightmare

Though Reizenstein's *tour de force imaginaire* has never been equaled by any single literary work about the city, the Katrina disaster signaled the high point in the overall flowering of the New Orleanian apocalyptic imaginary. This is true of both sides of apocalypse, the negative imagery of cataclysmic destruction and the positive imagery of rebirth and transfiguration. We might call the one-sidedly negative expression of this imaginary that was so common in the post-Katrina period "the official apocalypse" or "the apocalyptic urban nightmare."

President George W. Bush's notorious comments immediately after the disaster are very instructive. His words were part of a project of instrumentalizing apocalypse and, more specifically, part of the strategy of militarizing apocalypse. Bush describes a post-Katrina wasteland "as if" the region had been "obliterated by a—the worst kind of weapon you can imagine."[17] The worst kind of weapon one could imagine, if one happens to live on Planet Earth, is obviously a multimegaton nuclear warhead. Bush's message, thus spelled out, is an injunction to think that New Orleans was nuked. Useful conclusions follow from this apocalyptic thought experiment. First, a disaster of that imagined magnitude would certainly create a state of exception in which the legitimacy of extreme measures such as the displacement and disempowerment of masses of people and the extensive militarization would be beyond question. Second, the image of the city as a post-nuclear-holocaust tabula rasa plays into the larger agenda of reengineering New Orleans into a more gentrified "boutique city," following the demands of capital and assisted by the ideology of New Urbanism. Thus, the myth of a postapocalyptic social tabula rasa could obliterate consciousness of the interstices and antistices and, to whatever degree possible, annihilate them.

Bush concludes by saying, "now, we're going to try to comfort people in that part of the world." He (and his speech-writers) surely realized that a few more bumbling words on his part would hardly comfort anyone, so what could the actual message be here? If we parse Bush's statement, the first implication is that the overriding "recovery" strategy that most local citizens should expect would be fighting fire with rhetoric—though the present "fire" to be fought was primarily water, and the rhetoric was not very convincing. The second message was that the people of New Orleans were to be imagined as distant, alien others and treated accordingly. Almost any chief of state would refer to disaster victims from the same country as "fellow citizens," as fellow nationals ("Americans," "Mexicans," "Russians") or even as "brothers and sisters." So objectifying New Orleanians as foreigners ("people in that part of the world"), albeit in a patronizingly sympathetic tone, is particularly telling. If people in New Orleans are in "that part of the world," they are by definition not in "our" part of the world, but somewhere else. Bush's comments thus reveal his position as speaking unambiguously from within and on behalf of the core, marking New Orleans as within the semiperiphery of the world system while defining its place in the dominant social imaginary at that precise moment as decidedly peripheral.

The mainstream media worked diligently to propagate a complementary apocalyptic urban nightmare scenario. Several days after the flooding, Maureen Dowd in the *New York Times* lamented the supposed fact that "America [was] once more plunged into a snakepit of anarchy, death, looting, raping, marauding thugs, suffering infrastructure, a gutted police force, insufficient troop levels, and criminally negligent government planning."[18] The same image recurs in Allen G. Breed's Associated Press report on "New Orleans in the throes of Katrina, and apocalypse."[19] Breed arrived two days before Katrina, and shortly after the disaster, he concluded that "a walk through New Orleans is a walk through hell," albeit "punctuated by moments of grace." He states that "there is nothing to correct wild reports that armed gangs have taken over the convention center. That two babies had their throats slit in the night. That a 7-year-old girl was raped and killed at the Superdome."

There was nothing to correct this mainstream version other than the accurate information that emerged well after the image of New Orleans as "urban hell" had deeply penetrated the American social imagination.

Government officials also reinforced that image. Federal Emergency Management Agency director Michael Brown spoke of the difficulties of working in New Orleans as "conditions of urban warfare."[20] Local officials likewise contributed to creating this scenario. In an interview with Oprah Winfrey, a weeping chief of police Eddie Compass lamented conditions at the Superdome, saying, "We had babies in there. Little babies getting raped." Mayor Ray Nagin elaborated, informing Oprah that people "were trapped" and as a result "got to this almost animalistic state. . . . We have people standing out there, that have been in that frickin' Superdome for five days watching dead bodies, watching hooligans killing people, raping people. That's the tragedy. People are trying to give us babies that were dying."[21] So goes the story of the terrifying outbreak of asymmetrical warfare in the remote third-world banana republic of Bigeasia.

While there was tragic violence in the city, it was minimal in comparison to that imagined in the urban apocalypse scenario. The claims about violence in the Superdome and the Ernest N. Morial Convention Center, which became shelters for tens of thousands of citizens seeking refuge, were soon debunked. However, as Isak Winkel Holm notes, in order to justify a "large military operation, unprecedented on American soil," it was necessary to transform the citizens of New Orleans from "disaster victims" into "urban insurgents," so that Katrina was turned into "a natural disaster and a cultural disaster at the same time." It was "an example of cultural framing of a disaster with disastrous consequences."[22]

Apocalyptic Utopia

While mainstream media and government officials (in effect, the representatives of capital, the state, and white patriarchy) were presenting their image of apocalypse, a quite different one was emerging on the grassroots level. It was an image that accords with the deeper spiritual and political dimensions of apocalypse going back to ancient times. Hurricane Katrina (or, more accurately, the flood waters that followed) leveled that which stands, including social hierarchy, the state, and capital. What resulted was a "state of exception" in a very liberatory sense, a gap in history in which citizens who remained found themselves in the extraordinary position of being a community of equals faced with the task of determining the destiny of their community, including defend-

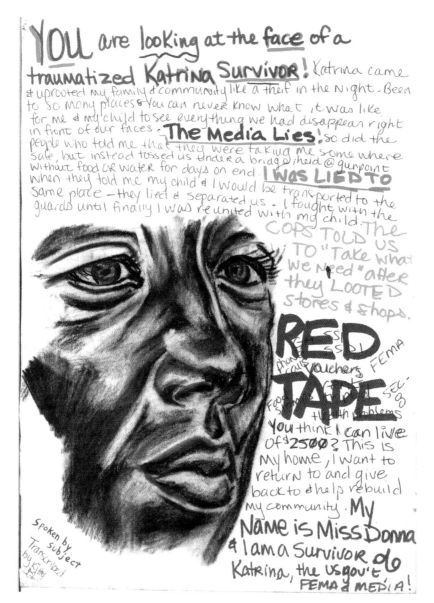

Figure 13.4. *My Name Is Miss Donna.* A traumatized Katrina survivor, one of many, exposes the cracks in the systems that conceal the reality of being even from ourselves, at least until apocalypse restores the possibilities of resurrection. Francesco Di Santis, *The Post-Katrina Portraits* (New Orleans: Di Santis and Latta, 2007). This image is a Portrait Story; to learn more about Portrait Stories, please visit http://portraitstoryproject.org/.

ing it from a range of threats—from demolition and ethnic cleansing, to capitalist plunder and state repression.

Francesco Di Santis, an "embedded artist," "visual folklorist," and anarchist activist, came to New Orleans on September 11, 2005, less than two weeks after the hurricane, to work in the recovery and to participate in liberatory social transformation. I met him a week later, when we were members of an affinity group working together in the Upper Ninth Ward. At that time Francesco was already talking to survivors and volunteers and sketching their portraits. Over the next several years, he created the Post-Katrina Portrait Project, a collection of several thousand images.[23] On each portrait, the subject wrote or dictated to a volunteer his or her post-Katrina narrative. These portraits recount the real-world apocalyptic history of dystopian destruction and devastation on the one hand, and of utopian creation and communal liberation on the other.

One of the volunteers describes the dark night of the soul, the traditional path to a breakthrough in both Western and Asian spiritual practice. "Last night, I woke to the shaking of my room. The walls were rattling and the whole house moved. I clung to my bed. The earth was quaking and I thought, 'this is it.' Pieces of the world were coming apart and I tried to grasp onto the remaining fragments of reality—before it was all gone. I woke again." This is the classic apocalyptic experience of the world coming apart and collapsing. A survivor who went through many terrifying experiences says, "You can never know what it was like for me and my child to see everything disappear right in front of our faces." This is the apocalyptic experience of the collapse of the everyday world. Many post-Katrina stories recount feelings of absolute abandonment, abject despair, and devastating fear of death and apocalyptic destruction.

This part of the post-Katrina story is well-known, though not so often through the direct testimony of those who experienced it or with the depth that such witnesses convey. What is amazing and inspiring is how so many of the portrait stories recount the other face of apocalypse: of ultimate redemption, of restoration, of hope, and of the surging up of utopian possibilities in New Orleans. One survivor says, "Sometimes it takes the complete stripping of your home or possessions to really see what life's about." Another volunteer observes, "Out of deep hurt can come beautiful transformation personally and collectively."

It is striking that so many described what was occurring in terms of a "crack" in the structure of history and in everyday reality. One volunteer says that "what matters most" in the Katrina experience is that there was a "system crack" in which new realities had become possible, and "we now have the chance to help enact a transformation." The community becomes a focal point of larger social transformation, so that through "all points radiating outward from our swampy heaven," we can know that "a paradigm shift is possible." The crack symbolizes the brokenness of the system, of the community, and of the lives of people, but it also signifies an opening through which germinating forces of creativity, imagination, love, and radical possibility are liberated. The crack thus signifies the becoming-antistitial of the interstitial.[24]

Scott Crow, cofounder of the Common Ground Collective, created in the immediate wake of the disaster, summarized the work of the organization using precisely this imagery. His account clearly points out the interstitial and antistitial nature of the "crack"—a space that first opens up in the midst of "that which stands" and then proceeds to threaten the standing of "that which stands in the way." In Scott's own words, "We had created a crack in history. We had revealed the lies, corruption, and failures of the state, and, without hesitating, we had done something about it. I had seen a transition from hopelessness to hope as thousands of people answered the call to come to the Gulf."[25] One might even say that the radically antistitial project of the Common Ground Collective was to expand that small systemic crack into a great gulf through which freedom surges forth and sweeps away the forces of domination. We were involved in a Gulf War of the Spirit, a war at the heart of the abyss.

As Di Santis explains, "Since Katrina, New Orleans has only become more of itself, relentlessly perpetuating its own follies and glories so profoundly endemic to it since French imperialists first settled a port city among the swamps of the Mississippi delta." These follies are the strategies of domination, of the state and stases, that Reizenstein had already delineated as early as the 1850s and that have become "more of themselves" most horrifically by policies of exclusion, ethnic cleansing, and effective denial of the "right of return." The glories are expressed above all in in the flowering of cultural and communitarian creativity in which the community of liberation and solidarity, the beloved community, has continually become "more of itself" in pursuing its destiny.

The Coming Apocalypse

Will New Orleans fulfill its apocalyptic promise? The answer is "probably," "inevitably," and "possibly," depending on which moment of apocalypse we have in mind.

First, it is highly probable that an apocalyptic disaster, the Big One, will arrive during the brief remaining period of human habitation. Measures to improve levees and drainage will be of limited help, but continued coastal erosion will aggravate the catastrophic effects when the fateful time comes.

Second, it is inevitable, barring a global social revolution that fundamentally changes the ecocidal course of world history, that New Orleans will meet its final apocalyptic fate before long. It will, probably within the

Figure 13.5. Fence posts in flood waters. Photograph © David Rae Morris, 2005.

next century, become a new Atlantis, sinking beneath the rising seas, along with much of Florida, most of Bangladesh, and many other of the world's coastal regions. In the ultimate irony, the sea will occupy Wall Street.

And finally, it remains possible that New Orleans will realize its apocalyptic utopian dream. It is possible that what is entirely impossible according to the dominant ideology, imaginary, and ethos, will occur: that New Orleans will fulfill its world-historical and Earth-historical revolutionary and regenerative destiny, and that its transformative apocalyptic message of creative destruction will spread to the larger world.

Over a decade after Hurricane Katrina, New Orleans is at a critical cultural moment. The relatively depopulated city[26] has remained the site of an extraordinary heritage of highly particularized and communally rooted, yet radically creative and imaginatively diverse, culture. To this milieu has been added an influx of young activist volunteers, artists, musicians, poets, urban homesteaders, political radicals, spiritual seekers, and visionaries. As a result, it is the locus of perhaps the greatest concentration of interstitial, and more significantly, incipiently antistitial culture. At such a moment of ethotic intensity, apocalyptic possibility appears, the missing circle of the real begins to emerge out of the mysterious crescent.

Faith in this possibility, the one expressed over a century and a half ago in Reizenstein's vision of cataclysmic liberation, lives on. This passion of creative destruction, the antistitial quest to liberate humanity and nature from the nihilistic and egoistic forces that are destroying everything of value, is expressed in a recent issue of the local publication *Uncontrollable*:

> Here we must and may only forge a liberation that is grounded in New Orleans' glorious, incomparable, horrifying and boundlessly rich history and particularities. As we eat New Orleans food, as we sing New Orleans songs, we build a New Orleans destruction of the state and capitalism. In all we do and all we attempt, we honor her. We live for her, we fight for her, we sacrifice everything for her—our mother—our city—our goddess—our home—New Orleans.[27]

As we gaze out across the gaping abyss of late modernity, not with our merely corporeal eye, but with the eye of the apocalyptic imagination, we envision the mysteries of New Orleans, as they can never be, but nevertheless must be, fully revealed and perfectly realized.

NOTES

1. Elisée Reclus, *A Voyage to New Orleans*, ed. John Clark and Camille Martin, (Thetford, VT: Glad Day Books, 2003), 35.

2. *Online Etymology Dictionary*, s. v. "interstice," accessed July 25, 2016, http://www.etymonline.com/index.php?term=interstice.

3. *Merriam-Webster Dictionary*, s. v. "static," accessed July 25, 2016, http://www.merriam-webster.com/dictionary/static.

4. On the importance of "the outside" and the outsider within, see Andrei Codrescu, *The Disappearance of the Outside: A Manifesto for Escape* (St. Paul: Ruminator Books, 2001).

5. This is, not so incidentally, the Heraclitean dialectical position: between land and sea, in the subtropics, on the fringes of empire, in a period of world-historical transformation. See Max Cafard, *Lightning Storm Mind: Pre-Ancientist Meditations* (New York: Autonomedia, 2017).

6. *Merriam-Webster Dictionary*, s. v. "apocalypse," accessed July 19, 2016, http://www.merriam-webster.com/dictionary/apocalypse.

7. One of the great books about the city is, in fact, *A Walk on the Wild Side*, by Nelson Algren (New York: Farrar, Straus and Giroux, 1956).

8. Eric Bookhardt, "The Jungle is Near: Culture and Nature in a Subtropical Clime," in *Mesechabe* 2 (1988–89), 1–5.

9. A reference to HRI Properties, one of the leading local real estate development corporations, and its CEO, Maurice Pres Kabacoff.

10. The connections between the anarchic carnivalesque here and Mikhail Bakh-

tin's analysis will be obvious. See Max Cafard, for example, in "Laughing Matters; or, In Praise of Folly," in *Surregional Explorations* (Chicago: Charles H. Kerr, 2012), 162–73. In Bakhtin's classic work, *Rabelais and His World* (Bloomington: Indiana University Press, 1984), he develops several themes that are echoed in the present discussion. Despite some commonalities, the fundamental difference between Bakhtin's concept of carnival and the one here concerns its ephemerality. For Bakhtin, "the feast was a temporary suspension of the entire official system with all its prohibitions and hierarchic barriers. For a short time life came out of its usual, legalized and consecrated furrows and entered the sphere of utopian freedom," ibid., 89. Bakhtin's carnival thus resembles Hakim Bey's "Temporary Autonomous Zone" in *T.A.Z.: The Temporary Autonomous Zone, Ontological Anarchy, Poetic Terrorism* (New York: Autonomedia, 1991), 93–143. The present analysis focuses on carnival as the realm in which ephemeral freedom is realized but relates that moment to the larger carnivalesque reality of a culture that has a dialectically ironic and ongoing relationship to the dominant order—we might say, "structural" in the very urge toward destructurization.

11. Baron Ludwig von Reizenstein, *The Mysteries of New Orleans* (1855), trans. and ed. Steven Rowan (Baltimore: Johns Hopkins University Press, 2002).

12. Ibid., xxviii–xxix.

13. Ibid., 130.

14. Ibid., 130.

15. Ibid., 189.

16. Ibid., 150–51.

17. "President Arrives in Alabama, Briefed on Hurricane Katrina," White House, September 02, 2005, accessed July 25, 2016, http://georgewbush-whitehouse.archives.gov/news/releases/2005/09/20050902-2.html.

18. Maureen Dowd, "United States of Shame," *New York Times*, September 3, 2005, accessed 25 July 2016, http://www.nytimes.com/2005/09/03/opinion/03dowd.html?_r=0.

19. Allen G. Breed, "New Orleans in the Throes of Katrina, and Apocalypse," USA Today, accessed July 25, 2016, http://usatoday30.usatoday.com/news/nation/2005-09-02-katrinawalkthroughhell_x.htm.

20. "Relief Workers Confront 'Urban Warfare,'" CNN, September 1, 2005, accessed July 25, 2016, http://www.cnn.com/2005/WEATHER/09/01/katrina.impact/.

21. CNN transcript from Anderson Cooper report, September 28, 2005, accessed July 25, 2016, http://transcripts.cnn.com/TRANSCRIPTS/0509/28/asb.02.html.

22. Isak Winkel Holm, "The Cultural Analysis of Disaster," in *The Cultural Life of Catastrophes and Crises*, ed. Carsten Meiner and Kristin Veel (Berlin: Walter de Gruyter, 2012), http://curis.ku.dk/ws/files/46389505/Cultural_Analysis_of_Disaster.pdf.

23. See Francesco Di Santis, *The Post-Katrina Portraits* (New Orleans: Di Santis and Latta, 2007), in which about 350 of the portraits are reproduced. Thousands were put on the walls of Common Ground Collective sites. Some were collected and put in the Historic New Orleans Collection, but a large number were lost when the sites were closed. A selection, accessed July 25, 2016, can be found online at https://www.flickr.com/photos/postkatrinaportraits/.

24. I have attempted to tell part of this story in a series of articles related to post-Katrina New Orleans. See John Clark, "New Orleans: Do You Know What It Means?," *New: Translating Cultures / Cultures Traduites* 2 (2006) https://www.academia.edu/2559184/_New_Orleans_Do_You_Know_What_It_Means_Reflections_on_Disaster_; "A Letter from New Orleans: Reclusian Reflections on an Unnatural Disaster,"

Capitalism Nature Socialism 17, no. 1 (March 2006): 7–18, https://www.academia
.edu/2540532/_A_Letter_from_New_Orleans_Reclusian_Reflections_on_an_Unnat
ural_Disaster_; and "Postscript to a Letter from New Orleans," *Perspectives on
Anarchist Theory* (Fall 2006), accessed July 25, 2016, http://divergences.be/spip
.php?article1485&lang=fr.

25. Scott Crow, *Black Flags and Windmills: Hope, Anarchy, and the Common
Ground Collective* (Oakland, CA: PM Press, 2014), 165.

26. While in 2013 the metropolitan area had 92 percent of its pre-Katrina population, New Orleans itself had a population of only 379,000, as compared to 485,000
before Katrina, and a high of 627,000 in the 1960 census. United States Bureau of the
Census, "State & County QuickFacts," accessed July 25, 2016, http://quickfacts.census
.gov/qfd/states/22/2255000.html.

27. *Uncontrollable* 2 (Winter 2013/14), 1.

INTERSPACE SEVEN ⚜

In highlighting the political stakes of using interstitial space as an interpretive lens on New Orleans, John Clark's manifesto reveals many of the aesthetic, social, and historical concerns that weave throughout this collection. All the essayists are drawn to the idiom of spatial in-betweenness as a distinctive way of describing, analyzing, criticizing, or celebrating different relations of freedom and constraint, inclusion and exclusion, tradition and change, and fantasy and reality, located in New Orleans. At the same time, while elaborating on Clark's notion of the antistitial, these essays also offer other senses of how in-between spaces relate to the city's history. If sweet spots can press toward radical destruction, they can also dynamically exploit, amend, and transform the conditions between which they stand. Why is it that New Orleans always seems about to end yet never does? For Mac Heard, as for our contributors, this elusive but ongoing interplay between the city's in-between spaces and the multiple responses that they evoke may be one factor that helps to account not only for New Orleans's complex attraction but also for the city's historically striking ability to reinvent and adapt itself to natural and social challenges. In this still evolving post-Katrina moment, the question for all of us may not be, When will densely human spaces like New Orleans implode? but rather, What long-standing cultural strategies can be newly mobilized to reimagine their futures?

Bibliography

Ackerman, Diane. *Deep Play*. New York: Vintage, 2011.

Adams, Don, and Arlene Goldbard. "Cultural Democracy: Introduction to an Idea." Last modified 1998. http://www.wwcd.org/cd2.html.

Arabindan-Kesson, Anna. "Threads of Empire: The Visual Economy of the Cotton Trade in the Indian and Atlantic Ocean Worlds, 1840–1900." PhD diss., Yale University, 2014.

Armstrong, Louis. *Satchmo: My Life in New Orleans*. New York: Prentice Hall, 1954. Reprint with introduction by Dan Morgenstern, Cambridge, MA: Da Capo Press, 1986.

Augé, Marc. *Non-places: Introduction to an Anthropology of Supermodernity*. New York: Verso Books, 1995.

Bachand, Marise. "Gendered Mobility and the Geography of Respectability in Charleston and New Orleans 1790–1861." *Journal of Southern History* 81, no.1 (2015): 41–78.

Bachelard, Gaston. *The Poetics of Space*. Translated by Maria Jolas. Boston: Beacon Press, 1969.

Bacot, Barbara SoRelle. "The Plantation." In *Louisiana Buildings, 1720–1940: The Historic American Buildings Survey*, edited by Jessie Poesch and Barbara SoRelle Bacot, 87–173. Baton Rouge: Louisiana State University Press, 1997.

Bakhtin, Mikhail. *Rabelais and His World*. Bloomington: Indiana University Press, 1984.

Baptist, Edward E. *The Half Has Never Been Told: Slavery and the Making of American Capitalism*. New York: Basic Books, 2014.

Barton, Craig Evan, ed. *Sites of Memory: Perspectives on Architecture and Race*. New York: Princeton Architectural Press, 2001.

Baudrillard, Jean. *Simulacra and Simulation*. Ann Arbor: University of Michigan Press, 1994.

Bechet, Sidney. *Treat It Gentle: An Autobiography*. New York: Hill and Wang, 1960.

Beckert, Sven. *Empire of Cotton: A Global History*. New York: Alfred A. Knopf, 2014.

Bellocq, E. J. *Bellocq: Photographs from Storyville, the Red-Light District of New Orleans*. New York: Random House, 1996.

Berliner, Paul F. *Thinking in Jazz: The Infinite Art of Improvisation*. Chicago: University of Chicago Press, 1994.

Berquin Duvallon, Pierre-Louis, *Travels in Louisiana and the Floridas in the Year 1802, Giving a Correct Picture of Those Countries. Translated by John Davis*, New York, 1806.

Belsey, Catherine. "Quality Beyond Measure: Architecture in the Lacanian Account of Culture." In *Quality Out of Control: Standards for Measuring Architecture*, edited by Allison Dutoit, Juliet Odgers, and Adam Scharr, 188–97. London: Routledge, 2010.

Benfey, Christopher. *Degas in New Orleans: Encounters in the Creole World of Kate*

Chopin and George Washington Cable. New York: Alfred A. Knopf, 1997.

Bey, Hakim. *T.A.Z.: The Temporary Autonomous Zone, Ontological Anarchy, Poetic Terrorism*. New York: Autonomedia, 1991.

Boggs, Jean Sutherland, Douglas W. Druick, Henri Loyrette, Michael Pantazzi, and Gary Tinterow. *Degas, 1834–1917*. New York: Metropolitan Museum of Art, 1988.

———. "New Orleans and the Work of Degas." In *Degas and New Orleans: A French Impressionist in America*. Edited by Gail Feigenbaum et al., 105–264. New York: Rizzoli, distributed for the New Orleans Museum of Art and Ordrupgaard, Copenhagen, 1999.

Bontemps, Arna, and Langston Hughes, eds. *The Book of Negro Folklore*. New York: Dodd, Mead, 1958.

Bookhardt, Eric. "The Jungle is Near: Culture and Nature in a Subtropical Clime." *Mesechabe* 2 (1988–89): 1–5.

Brasseaux, Carl, and Glenn Conrad, eds. *The Road to Louisiana: The Saint-Domingue Refugees, 1792–1809*. Lafayette: University of Southwestern Louisiana, 1992.

Brown, Marilyn R. *Degas and the Business of Art: A Cotton Office in New Orleans*. University Park: Pennsylvania State University Press for College Art Association, 1994. Reissued in 2010 as an ACLS Humanities E-Book: https://quod.lib.umich.edu/cgi/t/text/text-idx?c=acls;idno=heb04023.

———. "Documentation: The DeGas-Musson Papers at Tulane University." *Art Bulletin* 72, no. 1 (1990): 118–30.

Brown, Theodore Dennis. "A History and Analysis of Jazz Drumming to 1942." PhD diss., University of Michigan, 1976.

Brunn, H. O. *The Story of the Original Dixieland Jazz Band*. Baton Rouge: Louisiana State University Press, 1960.

Campanella, Richard. *Bourbon Street: A History*. Baton Rouge: Louisiana State University Press, 2014.

———. *Geographies of New Orleans: Urban Fabrics before the Storm* (Lafayette: Center for Louisiana Studies, 2006.

———. "On the Structural Basis of Social Memory: Cityscapes of the New Orleans Slave Trade, Part I." *Preservation in Print*, March 2013. http://www.prcno.org/programs/preservationinprint/piparchives/2013%20PIP/March%202013/19.html

———. "On the Structural Basis of Social Memory: Cityscapes of the New Orleans Slave Trade, Part II." *Preservation in Print*, April 2013: 18–19.

———. "Remembering the Old French Opera House: The Bourbon Street Landmark (1859–1919) Testifies to the Cultural Power of Old Buildings, and the Significance of Their Loss." *Preservation in Print*, February 2013: 16–18.

———. *Time and Place in New Orleans: Past Geographies in the Present Day*. New Orleans: Pelican, 2002.

———. "Why Prytania Jogs at Joseph," *Preservation in Print*, October 2013: 18–19.

Caponi, Gena Dagel. *Signifyin(g), Sanctifyin', and Slam-Dunking: A Reader in African American Expressive Culture*. Amherst: University of Massachusetts Press, 1999.

Cazayoux, Edward Jon. *A Manual for the Environmental & Climatic Responsive Restoration & Renovation of Older Houses in Louisiana*. Baton Rouge: Energy Section, Technology Assessment Division, Louisiana Department of Natural Resources, 2003.

Cafard, Max [John Clark]. "Laughing Matters; or, In Praise of Folly." In *Surregional Explorations*, 162–73. Chicago: Charles H. Kerr, 2012.

Csikszentmihalyi, Mihaly. *Flow: The Psychology of Optimal Experience*. New York: Harper Perennial Modern Classics, 2008.

Clark, John. "New Orleans: Do You Know What It Means?" *New: Translating Cultures / Cultures Traduites* 2 (2006).

———. "A Letter from New Orleans: Reclusian Reflections on an Unnatural Disaster." *Capitalism Nature Socialism* 17, no. 1 (March 2006): 7–18.

———. "Postscript to a Letter from New Orleans." *Perspectives on Anarchist Theory*, Fall 2006. http://divergences.be/spip.php?article1485&lang=fr. Accessed 25 July 2016.

Clayson, Hollis. "Threshold Space: Parisian Modernism Betwixt and Between (1869 to 1891)." In *Impressionist Interiors*, 14–29. Dublin: National Gallery of Ireland, 2008.

Codrescu, Andrei. *The Disappearance of the Outside: A Manifesto for Escape.* St. Paul: Ruminator Books, 2001.

Colton, Craig E. *Unnatural Metropolis.* Baton Rouge: Louisiana State University Press, 2006.

Copeland, Huey. *Bound to Appear: Art, Slavery, and the Site of Blackness in Multicultural America.* Chicago: University of Chicago Press, 2013.

Coyle, Katy, and Nadiene Van Dyke. "Sex, Smashing, and Storyville in Turn-of-the-Century New Orleans: Reexamining the Continuum of Lesbian Sexuality." In *Carryin' On in the Lesbian and Gay South*, edited by John Howard, 54–72. New York: New York University Press, 1997.

Crow, Scott. *Black Flags and Windmills: Hope, Anarchy, and the Common Ground Collective.* Oakland, CA: PM Press, 2014.

Crutcher, Michael E., Jr. *Tremé: Race and Place in a New Orleans Neighborhood.* Athens: University of Georgia Press, 2010.

Curtain, Philip D. *The Rise and Fall of the Plantation Complex: Essays in Atlantic History.* Cambridge: Cambridge University Press, 1998.

Curtis, Nathaniel Cortlandt. *New Orleans: Its Old Houses, Shops and Public Buildings.* Philadelphia: J. B. Lippincott, 1933.

Davis, Thadious. *Southscapes: Geographies of Race, Region, and Literature.* Chapel Hill: University of North Carolina Press, 2011.

Davis, James F. *Who Is Black? One Nation's Definition.* University Park: Pennsylvania State University Press, 1991.

Dawdy, Shannon Lee. *Building the Devil's Empire: French Colonial New Orleans.* Chicago: University of Chicago Press, 2008.

———. *Madame John's Legacy (16OR51) Revisited: A Closer Look at the Archeology of Colonial New Orleans.* New Orleans: Greater New Orleans Archaeology Project, 1998.

Defrantz, Thomas F. *Dancing Many Drums: Excavations in African American Dance.* Madison: University of Wisconsin Press, 2001.

Dessens, Nathalie. *From Saint-Domingue to New Orleans: Migration and Influences.* Gainesville: University Press of Florida, 2007.

Dinerstein, Joel. "Second-Lining Post-Katrina: Learning Community from the Prince of Wales Social Aid & Pleasure Club." *American Quarterly* 61, no. 3 (2009): 615–37.

———. *Swinging the Machine: Modernity, Technology, and African American Culture between the World Wars.* Amherst: University of Massachusetts Press, 2003.

Di Santis, Francesco. *The Post Katrina Portraits.* New Orleans: Di Santis and Latta, 2007.

Dodds, Warren "Baby." *The Baby Dodds Story.* Edited by Larry Gara. Rev. ed. Baton Rouge: Louisiana State University Press, 1992.

Dominguez, Virginia R. *White by Definition: Social Classification in Creole Louisiana.* New Brunswick: Rutgers University Press, 1986.

Douglas, Lake. *Public Spaces, Private Gardens: A History of Designed Landscapes in New Orleans.* Baton Rouge: Louisiana State University Press, 2011.

Dufour, Charles L. "Pie." *Women Who Cared: The 100 Years of the Christian Woman's Exchange.* New Orleans: Christian Woman's Exchange, 1980.

Durkheim, Émile. *Elementary Forms of the Religious Life*, 1912. Translated by Karen E. Fields. New York: Free Press, 1995.

Eckstein, Barbara. *Sustaining New Orleans: Literature, Local Memory, and the Fate of a City.* New York: Routledge, 2006.

Edwards, Jay D. "The Origins of Creole Architecture." *Winterthur Portfolio* 29, no. 2/3 (1994): 155–89.

———. "Shotgun: The Most Contested House in America." *Buildings & Landscapes* 16, no. 1 (2009): 62–96.

Eisenman, Peter. "Processes of the Interstitial: Spacing and the Arbitrary Text." In *Blurred Zones: Investigations of the Interstitial: Eisenman Architects, 1988–1998*, edited by Peter Eisenman et al., 94–101. New York: The Monacelli Press, 2003.

Ellis, Scott. *Madame Vieux Carré: The French Quarter in the Twentieth Century.* Jackson: University Press of Mississippi, 2010.

Evans, Freddi Williams. *Congo Square: African Roots in New Orleans.* Lafayette: University of Louisiana at Lafayette Press, 2011.

Federal Writers' Project of New Orleans. *New Orleans City Guide.* 1938, reprinted with an introduction by Lawrence N. Powell, New Orleans: Garrett County Press, 2009.

Feigenbaum, Gail. "Edgar Degas, Almost a Son of Louisiana." In *Degas and New Orleans: A French Impressionist in America.* Edited by Gail Feigenbaum et al., 3–23. New York: Rizzoli, distributed for the New Orleans Museum of Art and Ordrupgaard, Copenhagen, 1999.

Ferguson, Mary S. "Boarding Homes and Clubs for Working Women." *Bulletin of the Department of Labor* III, no. 15: 141–96. Washington, DC: Government Printing Office, 1898.

Freud, Sigmund. "The Uncanny." In *The Uncanny*, edited by David McLintock and Hugh Haughton, 121–51. London: Penguin Books, 2003.

Fuss, Diana. *The Sense of an Interior: Four Writers and the Rooms that Shaped Them.* New York: Routledge, 2004.

Galsworthy, John. "That Old-Time Place." In *The Inn of Tranquility and Other Impressions, Poems.* Vol. 15 of *The Works of John Galsworthy.* New York: Charles Scribner's Sons, 1923.

Gaudin, Wendy Ann. "Autocrats and All Saints: Migration, Memory, and Modern Creole Identities." PhD diss., New York University, 2005.

Genovese, Eugene D. *The Political Economy of Slavery: Studies in the Economy and Society of the Slave South*, 2nd ed. Middletown, CT: Wesleyan University Press, 1989.

Goffman, Erving. *Stigma.* Englewood Cliffs, NJ: Prentice Hall, 1963.

Goldin, Claudia. "The Work and Wages of Single Women, 1870–1920." *Journal of Economic History* 40, no.1 (March 1980): 81–88. http://www.jstor.org/stable/2120426.

Gordon, Alastair. *Naked Airport: A Cultural History of the World's Most Revolutionary Structure.* New York: Metropolitan Books, 2004.

Gottschild, Brenda Dixon. *The Black Dancing Body: A Geography from Coon to Cool.* New York: Palgrave MacMillan, 2005.

Guérin, Marcel, ed. *Degas Letters.* Translated by Marguerite Kay. Oxford: Bruno Cassirer, 1947.

———, ed. *Lettres de Degas.* Paris: Bernard Grasset, 1945.

Gindin, James. *John Galsworthy's Life and Art: An Alien's Fortress.* Ann Arbor: University of Michigan Press, 1987.

Hansen, Karen V. "Feminist Conceptions of Public and Private: A Critical Analysis." *Berkeley Journal of Sociology* 32 (1987): 105–28.

Hazeldine, Mike, ed. and comp. *Bill Russell's American Music*. New Orleans: Jazzology Press, 1993.

Hazzard-Gordon, Katrina. *Jookin': The Rise of Social Dance Formations in African-American Culture*. Philadelphia: Temple University Press, 1992.

Heard, Malcolm. *French Quarter Manual: An Architectural Guide to New Orleans's Vieux Carré*. Jackson: University Press of Mississippi, 1997.

Hearn, Lafcadio. "Old-Fashioned Houses," January 12, 1881. In S. Frederick Starr, ed., *Inventing New Orleans: Writings of Lafcadio Hearn*, 176–79. Jackson: University Press of Mississippi, 2001.

Heynen, Hilde. "Modernity and Domesticity: Tensions and Contradictions." In *Negotiating Domesticity: Spatial Productions of Gender in Modern Architecture*, edited by Hilde Heynen and Gülsüm Baydar, 1–29. London: Routledge, 2005.

Hill, Joseph A. *Women in Gainful Occupations, 1870–1920*. Washington, DC: Government Printing Office, 1929.

Hirsch, Arnold R. and Joseph Logsdon, eds. *Creole New Orleans: Race and Americanization*. Baton Rouge: Louisiana State University Press, 1992.

Holm, Isak Winkel. "The Cultural Analysis of Disaster." In *The Cultural Life of Catastrophes and Crises*. Edited by Carsten Meiner and Kristin Veel, 15–32. Berlin: Walter De Gruyter, 2012.

Hobbs, Robert, et al. *30 Americans: Rubell Family Collection*. New York: Distributed Art Publishers, 2011.

Hobson, Vic. *Creating Jazz Counterpoint: New Orleans, Barbershop Harmony, and the Blues*. Jackson: University Press of Mississippi, 2014.

Hogue, James. *The Uncivil War: Five New Orleans Street Battles and the Rise and Fall of Radical Reconstruction*. Baton Rouge: Louisiana State University Press, 2006.

Huizinga, Johann. *Homo Ludens: A Study of the Play-Element in Culture*. London: Routledge, 1949.

Johnson, Jerah. *Congo Square in New Orleans*. New Orleans: Louisiana Landmark Society, 1995.

———. "New Orleans's Congo Square: An Urban Setting for Early Afro-American Culture Formation." *Louisiana History: The Journal of the Louisiana Historical Association* 32, no. 2 (Spring 1991): 117–57.

Johnson, Walter. *River of Dark Dreams: Slavery and Empire in the Cotton Kingdom*. Cambridge, MA: Belknap Press of Harvard University Press, 2013.

———. *Soul by Soul: Life inside the Antebellum Slave Market*. Cambridge, MA: Harvard University Press, 1999.

Joyce, John J., Jr., Bruce Boyd Raeburn, and Anthony M. Cummings, eds. *Sam Morgan's Jazz Band: Complete Recorded Works in Transcription*. Middleton, WI: A-R Editions, 2012.

Kasarda, John D., and Greg Lindsay. *Aerotropolis: The Way We'll Live Next*. New York: Farrar, Straus and Giroux, 2011.

Keil, Charles. *Urban Blues*. Chicago: University of Chicago Press, 1966.

Keil, Charles, and Steven Feld, eds. *Music Grooves: Essays and Dialogues*. Chicago: University of Chicago Press, 1994.

Kendall, John. *History of New Orleans*. New York: Lewis Publishing, 1922. Reproduced by William P. Thayer on *Bill Thayer's Website*. http://penelope.uchicago.edu/Thayer/E/Gazetteer/Places/America/United_States/Louisiana/New_Orleans/_Texts/KENHNO/43*.html

Kirkland, Elizabeth. "A Home Away from Home: Defining, Regulating, and Challenging Femininity at the Julia Drummond Residence in Montreal, 1920–1971." *Urban History Review* 34 (2006): 3–16.

Laguerre, Michel. *Diasporic Citizenship: Haitian Americans in Transnational America.* New York: St. Martin's Press, 1998.

Landau, Emily Epstein. *Spectacular Wickedness: Sex, Race, and Memory in Storyville, New Orleans.* Baton Rouge: Louisiana State University Press, 2013.

Latrobe, John H. B. *Southern Travels: Journal of John H. B. Latrobe 1834.* Edited by Samuel Wilson, Jr. New Orleans: Historic New Orleans Collection. 1986.

Latrobe, Benjamin Henry. *Impressions Respecting New Orleans: Diary & Sketches, 1818–1820.* New York: Columbia University Press, 1951.

Lawrence, Jeanne Catherine. "Chicago's Eleanor Clubs: Housing Working Women in the Early Twentieth Century." *Vernacular Architecture Forum* 8 (2000): 219–47.

Lefebvre, Henri. *La production de l'espace.* 1974. Translated by Donald Nicholson-Smith as *The Production of Space* (Oxford: Oxford University Press, 1991).

Lemann, Bernard. *The Vieux Carré—A General Statement.* New Orleans: School of Architecture, Tulane University, 1966.

Lewis, Peirce F. *New Orleans: The Making of an Urban Landscape*, 2nd ed. Santa Fe, NM: Center for American Places; Charlottesville: University of Virginia Press, 2003.

———. "The Stages of Metropolitan Growth: The Street Pattern." In *New Orleans: The Making of an Urban Landscape*, 2nd ed., 47–49. Santa Fe, NM: Center for American Places; Charlottesville: University of Virginia Press, 2003.

Lopate, Phillip. *Waterfront: A Walk Around Manhattan.* New York: Anchor Books, 2004.

Long, Alecia P. *The Great Southern Babylon: Sex, Race, and Respectability in New Orleans, 1865–1920.* Baton Rouge: Louisiana State University Press, 2004.

Louis Armstrong in His Own Words: Selected Writings. Edited by Thomas Brothers. Oxford: Oxford University Press, 1999.

Loyrette, Henri. *Degas.* Paris: Fayard, 1991.

Loyer, François. *Paris Nineteenth Century: Architecture and Urbanism.* New York: Abbeville Press, 1988.

Malone, Jacqui. *Steppin' on the Blues: The Visible Rhythms of African American Dance.* Urbana: University of Illinois Press, 1996.

Massey, Doreen. *For Space.* London: Sage Publications, 2005.

———. *Space, Place, and Gender.* Minneapolis: University of Minnesota Press, 1994.

Masson, Ann. "J. N. B. de Pouilly," June 4, 2013. In *KnowLA: The Digital Encyclopedia of Louisiana History and Culture*, edited by David Johnson. Louisiana Endowment for the Humanities, 2010. http://www.knowla.org/entry/473.

McCusker, John. *Creole Trombone: Kid Ory and the Early Years of Jazz.* Jackson: University Press of Mississippi, 2012.

McInnis, Maurie D. *Slaves Waiting for Sale: Abolitionist Art and the American Slave Trade.* Chicago: University of Chicago Press, 2011.

McMullen, Roy. *Degas: His Life, Times, and Work.* London: Secker & Warburg, 1985.

Metzer, David. "Reclaiming Walt: Marc Blitzstein's Whitman Settings." *Journal of the American Musicological Society* 48, no. 2 (Summer 1995): 240–71.

Monson, Ingrid T. *Saying Something: Jazz Improvisation and Interaction.* Chicago: University of Chicago Press, 1996.

Nora, Pierre. "Between Memory and History: Les Lieux de Mémoire." *Representations* 26 (Spring 1986): 7–24.

Northup, Solomon. *Twelve Years a Slave*. 1853. Mineola, NY: Dover Publications, 2000.

Ockman, Joan. "*The Poetics of Space*, by Gaston Bachelard." "Representations/Misrepresentations and Reevaluations of Classic Books," special issue, *Harvard Design Magazine* 6 (1998).

O'Donovan, Susan Eva. *Becoming Free in the Cotton South*. Cambridge, MA: Harvard University Press, 2007.

Officer, Lawrence H., and Samuel H. Williamson. "The Annual Consumer Price Index for the United States, 1774–2015." MeasuringWorth, 2017. http://www.measuring worth.com/uscpi/.

Oswell, Paul. *New Orleans Historic Hotels*. Charleston, SC: History Press, 2014.

Pactor, Andrea. *A Sense of Place: A Short History of Women's Philanthropy in America*. Indianapolis: Lilly Family School of Philanthropy, Indiana University, 2010. http://www.cfgnh.org/Portals/0/Uploads/Documents/Public/A-Sense-of-Place-FINAL.pdf

Parham, Angel Adams. *American Routes: Racial Palimpsests and the Transformation of Race* New York: Oxford University Press, 2017.

Piketty, Thomas. *Capital in the Twenty-First Century*. Cambridge, MA: Belknap Press of Harvard University Press, 2014.

Pollock, Griselda. *Vision and Difference: Femininity, Feminism, and the Histories of Art*. London: Routledge, 1988.

Powell, Lawrence N. *The Accidental City: Improvising New Orleans*. Cambridge, MA: Harvard University Press, 2012.

"The Present State of the Country . . . of Louisiana . . . by an Officer at New Orleans to his Friend at Paris." In *Narratives of Colonial America, 1704–1765*. Edited by Howard H. Peckham, 61–62. Chicago: Lakeside Press, 1971.

Raeburn, Bruce Boyd. "Dancing Hot and Sweet: New Orleans Jazz in the 1920s." *Jazz Archivist* VII, no. 1–2 (December 1992): 10–13.

———. "Stars of David and Sons of Sicily: Constellations beyond the Canon in Early New Orleans Jazz." *Jazz Perspectives* 3, no. 2 (August 2009): 123–52.

Rasula, Jed. "The Media of Memory: The Seductive Menace of Records in Jazz History." In *Jazz among the Discourses*, edited by Krin Gabbard, 134–62. Durham: Duke University Press, 1995.

Réclus, Elisée. *A Voyage to New Orleans*. 1855. Edited and translated by John Clark and Camille Martin. Thetford, VT: Glad Day Books, 2004.

Redmon, David. "Playful Deviance as an Urban Leisure Activity: Secret Selves, Self-Validation, and Entertaining Performances." *Deviant Behavior* 24, no. 1 (2003): 27–51.

Reynolds, John S. *Courtyards: Aesthetic, Social, and Thermal Delight*. New York: John Wiley & Sons, 2002.

Rice, Charles. *The Emergence of the Interior: Architecture, Modernity, Domesticity*. London: Routledge, 2007.

Rich, Nathaniel. "Jungleland: The Lower Ninth Ward in New Orleans Gives New Meaning to 'Urban Growth.'" *New York Times Magazine*, March 21, 2012.

Robinson, Eugene. *Disintegration: The Splintering of Black America*. New York: Doubleday, 2010.

Rose, Al. *Storyville, New Orleans*. Tuscaloosa: University of Alabama Press, 1974.

Reizenstein, Ludwig von. *The Mysteries of New Orleans*. 1855. Translated and edited by Steven Rowan. Baltimore: Johns Hopkins University Press, 2002.

Rosner, Victoria. *Modernism and the Architecture of Private Life*. New York: Columbia University Press, 2005.

"Royal Orleans History." Omni Hotels and Resorts. http://www.omnihotels.com/hotels/new-orleans-royal-orleans/property-details/history. Accessed November 14, 2016.

Sakakeeny, Matt. *Roll with It: Brass Bands in the Streets of New Orleans*. Durham: Duke University Press, 2013.

Salvaggio, Ruth. "Eating Poetry in New Orleans." In *Southern Foodways*, edited by David Davis and Tara Powell, 105–23. Jackson: University Press of Mississippi, 2014.

Sander, Kathleen Waters. *The Business of Charity: The Woman's Exchange Movement, 1832–1900*. Urbana: University of Illinois Press, 1998.

Sanforth, Deirdre. *Romantic New Orleans*. New Orleans: Pelican, 1979.

Saxon, Lyle. *Fabulous New Orleans*. 1928. Repr. New Orleans: Pelican, 1989.

Schafer, Judith Kelleher. *Brothels, Depravity, and Abandoned Women: Illegal Sex in Antebellum New Orleans*. Baton Rouge: Louisiana State University Press, 2009.

Scharr, Adam. "Introduction: A Case for Close Reading." In *Reading Architecture: Researching Buildings, Spaces, and Documents*, 2–12. London: Routledge, 2012.

Scott, Anne Firor. *The Southern Lady: From Pedestal to Politics 1830–1930*. Chicago: University of Chicago Press, 1970.

Shapiro, Nat, and Nat Hentoff. *The Story of Jazz as Told by the Men Who Made It: Hear Me Talkin' To Ya*. New York: Rinehart, 1955. Repr. New York: Dover, 1966.

Sidlauskas, Susan. *Body, Place, and Self in Nineteenth-Century Painting*. Cambridge: Cambridge University Press, 2000.

Solnit, Rebecca, and Rebecca Snedeker, eds. *Unfathomable City: A New Orleans Atlas*. Berkeley: University of California Press, 2013.

Soja, Edward. *Postmodern Geographies: The Reassertion of Space in Critical Social Theory*. London: Verso Books, 1989.

———. *Thirdspace: Journeys to Los Angeles and Other Real-and-Imagined Places*. Oxford: Basil Blackwell, 1996.

Sommer, Robert. *Tight Spaces: Hard Architecture and How to Humanize It*. Englewood Cliffs, NJ: Prentice Hall, 1974.

Stieber, Nancy. Introduction to "Learning from Interdisciplinarity," special issue, *Journal of the Society of Architectural Historians* 64, no. 4 (2005): 417–18.

Strachen, Ian Gregory. *Paradise and Plantation: Tourism and Culture in the Anglophone Caribbean*. Charlottesville: University of Virginia Press, 2003.

Stoler, Ann Laura. *Race and the Education of Desire. Foucault's History of Sexuality and the Colonial Order of Things*. Durham: Duke University Press, 1995.

Sublette, Ned. *The World That Made New Orleans: From Spanish Silver to Congo Square*. Chicago: Lawrence Hill Books, 2008.

Thompson, Robert Farris. *Aesthetic of the Cool: Afro-Atlantic Art and Music*. Pittsburgh, PA: Periscope, 2011.

Touré. *Who's Afraid of Post-Blackness? What It Means to Be Black Now*. New York: Free Press, 2011.

Tregle, Joseph, Jr. "Creoles and Americans." In *Creole New Orleans: Race and Americanization*, edited by Arnold R. Hirsch and Joseph Logsdon, 131–185. Baton Rouge: Louisiana State University Press, 1992.

Tuan, Yi-Fu. *Space and Place: The Perspective of Experience*. Minneapolis: University of Minnesota Press, 1977.

Turino, Thomas. *Music as Social Life: The Politics of Participation*. Chicago: University of Chicago Press, 2008.

Turner, Victor. *The Ritual Process: Structure and Anti-Structure.* 1969. Repr. New York: Aldine Transaction, 1995.

Van Zante, Gary. *New Orleans, 1867: Photographs by Theodore Lilienthal.* London: Merrell, 2008.

Velez, Sebastian. "Evasive Ground: Axioms of New Orleans's Morphology" and "Fragmentation." In *New Orleans: Strategies for a City in Soft Land*, edited by Joan Busquets and Felipe Correa. Cambridge, MA: Graduate School of Design, Harvard University, 2005.

Verderber, Stephen, and David J. Fine. *Healthcare Architecture in an Era of Radical Transformation.* New Haven: Yale University Press, 2000.

"Wall Down." *Preservation in Print*, May 2013: 16.

Walters Art Museum. *The Age of Impressionism: European Paintings from Ordrupgaard, Copenhagen.* Baltimore: Walters Art Museum, 2002.

Waters, Mary, Philip Kasinitz, and Asad L. Asad. "Immigrants and African Americans." *Annual Review of Sociology* 40 (2014): 369–90.

Womack, Ytasha. *Post Black: How a New Generation Is Redefining African American Identity.* Chicago: Chicago Review Press, 2010.

Welter, Barbara. "Cult of True Womanhood: 1820–1860." *American Quarterly* 18 (1966): 151–74.

Wetzel, James R. "American Families: 75 Years of Change." *Monthly Labor Review* 1, no. 13 (1990): 4–13.

White, Shane, and Graham White. *Stylin': African American Expressive Culture from Its Beginnings to the Zoot Suit.* Ithaca: Cornell University Press, 1998.

Willinger, Beth. "The Women of the New Orleans Christian Woman's Exchange (1881-Present): From 'Helping Women Who Help Themselves' to a Mission of Historic Preservation." In *Louisiana Women: Their Lives and Times*, vol. 2, edited by Shannon Frystak and Mary Farmer Kaiser, 308–34. Athens: University of Georgia Press, 2016.

Wiltz, Christine. *The Last Madam: A Life in the New Orleans Underworld.* New York: Faber and Faber, 2000.

Winslow, Marshall, and Jean Stearns. *Jazz Dance: The Story of American Vernacular Dance* New York: Da Capo Press, 1968.

Wischermann, Ulla, and Ilze Klavina Mueller. "Feminist Theories on the Separation of the Private and the Public: Looking Back, Looking Forward." *Women in German Yearbook* 20 (2004): 184–97.

Wilson, Samuel, Jr. *The Creole Faubourgs*, vol. 4 of *New Orleans Architecture*. New Orleans: Pelican, 1974.

———. *The Architecture of Colonial Louisiana: Collected Essays of Samuel Wilson, Jr. F.A.I.A.*, edited by Jean M. Farnsworth and Ann M. Masson. Lafayette: Center for Louisiana Studies, University of Southwestern Louisiana, 1987.

Woodward, C. Vann. *The Strange Career of Jim Crow*, 3rd ed. New York: Oxford University Press, 1974.

Young, Marnin. "Capital in the Nineteenth Century: Edgar Degas's Portraits at the Stock Exchange in 1879." *Nonsite* 14 (December 15, 2014). http://nonsite.org.

Žižek, Slavoj. *The Parallax View.* Cambridge, MA: MIT Press, 2009

———. "Architectural Parallax: Spandrel and Other Phenomena of Class Struggle," lecture delivered at Jack Tilton Gallery, New York City, April 23, 2009, as discussed by Lahiji Nadir, "In Interstitial Space: Žižek on 'Architectural Parallax,'" *International Journal of Žižek Studies* 3, no. 3 (2009): 1–19.

About the Contributors

Carrie Bernhard is the director of the Lime Agency for Sustainable Hot/Humid Design, a nonprofit research and outreach organization dedicated to geographically responsive architectural and urban design in hot, humid tropical and subtropical regions. She is also a partner of Prosus Design, an architectural design office that focuses on small-scale design projects specific to the unique environment of New Orleans. She is the author of several publications about New Orleans architecture including, as a contributor, *Architecture in Times of Need: Make It Right—Rebuilding New Orleans' Lower Ninth Ward*.

Scott Bernhard, AIA, is the Jean and Saul A. Mintz Associate Professor at the Tulane School of Architecture in New Orleans, where he has been a member of the faculty for over twenty-five years. He has served as both associate dean and interim dean of the school and was director of the Tulane City Center from 2007 to 2012. The recipient of numerous design and teaching awards, he is a licensed architect and principal of a small collaborative research and design practice focused on building in the climate and context of New Orleans. His current research and publication includes work on the complexities of the urban fabric in New Orleans, on the relationship between architecture and social entrepreneurship, and on authenticity in architecture.

Barbara Brainard was awarded two Pollock-Krasner Foundation grants (2005, 2007), and a Louisiana Division of the Arts Fellowship (1999). Her work has been published in *New American Paintings, Louisiana Literature* and the *New Orleans Review*. Her monotypes are archived at the Drawing Center Viewing Program, the Los Angeles Printmaking Society, Rutgers University, and the New Orleans Museum of Art. She is an assistant professor at Loyola University New Orleans and is represented by Cole Pratt Gallery in New Orleans.

Marilyn R. Brown is professor emerita of art history in the Department of Art & Art History at the University of Colorado, Boulder, and in the Newcomb Art Department at Tulane University in New Orleans, where she previously taught for twenty-seven years. She is author of *Degas and the Business of Art: A Cotton Office in New Orleans* (Pennsylvania State University Press and College Art Association, 1994; ACLS e-book, 2010). Her edited volume *Picturing Children: Constructions of Childhood between Rousseau and Freud* (2002) was reissued in paperback by Routledge in 2017. She received the Interdisciplinary Nineteenth-Century Studies Essay Prize and the Nineteenth Century Studies Association Article Prize for "'Miss La La's' Teeth: Reflections on Degas and 'Race,'" *Art Bulletin* (December 2007). Her new book, *The 'Gamin de Paris' in Nineteenth-Century Visual Culture: Delacroix, Hugo, and the French Social Imaginary*, was published by Routledge in 2017.

Richard Campanella, a geographer with the Tulane School of Architecture, is the author of ten books and over two hundred articles about New Orleans geography, history, architecture, and culture. The only two-time winner of the Louisiana Endowment for the Humanities Book of the Year Award, Campanella has also received the Louisiana Literary Award, the Williams Prize, and the Tulane Honors Professor of the Year Award. In 2016, the government of France named Campanella a Knight of the Order of the Academic Palms.

John P. Clark is a native of the island of New Orleans, where his family has lived for twelve generations. He is director of La Terre Institute for Community and Ecology, which sponsors programs aimed at social and ecological regeneration and the creation of a cooperative, nondominating earth community. He is also professor emeritus of philosophy at Loyola University New Orleans. His most recent books are *The Impossible Community* (2013), *The Tragedy of Common Sense* (2016) and, as Max Cafard, *Lightning Storm Mind* (2017). He writes blogs for Changing Suns Press and PM Press. Over three hundred of his texts can be found at http://loyno.academia.edu/JohnClark. He is active in the radical ecology and communitarian anarchist movements and is a member of the Industrial Workers of the World.

Joel Dinerstein is professor of English and the former executive director of the New Orleans Center for the Gulf South at Tulane University. He is the author of *Swinging the Machine: Modernity, Technology and African American Culture between the World Wars* (2003), an award-winning cultural study of jazz and industrialization.

He is also the author of three books on the history of the concept of cool in American culture: *American Cool, Coach: A Story of New York Cool*, and *The Origins of Cool in Postwar America* (2016). He has been a consultant on jazz and popular music for HBO's *Boardwalk Empire*, Putumayo Records, and the National Endowment for the Humanities.

Barbara C. Ewell is emerita professor and former Dorothy H. Brown Distinguished Professor of English at Loyola University New Orleans. She has written and published on topics ranging from Renaissance poetry and feminist pedagogy to southern literature and women writers. She is author of *Kate Chopin* (1985) and has coedited several volumes, including (with Dorothy Brown) *Louisiana Women Writers* (1992), (with Pamela Menke) *Southern Local Color: Stories of Region, Race and Gender* (2002); and (with Jorge Aguilar Mora and Josefa Salmón) *The Anthology of Spanish American Thought and Culture* (2017).

Pableaux Johnson is a New Orleans–based photographer, journalist, and author. He is currently at work on several bodies of work documenting New Orleans's distinctive street culture, including the black Mardi Gras Indians and the city's social aid and pleasure clubs. His writing and photographic work appear in the *New York Times* and *Garden & Gun*. Johnson is currently touring the United States with his food and travel project the *Red Beans Road Show* (www.redbeansroadshow.com).

John P. Klingman holds a Favrot Professorship in Architecture at Tulane University. His upper-level design studios relate architectural design to issues of water engagement. In 2001 he received the President's Award for Outstanding Teaching. As an architect, he has consulted on projects in the city, including the US Custom House with Waggonner and Ball Architects, and on Tulane's uptown campus. He has been a member of the Architectural Review Committee of the New Orleans Historic Districts Landmarks Commission since 1995. Since 1997 he has written an annual "Best of New New Orleans Architecture" article for *New Orleans Magazine* and his *New in New Orleans Architecture* (2012) highlights eighty outstanding contemporary projects. He is the editor with Malcolm Heard and Bernard Lemann of *Talk about Architecture: A Century of Architectural History at Tulane*

Angel Adams Parham is associate professor of sociology at Loyola University New Orleans. She has published numerous essays on the intersection of race, migration, identity, and national belonging. She has a particular interest in the ways communities and cultures of the US South and the Caribbean have been mutually constituted by transnational flows of people and ideas in the past and the present and how those movements enlarge our understanding of what it means to be "American." Her book, *American Routes: Racial Palimpsests and the Transformation of Race* (2017) compares the immigration to the United States of nineteenth-century whites and free blacks from colonial Saint-Domingue. She is now at work on a new book manuscript entitled "A Place to Remember," which builds on the *lieux de souvenir* concept examined in this volume in order to explore concrete social and cultural connections between sites in the US South and the Caribbean.

Bruce Boyd Raeburn is director of Special Collections and curator of the Hogan Jazz Archive at Tulane University. He is the author of *New Orleans Style and the Writing of American Jazz History* and has published widely on the early development of New Orleans jazz, jazz historiography, and the impact of Hurricane Katrina on the New Orleans jazz scene. Raeburn has also worked professionally as a drummer in New Orleans for the past forty-six years, performing with artists such as Clark Vreeland, James Booker, Earl King, the Pfister Sisters, and many others.

Ruth Salvaggio is professor of English and comparative literature at the University of North Carolina at Chapel Hill, where she teaches courses in early Atlantic literatures, feminist theory, and poetry. She is the author of several books and essays, including works on New Orleans. Her book, *Hearing Sappho in New Orleans: The Call of Poetry from Congo Square to the 9th Ward* (Louisiana State University Press, 2012) uses Sappho's fragments as a guide to the forgotten and fragmented poetic history of the city. Her essays on New Orleans gravitate around varied kinds of recuperative poetics in the city.

Christopher Schaberg is associate professor of English and environmental studies at Loyola University New Orleans, and founding coeditor of Bloomsbury's Object Lessons series. He is the author of *The Textual Life of Airports: Reading the Culture of Flight* (Continuum, 2011; Bloomsbury, 2013), *The End of Airports* (Bloomsbury, 2015), and *Airportness: The Nature of Flight* (Bloomsbury, 2017).

Teresa A. Toulouse is newly retired professor of English at the University of Colorado, Boulder and professor emerita at Tulane University, where she taught for twenty-nine years and served as long-time director of the American studies program. A scholar of American literature and culture, she is author and editor of many essays and three books on colonial and antebellum New England writers. She has recently coedited a volume of essays for *English Language Notes* on environmental trajectories in the humanities and is currently writing a monograph comparing colonial American devotional styles and practices. She was privileged to teach New Orleans as a Cultural System with Mac Heard.

Beth Willinger, a sociologist and feminist scholar, is former executive director of the Newcomb College Center for Research on Women and founding director of the women's studies program at Tulane University. Her research on women's lives has examined the past as well as the present, particularly in her work on the history of the Christian Woman's Exchange and as coeditor with Susan Tucker of *Newcomb College, 1886–2006* (Louisiana State University Press, 2012). She is editor of *Katrina and the Women of New Orleans* (2008) and produces regular reports on the status of women in New Orleans and Louisiana.

Index

References to illustrations appear in **bold**.